THE
BLAST
OF WAR

The royalist pamphlet Mercurius Rusticus, *1643*

THE
BLAST
OF WAR

DESTRUCTION IN THE
ENGLISH CIVIL WARS

STEPHEN PORTER

Front cover image: Blackbeck, 'Storm clouds forming over Corfe Castle ruins and countryside'. (Getty Images)

First published by Sutton Publishing Ltd, 1994
This edition published by The History Press, 2011

The History Press
The Mill, Brimscombe Port
Stroud, Gloucestershire, GL5 2QG
www.thehistorypress.co.uk

British Library Cataloguing in Publication Data.
A catalogue record for this book is available from the British Library.

ISBN 978 0 7524 6116 8

Printed in Great Britain
Manufacturing managed by Jellyfish Print Solutions Ltd

Contents

List of Illustrations

Photographs and illustrations are reproduced by kind permission of the following: Ashmolean Museum, Oxford, 1, 2, 8, 9, 11–14, 19, 22, 31, 38, 39, 59; Berkshire County Reference Library, 18; Bodleian Library, Oxford, 4 (MS. Top. Bucks. b.6), 37 (MS Ashmole 1521, p. 147); British Library, 6 (1608/624), 7 (1397/D2), 16 (E245/8), 17 (E293/27), 21 (E453/18), 29 (E99/14), 58; Cambridge University Collection of Air Photographs, 30, 32; Syndics of Cambridge University Library, 25, 34; Chester City Council, Dept of Leisure Services, 24, 44; Exeter Museums Archaeological Field Unit, 10; Gloucestershire Record Office, 42; Hereford City Council, 20; Humphrey Household, 3; Joan Johnson, 27; Anthony Kersting, 41; Leicestershire Libraries, 35; Liverpool Record Office, 56; National Monuments Record, Royal Commission on the Historical Monuments of England, 28, 40, 47–51, 53–5, 57; Oxfordshire County Council, 26; author's collections, 52

Foreword

The Civil War in Britain in the mid-seventeenth century has been studied from many different viewpoints, and at no time more intently than in the last fifty years. But the material damage caused by the war has been taken for granted as a feature seen at a distance in the landscape, and never thoroughly examined at close quarters. That blurred view has now been clarified, and far more detail delineated in Stephen Porter's book. Through a sequence of accidental circumstances, which he explains in his Preface, the author gained an unrivalled knowledge of the contents of our local archive offices throughout England, and because his researches were centred on the seventeenth century, this subject confronted him, demanding to be studied in its many local and general aspects.

A survey of the destruction wrought in time of war, in fact, makes a timely appearance, for little imagination is needed nowadays to bring the documents to life. Few people in twentieth-century Britain lack experience in their families of the loss of life and property wrought by war, and now that the television screen familiarizes everyone with the actual sights of war, thrusting us on to devastated streets only a few hours after the firing has ceased, the reality lives under our eyes. A once remote experience is ever present, as war is waged somewhere in every continent of the world.

The historical documents, in consequence, have an immediacy which they once lacked, and many of those which Stephen Porter has uncovered will remain long in memory, like the account of a soldier returning to Hereford, only to find his landlady dead from grief at the ruin of her home. Other details hold fresh meaning, when, for example, they explain why a familiar local church was rebuilt, even moved to a new site, because it was damaged in the Civil War.

The context in which wars are fought constantly changes, with the result that major differences of style were introduced in the 1640s by 'the military revolution' that had been under way from the sixteenth century onwards. The new technology was a European phenomenon, brought to England by experienced professional soldiers and by books of instruction. But while Englishmen read the books, and contemplated using their knowledge one day in the Low Countries, perhaps also against Scotland or Ireland, they can never have foreseen using it against their fellows in English towns and villages. Yet so it happened: mortars were wheeled into towns, terrifying the population 'at the strangeness thereof', heated shot was fired from cannons and muskets, fire darts were directed at thatched roofs to set them alight. The personal injuries, the taxing of medical skills, the ruined lives, lurk between the lines of many pages, and leave the reader reflecting on further themes.

Some towns underwent the horrors of siege, and occupation at different times by more than one side, Newark perhaps suffering among the worst. Along with this went pillaging, wanton destruction of houses in retribution, and the blocking of water supplies; it all has a familiar ring. The present misery of Yugoslavia reverberates in these pages, mingling the same sufferings of two wars, though the two experiences are separated in time by three and a half centuries. Where did the homeless find shelter when 144 houses were burned down in Beaminster, 300 were destroyed in Oxford, and 241 in Gloucester? Plainly, the unthinkable became thinkable when buildings in the cathedral close at Exeter were used to house those without a roof over their heads, and finally the corporation bought the deanery to divide into sixty tenements for the homeless poor. In Gloucester, a resourceful family went to live in a dovecote, sleeping more comfortably when once they were given permission to build a chimney. The reader may even smile in recognition at the familiarity of the scene, when sufferers waited ten, twenty, and thirty years for compensation, and some of Lancaster's buildings, standing in 1684, seem to include those hastily thrown up in the 1640s for temporary accommodation only.

As in all wars, some restraint was exercised by individuals, thinking rationally about a different future, and not wishing 'too many sad marks left of the calamity of this war'. It is satisfying that Stephen Porter can find some record of their brave stand.

Presumably, there will always be some who are exhilarated by the drama and excitement of war, and will respond to *The Call* of Thomas Osbert Mordaunt,

> Sound, sound the clarion, fill the fife!
> Throughout the sensual world proclaim,
> One crowded hour of glorious life
> Is worth an age without a name.

But this book penetrates beneath that brittle surface to give a more comprehensive, and more satisfying view than before of the deeper levels of the story during the English Civil War. Its mood matches that of the Quaker poet, John Scott of Amwell, Hertfordshire, when he made his powerful retort to Mordaunt:

> I hate that drum's discordant sound,
> Parading round, and round, and round:
> To me it talks of ravag'd plains,
> And burning towns, and ruin'd swains,
> And mangled limbs, and dying groans,
> And widows' tears, and orphans' moans;
> And all that Misery's hand bestows,
> To fill the catalogue of human woes.

Joan Thirsk

Preface

Strange as it may seem, this book has its origins in research undertaken more than twenty years ago into the pattern of farming in Huntingdonshire in the seventeenth and early eighteenth centuries. This small county contained only eight market towns, but two of them suffered from devastating fires, St Ives in 1689 and Ramsey in 1731. It was impossible to put these disasters into context, however, for no list of town fires existed. Having completed that research, it was then my good fortune to work as Joan Thirsk's research assistant for Volume V of *The Agrarian History of England and Wales*, a post which took me all over the country and enabled me to use many local history libraries to compile a list of fires. By that time similar work had been done by E.L. Jones and Michael Turner, and we pooled our findings and published a gazetteer of English urban fires for the period 1500–1900.

The gazetteer is of fires that began accidentally and excludes those started deliberately during the military operations of the 1640s. These clearly fell into a different and extensive category, and had proved more difficult to track down. Having identified the problem my good fortune continued, and I was able to work with Ian Roy and Ian Gentles on their separate studies of aspects of the Civil Wars. Both of them generously shared their extensive knowledge of the period with me and encouraged me to pursue my own researches into the destruction of property during the wars, which I was able to work up into a thesis under Ian Roy's supervision. The study was then further widened, from a consideration of urban destruction to that of the demolition of all buildings, in town and countryside, and it is the findings of this wider study which are presented here.

In carrying out a study which has lasted so long and involved visiting so many libraries and record offices, I have incurred numerous debts to archivists, librarians and scholars. I am particularly grateful to the archivists at the Hereford and Worcester, Gloucestershire, Chester, Devon, Somerset, Colchester and Lincolnshire record offices, and to the staff at the Bodleian Library, the Public Record Office, the British Library, the National Library of Wales, Oxford City Library, the libraries of the dioceses of Worcester and Exeter, and of Christ Church, Corpus Christi College, Magdalen College, Balliol College and Merton College, Oxford. The records of the Dean and Chapter of Carlisle and the Dean and Chapter of Worcester were consulted with their kind permission, and the Wase Collection with the kind permission of the President and Fellows of Corpus Christi College.

Much of the research was carried out while I was a member of the staff of the

History Department at King's College, London, and I am very grateful both for the opportunity to work in the college and the help and support which I received from other members of the department. The study would have been much more difficult if I had not had access to the Institute of Historical Research, and I am grateful to the staff for their help and for maintaining this invaluable research collection.

The Central Research Fund of the University of London generously supported the considerable amount of travel undertaken, and I am very grateful for a subvention from the Isobel Thornley Bequest Fund to the University towards the costs of publication.

I have benefited immeasurably from Ian Roy's expert advice and helpful encouragement over many years, and also from the opportunity which he gave me to work on the Civil War. I am also greatly indebted to Ian Gentles for employing me as his research assistant for his book on the New Model Army, research which alerted me to much new material.

Alan Everitt, Joan Thirsk and Barry Coward made constructive suggestions. E.L. Jones and Michael Turner shared their knowledge of town fires with me, and Peter Borsay kindly supplied me with information on Warwick.

My colleagues at the Survey of London provided references and checked out sites for me, and Alan Cox, John Greenacombe and Ann Robey were especially helpful. I am also grateful to Charmian Hearne for much sensible advice on the preparation of the text, and to Robert Tittler for his friendly encouragement and help.

My wife Carolyn has given many years of patient support. She not only packed the sandwiches but also came along to help to consume them, incidentally offering challenging observations on such matters as the capabilities of seventeenth-century artillery.

CHAPTER ONE

The European Context

. . . the miserable estate of Germany, wherein as in a glass you might see the, mournfull face of this our sister nation, now dumb with misery, and who knows how fast the cup may pass round? . . . For burning, pulling down, and ruining of churches, cities, villages, the like hath not been heard.
    Nehemiah Wallington, Historical Notices, *ed. R. Webb, I, 1869*

In 1653 a report was presented to the House of Commons pointing out that 'divers Petitions' had been sent in requesting assistance for those who had suffered 'in the burning, pulling down, and destroying, of their Houses and Goods'.[1] It stressed that the destruction had been carried out by both sides during the Civil War and that it had occurred 'in sundry Parts of the Nation'. The report was misleading only in its implication that the buildings had been destroyed by soldiers solely for defensive and preventive reasons 'to secure themselves and Garisons from the Prejudice they might receive by the Enemies possessing thereof'. In fact, there had also been destruction during offensive operations – assaults, bombardments and raids – and in accidental fires. A vivid picture of the aftermath of wartime destruction was provided by the inhabitants of Boarstall in Buckinghamshire, a few months after their village had been destroyed. Responding to a request for a summary of the effects of the war, they could only reply that they were unable to return 'any direct accoumpt by reason our houses with writings have beene consumed with fyer [and] we dispearsed soe that we are alltogether in a confusion'.[2]

It is not at all surprising that property was destroyed during the Civil Wars, for the practice of burning or demolishing buildings within enemy territory was as old as warfare itself,[3] and depriving a foe of the defence and shelter they could provide, as well as punishing a hostile population, were common military objectives. The extent of the losses during the English Civil Wars and the means of destruction were both characteristic of contemporary European conflicts. They reflected the stage then reached in the evolution of warfare, particularly the balance between attack and defence. Campaigns conducted by small, tightly disciplined armies that were self-contained and supported by well-organised commissariats, supplied from their own bases and operating independently of the civilian population, may have caused little destruction of property, but these were not the conditions in which any armies in Europe operated in the early seventeenth century.

The development in the late fifteenth century of mobile cannon trains had brought about a revolution in siege warfare. Castle and town walls designed to resist bombardment by medieval siege engines quickly succumbed to gunfire, and the masonry walls which had been the standard form of fortification throughout the Middle Ages no longer offered protection against even a modest siege train. Improvements in gunfounding and the manufacture of gunpowder during the sixteenth century increased the effectiveness of cannon as instruments of destruction. Completely new forms of defence had to be devised to counter the threat. The result was fortifications of much greater thickness than anything built hitherto, consisting of earthworks, faced with brick or stone, with a low profile that was designed to offer both the smallest possible target and the greatest possible resistance to an attacker's guns. The system also provided the defenders with wide fields of fire when replying to the besiegers' batteries and repelling assaults. Central to this system was the bastion, an arrowhead-shaped structure projecting forward from the line of the ramparts to allow enfilading fire along the face of the defences. The evolution of the new 'artillery defences' saw the construction of works of increasing complexity, usually incorporating a wet or dry ditch, fronted by the clear ground known as the *glacis*, and perhaps by other earthworks as well.

Because of these developments many towns had their defences remodelled, or they were fortified for the first time, with the bastioned trace, or *trace italienne*. The squat walls and their associated features covered much more land than the town walls and towers which they replaced. They were also expensive to build, and so their construction was not a step to be undertaken lightly.[4] Dutch towns possessed few bastioned fortifications before the 1570s, but thereafter, during the Eighty Years' War between the United Provinces and Spain, most of them were given the new style of defences, and a distinct pattern of earthwork fortifications and wet ditches evolved to suit the conditions there.[5] The success of the bastioned fortifications in nullifying attempts by attacking forces to take towns by assault produced long sieges, with the threat of starvation as the principal means of capture. Haarlem was besieged for thirty weeks in 1572–3 before surrendering to the Spanish army, the futile siege of Rouen lasted for twenty weeks in 1591–2, and the Spaniards' ultimately successful investment of Ostend for a staggering 167 weeks between July 1601 and September 1604. Besieging forces spent so long in their encampments that they not only constructed earthwork lines of circumvallation facing the town, to protect their batteries from the defenders' artillery fire and sallies, but also lines of counter-vallation facing the surrounding country as their own defence against a relieving army.

A corollary of the large-scale and prolonged sieges of the late sixteenth and early seventeenth centuries was larger armies than hitherto, operating well beyond the traditional campaigning season of the summer months. Not only were the field armies larger and more complex, but troops were also needed to garrison the fortified towns and other strong points which would require a considerable effort to recover if they were captured. There were 208 permanent garrisons held by over 33,000 men in the Spanish Netherlands in 1639.[6] The military's demands upon the civilian population grew as the numbers of troops and garrisons

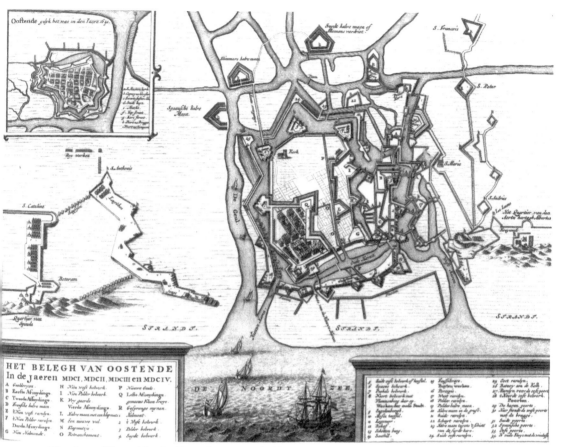

The siege of Ostend by the Spanish army in 1601–4 was one of the major sieges of the period, and both the defenders and besiegers constructed elaborate works. This strategically important town still had substantial fortifications in 1641

increased. They included high levels of taxation, fines imposed upon both individuals and communities, the impressment of men to serve as soldiers, the supply of horses, other livestock and provisions, and accommodation for the troops and their followers. Civilians were also the victims of casual and systematic plundering, high levels of mortality caused by the epidemic diseases spread by the armies, the disruption of trade, and the destruction of buildings and their contents. The control of resources and the denial of them to an enemy were important factors in an army's ability to wage war, and the need to maintain the armies was such that civilian resistance to the soldiers' demands could not be tolerated and was met with violence. Increased numbers of troops, the length of the campaigns, the duration of sieges, the stagnation in strategy which resulted, and the impact of warfare on the civilian population, were important elements in the transformation in the conduct of war that has been identified as a military revolution.[7]

The Elizabethan defences of Berwick-upon-Tweed are among the best sixteenth-century fortifications surviving in Europe. This view between two bastions shows how fire from artillery placed in the flankers could sweep the ground in front of the walls

The British Isles were on the periphery of these developments. The Elizabethan and Jacobean campaigns in Ireland resembled the continental wars to some extent, but the relatively small numbers of combatants and the guerrilla nature of much of the fighting limited the extent to which the features of the military revolution were introduced. There were no long and formal sieges necessitating the construction of the earthworks of the bastion trace, for example.[8] In England, new fortifications were constructed to protect the ports of Plymouth, Portsmouth and Hull, but the only complete bastioned defences were those erected at Berwick-upon-Tweed between 1558 and 1569, and they were already obsolescent when they were constructed.[9] Nevertheless, it is clear that the Civil War was not, and could not have been, fought in isolation from continental military developments. Inevitably, the current practices and technology of warfare were drawn upon by both sides. Points of contact between the British Isles and the continent in terms of military affairs were threefold: the interchange of personnel, the textbooks and other literature on the theories and practices of warfare, and the memoirs and reminiscences of those who had served in European armies.

Many British men served on the continent in the years preceding the Civil Wars. In the later years of Elizabeth's reign the armies in Ireland and the Low

Countries had contained considerable numbers of her subjects, while others had fought in the civil wars in France. The more pacific policy of the early Stuarts meant that those who wished to pursue a military career went increasingly into foreign service, especially in the Low Countries and Germany. The estimate that as many as 20,000 Britons served abroad in the years between the accession of Charles I and the outbreak of the Civil War may be on the low side. There was an average of 4,000 with the Spanish Army of Flanders during the 1630s and several times that number fighting in Germany.[10] Those who campaigned abroad can be roughly divided into two categories: the gentlemen volunteers and the professional soldiers.[11] Typically, the former served for relatively short periods, perhaps during a longer spell of travelling on the continent, while the latter may have campaigned abroad for many years, gaining wide experience of warfare. The difference between the two groups is shown in the contrasting careers of Henry Rich, Earl of Holland, and Philip Skippon. Rich 'betook himself to the war in Holland, which he intended to have made his profession; where, after he had made two or three campaigns, according to the custom of the English volunteers' he returned to England, while Skippon 'served very long in Holland, and from a common soldier had raised himself to the degree of captain and to the reputation of a good officer'.[12] Many British soldiers returned from the continent to enlist in the forces raised for the Bishops' Wars between England and Scotland, the campaigns in Ireland that began in 1641, and the Civil War itself. The royalists benefited from the expertise of such officers as Sir Arthur Aston, gained during service in the Russian, Polish and Swedish armies, and Sir Henry Gage, commander of the English regiment in the Army of Flanders. Because of his military career Gage had hardly set foot in England during the twenty years before the Civil War. He not only offered his own services to the king, but was instrumental in arranging for other English officers in the Spanish service to be released from their contracts in order to join the royalist armies.[13] The parliamentarians tended to draw recruits from among British soldiers with the Dutch forces, and the Scots soldiers abroad had generally, although not exclusively, served in the Danish and Swedish armies.[14]

Because of the return of such men, both sides in the Civil War contained many officers who had experience of European warfare. Some of them can fairly be classified as soldiers of fortune: roughly one in six of those who held field command in the royalist armies fell into that category.[15] Former colleagues from the continental wars found themselves ranged on opposite sides. The occasion during the siege of Worcester in 1646 when the royalist governor Henry Washington met with Colonel Henry Dingley and other parliamentarian officers during a truce, and shared a few hours drinking and reminiscing about 'being fellow soldiers in the Low Countries', may be only one of several such incidents during the Civil War.[16]

European experience amongst the rank and file soldiers was also highly valued, especially in the early stages of the conflict, when the armies had to be created from the newly raised levies and the militia. One Shropshire man served in the Low Countries, took the rank of sergeant in the militia on his return, and then enlisted in the king's army early in the Civil War, being made a sergeant 'because hee was a stout and experienced soldier'. He later became governor of a small royalist garrison in the county.[17] Such 'old soldiers' were appreciated for the knowledge and experience they could impart to their unseasoned comrades, and the practical information acquired through having taken part in military operations. There was movement in both directions during the war years, with the British contingents abroad not only supplying troops for the Civil War campaigns, but also recruiting from amongst the participants. In 1645 the English forces in the Dutch service applied to Parliament for permission to take recruits from the royalist prisoners, and they had a good pool to draw upon following the battle of Naseby.[18]

The influence of the professional soldiers increased steadily during the war, as those who held senior command chiefly on the strength of their social rank were replaced by professional officers. This process occurred in both the royalist and parliamentarian armies and was virtually completed by the time the 1645 campaigns began. The purge of the parliamentarian high command produced by the Self Denying Ordinance of April 1645 (which prevented members of both Houses of Parliament from holding military office) did remove some officers who had gained considerable military experience abroad before the war, such as Sir William Waller, but it also cleared the way for the career soldiers to take control. In the spring of 1645 the principal field armies were commanded by Prince Rupert, George Lord Goring, Sir Thomas Fairfax, the Earl of Leven, Edward Massey, Sydenham Poyntz and Bartholomew Vermuyden, all of whom had experience of continental warfare.

In addition to the British soldiers who returned to serve in the wars, there were the Europeans who crossed the Channel. They included private soldiers, such as the contingent of Frenchmen that served with Prince Maurice's army in the West Country in 1644, and the Dutch troops who fought in the parliamentarian armies.[19] There was also a significant number of experienced officers and specialists. For example, Adam Styall, a Bohemian, served as Physician General to the parliamentarian armies from 1642 until the end of 1645, first under the Earl of Essex and then in the New Model.[20] Both sides acquired the services of engineers and gunnery experts to supervise the construction of fortifications, the conduct of sieges and the operation of their artillery. The royalists employed the Walloon engineer Sir Bernard de Gomme, and Prince Rupert's staff included the Frenchman, Bartholomew de la Roche, a pyrotechnist, or, in the vocabulary of the time, fireworker.[21] For the first few months of the war the Earl of Essex's fireworker was William Roberts, but he was discharged in December 1642, and the post was then filled by Joachim Hane, a German.[22] The preference for foreign engineers continued throughout the war. Early in 1645 Sir Jacob Astley requested the services of an engineer for his army in the Welsh Marches and Prince Rupert recommended a Frenchman 'who has the reputation of being a good one'.[23] A few months later the parliamentarians complained of the 'greatest want . . . of good engineers' to serve with the New Model Army and asked if one could be recruited in the Low Countries, together with two 'skilful conductors' for directing siege operations. Peter Manteau Van Dalem, a Walloon or Dutchman, was eventually appointed as the army's Engineer-General.[24]

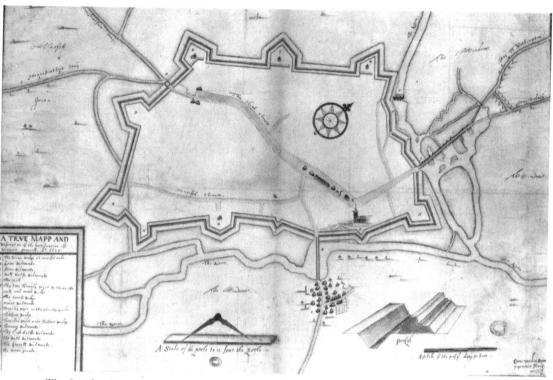

The fortifications shown on this plan of Newport Pagnell in 1644 indicate the strategic importance of this small Buckinghamshire town

As well as those who served on the staffs of the senior commanders, there were others who were appointed to individual garrisons. These had to have a range of skills. Captain Cornelius Vanderboone was 'engineer & master of the fireworks, petards, granadoes & mortar pieces' at Newport Pagnell.[25] Others were contracted directly to the civilian administrations of the towns, rather than through the army commands. Great Yarmouth hired a foreign professional to manage its defences.[26] Perhaps the best-known example is that of Johann Rosworm, a German engineer who had seen service in the Low Countries. He was hired by the citizens of Manchester in the summer of 1642 to organise the town's defences. This he did, directing the successful resistance to Lord Strange's forces. He was rewarded with an extended contract at an annual salary of £60, and it is because of his complaints regarding his pay arrears that so much is known about his six-year-long service there.[27]

Although there was a shortage of English soldiers with specialist skills, there had been a considerable interest in military affairs during the period before the Civil War. It was reflected in the establishment of military companies. The 'Society practising Armes in the Artillery Garden' in the City of London, founded in 1537, was revived in 1610, and similar companies were created in Westminster, Southwark and seven provincial towns during the next twenty years.

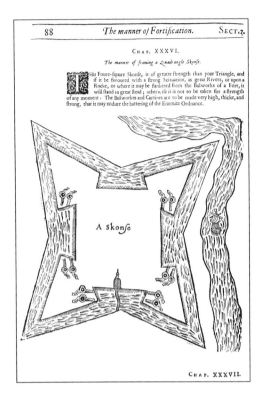

Robert Ward's Animadversions of Warre, *published in 1639, contains a wide-ranging account of military practices. His illustration of a 'Quadrangle Skonse' shows the typical bastion, the key element in the fortifications that were evolved in the sixteenth and seventeenth centuries to withstand artillery fire. The best surviving example, at Newark, is shown on p. 128*

They provided officers for the militia and took a practical interest in military training, as well as serving as forums in which the martial affairs and theories of the day could be debated. Their membership included the authors of some of the best training manuals of the period.[28]

Military literature was an expanding genre. Many of the textbooks and manuals of instruction published in England were direct translations of, or were based upon, foreign works. In addition to the books in English, the works of continental authors also circulated in their original languages. Although such books were largely theoretical, many authors illustrated their ideas with examples from contemporary warfare, and in some cases from personal experience. Some works covered the general conduct of warfare, while others specialised in such topics as fortification, artillery, pyrotechnics or drill. The interest in 'artificial fireworks' was such that some writers devoted a section of their work to the subject, and a number of books dealt almost exclusively with the topic. These included Thomas Malthus's *A Treatise of Artificial Fire-Workes* (1629), which described many of their military applications, and John Babington's *Pyrotechnia* (1635), which described fireworks for pleasure and entertainment.

There was a smaller literature on notable military actions, the experiences of individuals, or news of current events. Such works provided the reader with an impression of the conduct, rather than the theory, of warfare. In 1627 two English translations of Hugo's description of the siege of Breda appeared, one of which achieved considerable popularity,[29] and accounts of a number of the other major sieges of the period were published. Among the memoirs of Englishmen who had served abroad were Sir Roger Williams's narrative of the years he had spent campaigning in the Low Countries, which was published in 1618, and Sir Francis Vere's record of the same conflict, which did not appear in print until 1657.[30] Robert Monro's account of his experiences with the Scots regiment in the Swedish service in Germany was issued in 1637, at a time when there was much interest in those campaigns. It contained descriptions of the deliberate firing of a town to protect the castle which he was defending, the destruction of the suburbs of Frankfort-on-Oder before the siege in 1631, an accidental fire that began there when the city had been captured, and an example of the punitive burning of a town.[31] His lively account must have helped to give readers a vivid picture of operations in the German wars. Popular interest in the Thirty Years' War was also fuelled by a number of pamphlets published in London during the 1630s. The corantos and newsbooks of the period also carried news about battles and sieges, as well as other information on military matters.[32]

The reader was, therefore, well provided with material relating to military affairs. There was an increasing interest in the subject during the late 1630s, and the market for military books was clearly a growing one. In the first thirty-five years of the century, sixty such books were published in English, but between 1635 and 1642 a further thirty-three appeared. The Civil War period saw the re-issue of several earlier works, specifically aimed at the officer corps on both sides. Henry Hexham's *The Principles of the Art Militarie Practised in the Warres of the United Netherlands* and his *An Appendix of the Quarter for the ransoming of Officers of all Qualities, and Souldiers, concluded betweene the King of Spayne his side, and the side of the States General of the United Netherlands* were both published initially in 1637 and were re-issued in 1642 and 1643 respectively. Also in 1643, there was a new edition of Thomas Smith's *The Art of Gunnery*, which had first appeared in 1600, and of books by William Bourne, Gervase Markham, and William Barriffe, all first published before 1642. Bourne's *The Arte Of Shooting In Great Ordnance* had originally been published in 1587, and its 1643 edition was issued with Robert Norton's *The Gunners Dialogue*.[33]

The 1640s also produced new specialist books, using incidents from the Civil War as illustrative examples. They were drawn upon by David Papillon, an architect and military engineer of Huguenot extraction, whose *A Practicall Abstract of the Arts, of Fortification and Assailing* (1645) was dedicated to Sir Thomas Fairfax and dealt with an important aspect of the conflict. Papillon's view was that 'foreign fortifications' could not be fully reproduced in the circumstances of the English Civil War because there was not enough time or resources to erect or adequately garrison them. He also criticised the extent to which suburbs and hamlets close to fortifications had been destroyed during the Civil War, complaining that engineers were too ready to comply with 'those in authoritie, or with the selfe-conceited men of a Garrison'. But his supervision of the improvement of Gloucester's fortifications came after the city's suburbs had been destroyed. Another author whose information came from experience of the war was Nathaniel Nye, described as 'Mathematician, Master Gunner of the City of Worcester' on the title page of his *The Art of Gunnery*, published in 1647. This

Several books were published during the 1640s by those with practical experience of the Civil Wars. David Papillon was a military engineer who improved the fortifications at Gloucester

book contains much practical information on the use of artillery, and refers to his own experiences at the siege of Worcester in the previous year, incidentally providing evidence for the extent to which its suburbs had been destroyed.[34]

The number of works relating to warfare published both before and during the Civil War indicates that there was a considerable market amongst a readership that included not only the specialist, but also the amateur or 'armchair soldier'.[35] Most landed families possessed libraries of some kind by 1640 and, if Kent was at all typical, at least two-thirds of the urban gentry and professional men were book owners at the same date.[36] Because of the element of military instruction in the education of contemporary gentlemen, their collections commonly included some relevant titles. Many of those who provided the leadership in the coming conflict should have been aware of at least a part of the literature available, even if they lacked practical experience. Edward Harley, a future colonel in the parliamentarian forces, was one of those who felt the need to brush up on his knowledge of military practices as the war approached. His bookseller's account prepared in March 1642 shows that Harley had recently bought eleven books on military subjects, including Machiavelli's *The Art of War*, Hexham's *Military Discipline*, Monro's *Expedition with the Worthy Scots Regiment. . .* and, fresh from the press, John Cruso's *Castramentation, Or The Measuring Out Of The Quarters For The Encamping of an Army*.[37] The diary kept by Richard Symonds of the king's lifeguard of horse while on campaign includes references to Shute's *Heroicke Acts of his Excellencie of Prince Maurice of Nassau*, suggesting that either he had a copy of the book to hand, or was very familiar with its contents.[38]

Those with an informed interest in contemporary warfare would have been aware of the techniques employed and would have known the circumstances in which property was destroyed for military reasons. How this knowledge was translated into operational conduct is more uncertain. Clearly, commanders involved in a skirmish or battle lacked the time, and presumably the inclination, to consult their manuals for advice on the appropriate manoeuvre to adopt, but those employed in preparing the fortifications of a town or other garrison, or directing a besieging force, would be able to do so. Although constrained by circumstances and mindful of their own experiences and the advice of their officers, their knowledge of the practices of war, and of appropriate precedents, may have influenced them when faced with decisions regarding the destruction of buildings.

There was also a considerable output of newsbooks, pamphlets and broadsheets that must have done much to disseminate information on the methods of contemporary warfare. This brought the conduct of the wars in the Low Countries and Germany to the attention of a wider readership than just those with a specialist interest. An earlier generation had been engrossed with the wars in the Low Countries, and particularly the sack of Antwerp by mutinous Spanish troops in 1576 in the 'Spanish fury', when about 1,000 houses were destroyed and 8,000 lives were lost. Although the campaigns there remained of considerable interest to British observers when they resumed in 1621, and the region provided the yardstick by which fortifications were judged, popular attention switched to the Thirty Years' War and the progress of the fighting in Germany, especially during the 'Swedish phase' in the 1630s. The incident which attracted most notice and caused widespread horror was the burning of the protestant city of Magdeburg and the death of perhaps as many as 20,000 of its citizens, following its capture by Imperialist troops in 1631. Public consciousness in protestant Europe was profoundly affected by this catastrophe (more than 260 items relating to the disaster were published) and it was still a fairly fresh memory in the mid-1640s.[39] The events which followed the royalist capture of Leicester in 1645 were compared to it by parliamentarians, although the difference in scale was acknowledged.[40] Such publications as the newsletter *The Swedish Intelligencer* and Vincent's *The Lamentations of Germany*, which appeared in 1638, drew attention to the excesses of the soldiery in the continental wars.[41] To an avid reader such as the London puritan woodturner Nehemiah Wallington this literature provided ample evidence of the destructive potential of the imminent Civil War.[42] Evidence of the nature of the German wars also came from the testimony of refugees. As late as 1642 the London Drapers' Company gave £6 13s. 4d. to a citizen of Magdeburg 'after his long suffering, misery and sickness, which befell him in his hard usage upon the late lamentable bloody and cruel massacre'.[43]

Both those whose reading was confined to the more lurid propagandist material and the readers of military texts would have anticipated that the impact of the Civil War upon the civilian population would include the destruction of property. Their different perspectives and sources of information may have led them to a differing interpretation of the reasons for such destruction, however. The general reader of the news from Germany may have had the impression that what was to be expected was punitive, if not actually wanton, destruction carried out by a hostile soldiery whose wrath was chiefly directed against civilians. The more specialised student who had digested the professional literature, and someone who had experience of warfare, would have been aware that there were several circumstances which contained the potential for the destruction of property, that punitive burning was only one of them, and that preparations for the defence of a town or garrison were in fact a more common cause of the clearance of buildings.

To the vast majority of the population the destruction of property was one of the effects of the continental wars, drawn to their attention chiefly through occasional appeals for assistance contained in the charitable briefs read after divine service. Such pleas for aid were far outnumbered by petitions from individuals and communities in England whose houses had burnt down. Indeed, the destruction of buildings was generally associated not with the activities of soldiers, but with accidental fires, partly because it was so long since there had been any military campaigns on English soil. The rebellions in 1549 in Norfolk and the West Country culminated in the sieges of Norwich and Exeter, and in the course of those operations a considerable amount of property was burnt.[44] The only other incident during the period in which a town suffered as a result of military action came in July 1595, when a Spanish force landed from four galleys and burnt much of Penzance and Newlyn.[45] Thereafter, no conflict caused the destruction of property until the preparations at Newcastle-upon-Tyne to resist the Scottish forces during the Bishops' Wars.[46] There were, in contrast, twenty

THE

PRACTISE
of Fortification:

Wherein is fhewed the manner of
fortifying in all forts of fcituations , with
the confiderations to be vfed in delining,
and making of royal Frontiers, Skon-
ces , and renforcing of ould
walled Townes.

Compiled in a moft eafie, and compendious method,
by Paule Iue. Gent.

Imprinted at London by Thomas Orwin , for Thomas
Man, and Toby Cooke. 1589.

Paul Ive was a military engineer and the author
of this, the first book on fortification by an
Englishman

major town fires during the period 1580–1640, the most damaging ones being those at Nantwich in 1583, Darlington in 1585, Wolverhampton in 1590, Stratford-upon-Avon in 1594, 1595 and 1614, Tiverton in 1598 and 1612, Bury St Edmunds in 1608, Dorchester in 1613 and 1625, Wymondham in 1615, and at Banbury in 1628.[47]

The most common causes of these and many other fires were the widespread use of combustible building materials, particularly thatch, inadequate chimneys, the practice of trades with a high fire risk in unsuitable premises, and the stocks of fuel, corn and hay that were kept within the built-up area. Such disasters were widely interpreted as acts of God: to a puritan like Wallington they were punishments visited upon a sinful and wicked people and warnings to reform that should not be disregarded.[48] Despite such apparent fatalism, there was also an awareness that the dangers could be reduced, if not completely overcome. During the sixteenth and early seventeenth centuries many towns took steps to control fire hazards and orders were also made for the provision of fire-fighting equipment, which consisted of leather buckets, firehooks – used like grappling irons to unroof buildings – and ladders. In the course of the sixteenth century hand-held squirts were introduced and, a major innovation, in the second quarter of the seventeenth century the first fire-engines were brought into use, initially in London and then in provincial towns such as Norwich, Worcester and Devizes.[49]

Either as a result of the attention given to fire prevention – the Privy Council made a number of relevant orders during the early seventeenth century[50] – or simply because of good fortune, the years preceding the Civil War were relatively free from major fire disasters, despite a run of especially warm summers in the mid-1630s. In August 1633 a fire in the small Dorset town of Bere Regis burned down fifty houses, but the remainder of the decade passed without a serious blaze, and the next recorded one of any size occurred at Yeovil in July 1640, when eighty-three houses were burnt down.[51] The last major town fire before the Civil War destroyed a considerable number of buildings in the principal street of Stratford-upon-Avon in 1641, causing damage valued at £8,619.[52] Thus, both deliberate destruction during military operations and major fires were becoming increasingly remote by the early 1640s.

Those who anticipated a damaging Civil War must have been aware that such a situation was about to change. There was considerable apprehension in 1642 that the coming war would have an impact similar to the conflicts in Germany. While the more exaggerated fears born of the propagandist publications of the 1630s were not to be realised, many of the elements inherent in the nature of warfare in the mid-seventeenth century which had damaging effects upon the civilian population were to be reproduced during the wars in England and Wales. Once the campaigns in the autumn of 1642 had produced a stalemate, the initial war of movement became one where both sides sought to consolidate their hold on territory and resources, fortifying bases from which to do so. These had to be reduced one by one, and the war years were punctuated by more than 300 sieges, ranging from the capture of minor garrisons by relatively small forces to the formal investment of such well-defended towns as Hull, Newark, Worcester, Exeter, Chester, Newcastle-upon-Tyne and York.

The major sieges were substantial operations: the Scots' investment of Carlisle lasted for eight months in 1644–5 and the siege of Newark for more than five months in 1645–6. The parliamentarians managed to combine their armies and bring 30,000 men against York in 1644, and they concentrated 16,000 at the siege of Newark two years later.[53] These were unusually large forces at Civil War sieges, but are indicative of the numbers of men engaged in the fighting. It has been estimated that perhaps 10 per cent of adult males were under arms during the campaigning seasons of 1643, 1644 and 1645, with 20–25 per cent serving as soldiers at some stage of the conflict. The impression of a large-scale war is strengthened by the assessment that during the Civil War there were 85,000 deaths caused directly by military actions and at least 100,000 others attributable to disease.[54] Such a conflict, lasting for six years, was bound to have a significant impact on the population, which had to support the armies and garrisons with pay, provisions, transport and quarters. It also contained considerable potential for the destruction of property.

CHAPTER TWO

The Causes of Destruction

... when such an exigency happens, that a City must be fired, or both it and
the kingdom lost or hazarded, it is a foolish cruelty, not Christian mercy, to
be over-pitiful.
'The Trial of Colonel Nathaniel Fiennes, 1643': T.B. Howells, State Trials, *IV,*
1816

The English Civil War began with a series of sporadic and inconclusive
encounters in the summer of 1642. The raising of the king's standard at
Nottingham on 22 August was a symbolic act and did not mark the start of the
conflict. The first actions had taken place in July and preparations for the war,
which had come to be regarded as inevitable, had been going on for some time.
Many towns had anticipated the outbreak of hostilities by renewing their
magazines of arms and gunpowder and making preliminary arrangements for
defence.[1] These included the removal of structures close to the defences: in July
the corporation of Great Yarmouth ordered the demolition of buildings under the
town walls and in the suburbs.[2] The first sieges also took place in the summer
months. Early in July Sir John Hotham, the parliamentarian governor of Hull,
ordered that houses outside the walls should be destroyed, and the royalist
assailants burnt the mills, to deprive the defenders of their resources, and also
attempted to set the town on fire. The more formal siege of Hull in September
included a bombardment by the besiegers, and early in that month a
parliamentarian force captured Portsmouth after a brief investment, during which
they subjected the town to a cannonade that destroyed much of St Thomas's
church.[3]

   During the remainder of the summer and through the autumn the war began
to take shape, with efforts to gain control of territory, and plundering raids in
which money, arms, horses and other supplies were secured.[4] The early
manoeuvres of the field armies produced the battle of Edgehill on 23 October and
the subsequent royalist march on London that was checked at Turnham Green.
Parliamentarian propagandists drew parallels between the behaviour of the
royalist soldiers during their capture of Brentford, when some houses were set on

The Right Worshipfull Sr Iohn Hotham Kt Gouernour of Kingston vpon HVLL

Sir John Hotham was the governor of Hull during the royalist sieges of 1642. His improvements to the fortifications included the addition of earthworks to the town walls and the demolition of the suburbs

fire, and their incursions into Surrey, and the worst excesses of the continental wars.[5] As they withdrew along the Thames valley in mid-November, royalist troops burnt part of Sir Thomas Hampson's house at Taplow.[6] In the following month Prince Rupert's forces captured Marlborough and sacked it, setting houses on fire in the process.[7] Thus, all of the elements that were to lead to the destruction of property during the Civil War were present in its early months: the removal of buildings for defensive reasons, or to prevent the enemy from benefiting from them, and destruction during raids, other offensive operations and bombardments of besieged places. There was also the increased danger of accidental fires. While part of the Earl of Essex's army was billeted in Coventry at the end of August 1642, a fire broke out one night at a baker's close to the soldiers' magazine. It was extinguished 'and no great harme done' but, understandably, 'the citizens were much affrighted'.[8]

The garrisoning of many towns during the war led to the renovation and modernisation of their fortifications and in some places to the construction of completely new defences.[9] The walls and towers of some towns had not been maintained and so had fallen into disrepair, or they had been dismantled, while the moats and ditches had gradually filled up and the land had been made into gardens. Not all towns had allowed their defences to deteriorate, however, for town walls had a certain symbolic significance as a mark of urbanity, as well as a practical defensive function that had been put to the test at Exeter and Norwich during the rebellions in 1549. The walls at York were substantially intact, as were those at Hereford, for when Nehemiah Wharton, a London apprentice serving in the Earl of Essex's army, arrived there in September 1642 he found that the town was 'environed with a strong wall . . . with five gates'.[10] Where medieval walls were reasonably well preserved they could be incorporated into the new defences and shielded by a bank of earth thrown up against them, to absorb artillery fire and protect the masonry. If this proved inadequate and was penetrated, so that the walls were shattered, a similar lining of earth on the inside provided further protection. Redoubts or bastions were added, projecting from the walls, or standing some way forward of them, so that there was no dead ground and the whole of the defensive line was within reach of the defenders' guns. Outlying forts were built where necessary to incorporate features threatening to the defences if occupied by a hostile force. For example, at Worcester the 'Great Sconce' was built on a low hill to the south of the town, connected by bulwarks to the main perimeter, and there was a number of similar forts at York.[11] Such works required the removal of buildings that were close to or against the existing walls. It was also desirable that there should be an unobstructed passage along the inside of a wall, to allow the soldiers to patrol the whole perimeter and to make it easier for troops to be moved swiftly from one sector to another to reinforce threatened points during an assault. Such a gap also provided a distinct zone separating the areas under civilian control from those within the military's jurisdiction. For these reasons, buildings and trees along the lines of town walls were cleared away. In November 1642 an order was issued for the demolition of all the 'Sheds, on the Outside of the Walls' of the City of London. The width of the belt of cleared ground at Exeter was sixteen feet and it was ruled that all trees within that distance of the city walls were to be cut down.[12]

The legend on the map reads:

1 The Cathedral or Colledge Church
2 S.t Peters Church
3 S.t Andrews Church
4 S.t Martins Church
5 S.t Nicholas Church
6 S.t Clements Church
7 S.t Albans Church
8 S.t Gilos Church
9 Swithins Church
10 S.t Iohns
11 All S.tt Church
12 The Fort Royall
13 Castle hill
14 Byshops Palace
15 Castle Colledge
16 Sudbury
17 Sudbury
18 S.t Martin
19 Fore Gat
20 Friers G.
21 Frog-Ga
22 S.t Nighs Str
23 Friers St
24 Pitch Cr
25 Bridgcorn
26 The Water
27 The Key

An Exact Ground=Plot of y.e City of **WORCESTER**, *As it stood fortify'd 3.Sept.1651.*

The Civil War defences of Worcester comprised earthworks added to the city walls and a new fort and works on the south side of the city

The erection of new works also caused the destruction of property. The extensive features of the bastion trace occupied far more land than the medieval defences which they replaced or supplemented. Even the relatively unsophisticated earthwork fortifications characteristic of the smaller towns and villages often necessitated the clearance of some buildings before they could be raised, and at many places the initial works were later developed and extended. At Exeter, Gloucester and Bridgwater the ditches alone were thirty feet across and the bank and the *glacis* added considerably to the width.[13] Only rarely did the defensive lines lie so far from the built-up area that no property had to be demolished during their construction. Those at Bristol, Plymouth and Chester did not cut through the suburbs, but the very extensive fortifications at London required the removal of houses at Whitechapel, Shoreditch and Bloomsbury, and the large fort constructed on the east side of Magdalen Bridge at Oxford led to the demolition of a number of buildings.[14] Generally, the building of earthwork

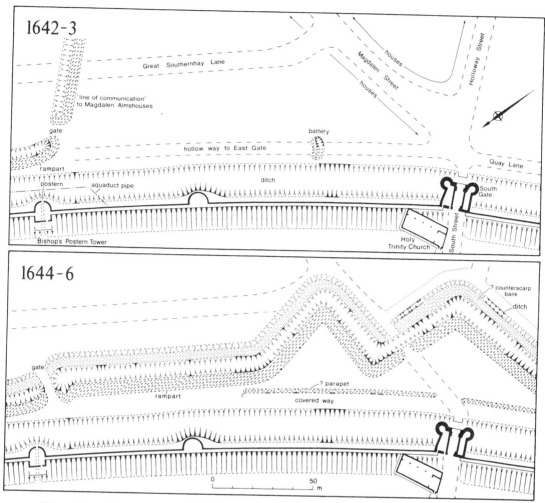

These plans of the defences at the South Gate, Exeter, in 1642–3 and their more extensive successors of 1644–6 are based upon evidence from excavations

defences could not be accomplished without the destruction of buildings, the demolition of fences and walls and the cutting down of hedges and orchards. Moreover, because the works were faced with turf to protect them against erosion, pasture land was spoiled over a much wider area than that actually occupied by the fortifications, and the growth of a new sward that was thick enough to be grazed may have taken several years. The land that was damaged in this way was of comparatively high value because of its proximity to the town, and so the costs to landowners and tenants was considerable. There were complaints from many places that the construction of earthworks had ruined gardens, orchards and pasture enclosures. Both the larger towns, such as Exeter, Bristol, Canterbury and Leicester, and the smaller ones, including Carmarthen, Barnstaple, Aylesbury and Olney, were affected in this way.[15]

The removal of property to provide the defenders with a clear field of fire around the fortifications produced destruction over a wider area. It was desirable to compel attackers to cross open ground when making an assault, exposing them to the defenders' fire. To leave buildings standing around the defences invited attacking troops to use the cover they provided to get close to the fortifications. The parliamentarian force which captured Malmesbury in 1644 made full use of the houses within pistol shot of the defences, 'by which meanes our men were brought safe under the shelter of their workes'.[16] It was obviously preferable to clear such buildings away so as not to help assailants making their approach. In some cases the removal of property and all other features that would assist an enemy or obstruct the defenders' fire was carried out with considerable thoroughness. At Bridgwater in 1645 the troops of the New Model preparing to attack the town found that the clearance had been so complete that there was 'not a clod' to provide them with cover.[17] This had a deterrent value, for assaults launched in such circumstances were likely to lead to a high number of casualties

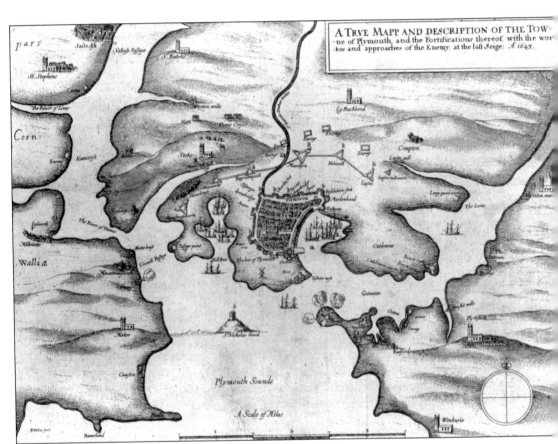

This plan of Plymouth in 1643, engraved by Wenceslaus Hollar, shows the extensive fortifications and the position of the besiegers' works and batteries

and for that reason troops were often understandably reluctant to take part. The royalists lost many men during their capture of Bristol in 1643, especially on the south side of the city, where the attack was made across 'a plain level before the line'. The loss of life amongst the soldiers on that occasion had an adverse effect upon the morale of the army, despite the ultimate success of the operation.[18]

The clearance of property around the defences had a number of other advantages for a garrison. By depriving besiegers of cover close to the fortifications, the effectiveness of their marksmen using small arms was reduced because they were compelled either to fire from a range where they were ineffective, or to use positions that exposed them to the defenders' own fire. For similar reasons it was difficult and hazardous to set up artillery batteries within an effective range. Where there was a lack of protection, a besieging army would dig trenches and use them to approach the fortifications, but they did not provide the same degree of shelter as did buildings or walls, were liable to flooding, and took time and labour to construct. Similar difficulties were encountered if it was decided to undermine the defences and explode a mine. This was one of the most promising methods available to besiegers and, by removing all cover close to the fortifications, defenders forced the miners to begin their tunnelling some distance away. The further that the tunnels had to be driven, the longer the work took and the greater the likelihood that the mining would be detected and defeated by counter-mining.

Another reason for the destruction of property around the defensive perimeter was that it deprived the besiegers of accommodation. A force that opted to undertake a siege rather than an assault needed quarters around the town or garrison that was besieged. The numbers to be accommodated could be considerable and included the various groups of camp followers as well as the soldiers themselves. But not all of a besieging force had to be quartered close by, for it was advisable to retain some of it in reserve, to keep communications open, prevent a relief army from interrupting the siege, and to bring in supplies. Pioneers building earthworks, artillerymen manning the batteries and troops stationed to repel sallies and ensure the effectiveness of the blockade would all have to be billeted close to the defences, however. If all of the buildings had been destroyed, alternative shelter had to be provided in tents or huts, which had a number of disadvantages. For one thing, they were insubstantial: the huts occupied by the Scottish troops besieging Newcastle-upon-Tyne were built of turf, clay, straw and wattles, and each hut contained just one room.[19] If the weather was fine such structures were not especially inconvenient, but when it was wet they were conducive to illness and low morale among the besieging troops. Conditions at the siege of Hull were so bad that an observer thought it was probable that the besiegers would rot before the besieged were starved.[20] Such an encampment was particularly inadequate in winter and the conditions for the soldiers quartered in it could be very unpleasant. Generally, it was recognised that 'frost and snow is ill for soldiers to lye in siege'.[21] An efficient governor would not only have destroyed buildings for some distance around before a siege began, but would also have removed the materials and cut down nearby woods, depriving the besiegers of fuel and forcing them to divert some of their time and energies to supplying their needs from further afield. Another drawback of a temporary encampment was that it was likely to be insanitary. The risk of typhus or other diseases breaking out amongst the troops was much greater when they were quartered in such conditions than when they were properly housed. There was also the danger of an accident, such as the fire which swept through the huts of the parliamentary army besieging Worcester in 1646.[22] The morale of a force that had to live in such conditions for any length of time was likely to be low and the number of desertions correspondingly high.

Some buildings gave particular problems to a garrison. This was especially true of churches, for their construction was such that they could be fortified as strong points from which operations could be launched against the defences, and they were capacious enough to house a considerable number of men. Those with towers provided ready-made observation posts, giving the besiegers vantage points from which to watch the defenders' movements and also useful positions for marksmen. It was even possible to manoeuvre the smallest artillery pieces on to church towers, and although the weight of the shot which they discharged made them no more than irritants to a garrison, governors were anxious to avoid

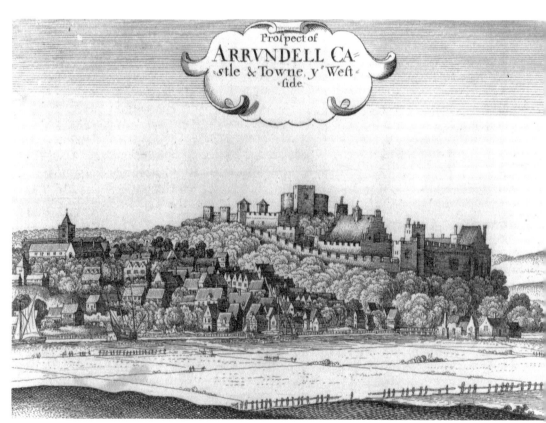

The parliamentarian besiegers of Arundel Castle used the church tower as a vantage point from which to fire at the defenders. Wenceslaus Hollar's view of the town is dated 1644

such irritations if possible. At Arundel in 1643 Waller's troops hauled two sakers (which fired balls of 5–6 lbs) up the tower of St Nicholas's church and they and 'divers musquetiers . . . played hotly on the enemy, which appeared on the top of the castle'. The tower of St John's church at Chester was not demolished and caused great inconvenience to the besieged during the siege of 1645–6, particularly through the musketeers who were posted there. Similarly, musket fire from the steeple of St Nicholas's church at Nottingham presented a serious difficulty to the defenders in the castle and made it hazardous for them to operate their battery.[23] Other substantially built structures which could be fortified or provide accommodation were potential liabilities. An example was the 'strong stone building' in the northern suburb of Worcester, which was said, surely with some exaggeration, to be able to hold 500 men.[24]

Where the removal of buildings was decided upon for these reasons, the suburbs beyond the defences were almost invariably destroyed. Sir Balthazar Gerbier likened the process to the amputation of a leg 'to save the body of a mortall Gangreen',[25] and that was not inappropriate, for the characteristic form of the early modern suburb was an elongated ribbon development extending some distance from the town. Most towns had at least one such suburb and the larger ones had several. Typical examples were the Foregate suburb on the north side of Worcester and those outside the New Gate and West Gate at Newcastle-upon-Tyne. Towns standing at the bridging point of a river commonly had a suburb on the far side of the bridge, such as Handbridge on the south side of the Dee at Chester, St Thomas's across the Exe Bridge at Exeter, and Frankwell on the west side and the Abbey Foregate district on the east side of Shrewsbury. The extended form of such suburbs meant that a long defensive line was required if they were to be enclosed within the fortifications. There were two important factors that militated against such a line. One was that it was expensive to build in terms of both labour and money. London's extensive fortifications consisted of two dozen forts connected by eleven miles of banks and ditches and they were made possible by its uniquely large labour force, with thousands – one report said 20,000 – turning out daily in the spring of 1643 to construct the earthworks. No other city could muster anything like that manpower, even when labour was brought in from the surrounding countryside.[26] Some contribution towards the cost of the materials and tools required could be obtained by taking a levy from those whose properties would be protected. The royalists at Oxford included the Holywell district within the city's fortifications, demanding £300 to help pay for the extra length of line required, justifying the impost on the grounds that if the area had been excluded the buildings there would have been demolished.[27] The second drawback of a long line was the large numbers of soldiers and of artillery pieces required to man it. The Venetian ambassador pointed out that London's long lines would be difficult to defend, for that reason.[28]

There was one consideration that favoured building the works some distance from a town, however, and that was to protect it from the besiegers' artillery fire and so reduce the risk of its being set on fire. This gave some reassurance to the townsmen, which may have been a factor to set against the military problems posed by a long line. Nevertheless, few places could justify such lengthy fortifications as those at London and Oxford,[29] the headquarters of the respective sides, Chester and Bristol. The line at Chester was later shortened to a more defensible length, but even so was breached without great difficulty during the parliamentarian assault in 1645.[30] The extent of Bristol's fortifications was determined by the need to incorporate the high ground on the north side of the city, which would have made the garrison's position untenable in enemy hands. The result was defences that were almost five miles long, and were so extensive that the parliamentarian garrison in 1643 was too small to be able to man them properly and so the soldiers 'stood very thin upon the line'.[31] The topography and the length of the fortifications made defence of the city difficult and the northern perimeter was breached during the assaults in 1643 and 1645. The example of Bristol shows why governors preferred to defend the shortest possible line, which in most places was achieved by excluding and clearing the suburbs. Only those few suburbs which lay laterally along the line of the walls, such as the housing in Gillygate at York, were safe from destruction in the light of such considerations.

The breadth of the cleared zone outside the defences was dictated partly by the terrain, but presumably it would have extended at least far enough from the fortifications to cover the range of the largest artillery pieces, and ideally would have been much wider than that. Buildings were cleared for 600 yards outside the Fore Gate at Worcester and for 750 yards from the East Gate at Exeter.[32] Contemporary writers recommended that structures, trees and hedges within half a mile of the defences should be removed.[33] The garrison in Lyme Regis regretted not destroying two farmhouses, one of them a quarter of a mile from the town and the other half a mile from it, because the besiegers fitted them up as bases for their operations. At Wallingford the royalist defenders were reported to have pulled down houses and cleared the ground to provide uninterrupted visibility for two miles on the west side of the town, and as the Oxford garrison prepared for a siege in 1645 it was said to be preparing to pull down all houses within three miles of the defences.[34]

It is clear from this that villages close to a defended town were also liable to suffer loss of property, for they could provide shelter and materials for a besieging force. Prince Rupert's preparations for a siege at Bristol in 1645 included the burning of Clifton to the north and Bedminster to the south of the city. The parliamentarians claimed that several other villages were only saved by the timely appearance of Fairfax's army.[35] Boughton and Chrisleton near to Chester were destroyed by the garrison in the course of the war, and the defenders of Wareham burned down nearby Stoborough.[36] Similarly, a force from King's Lynn attempted to burn down Gaywood, a mile away, where a part of the besieging force was billeted, and they did succeed in destroying an almshouse and a number of other houses.[37] These villages all lay within two or three miles of a fortified town, but places further away also suffered from this type of destruction. Royalist soldiers from Reading destroyed property at Twyford and Wokingham, respectively five and eight miles away, apparently in order to deprive the parliamentarians of quarters.[38]

Buildings which had escaped the defenders' clearances could nevertheless be removed by a besieging army when it arrived and conducted a regular siege.

*This detail from a plan illustrating the siege
of Newark in 1645–6 (see p. 84) shows the
defences constructed by the besiegers around
the village of Winthorpe*

While the besiegers would wish to preserve surviving buildings for their
magazines and quarters, the construction of their own earthworks was liable to
cause the destruction of some structures. Forts were built to protect the camps
and artillery batteries, both from sallies by the garrison and attacks from a
relieving army. They were connected by lines of banks and ditches, enclosing and
sealing off the besieged place. This led to the clearance of buildings and the
destruction of gardens, trees, walls and hedges to level the nearby ground, in the
same way as did the construction of the actual defences. Those Civil War sieges
that were major operations lasting for many weeks employed all the practices of a
formal siege of the period. Many of the lines and works were built in open
countryside or on land previously cleared by the defenders, although outlying
villages were seized and fortified, as were buildings that had not been removed.
The extensive earthworks constructed by the army besieging Newark in 1645–6
included four forts that enclosed villages within them. Similarly, the
parliamentarian army at Colchester in 1648 surrounded the town with forts,
capturing nearby Greenstead church before the defenders could destroy it, and
enclosing it in a star-shaped fort.[39] The effects of the construction of earthwork
fortifications therefore extended quite widely at those places which sustained a
major siege.

The besiegers also needed materials for the buildings they required for
accommodation and guardhouses, to replace those destroyed by the defenders.

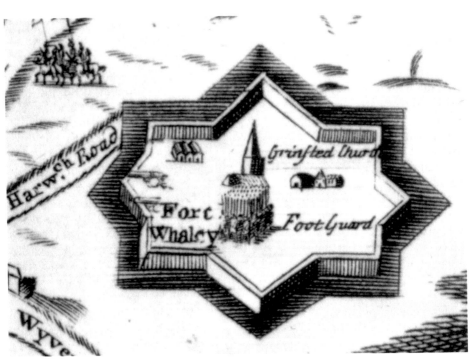

This detail from a siege plan of Colchester (see p. 44) shows Greenstead church, which was enclosed with earthwork defences by the parliamentarian army besieging Colchester in 1648

Some buildings may have survived the garrison's precautionary clearances, but were inconveniently sited, perhaps being too far from the besieged place to be useful. These could be demolished and reconstructed where they were needed. The owner of two houses a few miles from Bristol complained that although they had escaped the garrison's attentions, they were 'totally ruined' and their materials used to make huts for the soldiers of the New Model who had quartered close by while besieging the city. A parliamentarian soldier whose house near to Dartmouth was still standing when the New Model arrived before the town indignantly reported that it was then 'torn downe by our owne armey'.[40]

The defensive destruction considered so far has related to property that lay on or beyond the outer defences of towns. Damage was also done within towns and to villages that stood adjacent to a country garrison. Governors often fortified a stronghold either inside or on the edge of a town, to serve as a secure headquarters and magazine that could be administered separately from the town itself, and a place that could be defended if the town was captured or the garrison was insufficient to man its fortifications. The topography of some towns was such that they could not easily be fortified by the construction of earthworks, or their strategic importance was such that it was not deemed worthwhile to expend the effort required to provide them with such defences. Nevertheless, they could be held by the establishment of citadels. It was an advantage to the military if the stronghold lay outside the legal jurisdiction of the civic authorities, as Banbury

Castle did, for example. It was usually castles which were most suitable for such citadels, and they served that purpose at Bristol, Chester, Nottingham, Oxford, Scarborough, Dudley and Bridgnorth. Some had been converted into residences and the walls neglected, but they could be refortified fairly easily in most cases.

Where there was no castle, other buildings or groups served the purpose, provided that they were large enough, could be adapted for defence and stood some way apart from the main body of the town. Houses at Woodstock, Chipping Campden, Wellington and Faringdon were used in this way, and at Lichfield the cathedral close was a self-contained and defensible enclave that was used as a stronghold throughout the Civil War.[41] Churches, castles and houses in or close to country towns and villages were also fitted up as garrisons and some were given earthwork defences. At Highworth, Wiltshire, the church was protected by a line and bulwarks, and the royalist garrison at Shelford House in Nottinghamshire was protected by 'a very strong Bullworke, and a greate trench without, in most places wett at the bottome . . .'.[42] The works at Phyllis Court at Henley-on-Thames were extensive enough to have 300 foot and a troop of horse quartered within them. They were described as 'strong & regular, & the Thames brought rownd the fort, in a large graft [ditch]'.[43]

The removal of buildings from around such citadels was as necessary as was the clearance of suburban property – to deprive an enemy force of accommodation, cover, and shelter for undermining, and to allow the garrison a clear field of fire. There was an important difference, however, for while the destruction of suburbs left alternative accommodation within the defences, the removal of buildings around a citadel was likely to involve much of the urban area, or an entire village, leaving the garrison itself short of quarters and driving away the civilian population which serviced it. The space available within a citadel was necessarily limited and was restricted to the soldiery. Clearance in such circumstances was a very serious step. Most governors had to be content with removing the structures from the immediate vicinity of a stronghold as a first stage that could be extended if the place was threatened. In December 1642 the Common Council at Bristol agreed to investigate what could be done to compensate those whose 'houses or hovells' built 'against or about' the castle walls would have to be demolished.[44] At the same time as the suburbs of Bridgnorth were cleared, the houses that stood between the castle and the town were also pulled down, on the governor's instructions, and at Woodstock houses near the manor house were demolished.[45]

The constraints which applied when there was no threat to the place were removed once an enemy force threatened a siege or captured the town or village. Purely military considerations then came to the fore and much of the property close to the citadel was liable to be destroyed, preferably in advance or as the defenders withdrew within their perimeter. Twice during the war Lord Ogle found it impossible to hold Winchester against parliamentary forces and, as his troops retreated into the castle, they set fire to houses close by. It was that part of the city near to the castle which suffered the worst destruction, with the 'most part' of the parish of St Clement reported to be burnt by the end of the siege of 1645.[46] When the royalists penetrated the outer defences of Bristol during their assault in 1643, Nathaniel Fiennes, the governor, contemplated abandoning the city and holding out in the castle, which was fitted up as a citadel. This would have involved setting the city on fire, but Fiennes opted for surrender rather than continued resistance. He was later condemned for his decision on the grounds that it would have been preferable to burn 'the greatest part of the City . . . to preserve the castle and other parts of it' rather than yield the whole place. Prince Rupert followed the same course when faced with a similar situation there two years later, but on that occasion the royalist defenders had started a number of fires before their commander requested a parley, intending to cover their withdrawal into the castle should that prove necessary.[47]

Where the destruction was not completed before a garrison was besieged in its citadel, it faced the problem of destroying the remaining buildings during sallies or by firing projectiles into the buildings. These efforts had the benefit of harassing the besiegers as well as improving the security of the citadel, but the destruction caused was likely to be less complete than if it had been effected while the garrison was still in control. One attempt by the troops besieged in Knaresborough Castle to set fire to buildings in the town resulted in only one house being destroyed, for example.[48] Similarly, the defenders of Basing House managed to fire only one house during a night-time sally, but on the following night they were more successful and claimed to have 'fired all between us and the church'.[49] Beleaguered garrisons could destroy considerable amounts of property if their actions were well planned and efficiently executed: forty houses were burnt during a sally by the garrison of Holt Castle in Denbighshire, and the royalists in the castle at Bridgnorth had a spectacular success in burning down much of the town using artillery fire.[50] A great deal of property in Banbury was destroyed by the castle's defenders in the course of the war.[51] Such defensive destruction carried out to protect a citadel was potentially very damaging.

Some defensive destruction was done with little or no preparation if a force was surprised, perhaps in an unfortified place. In such circumstances the soldiers improvised defensive positions by pulling down buildings to barricade streets. This gave time for a withdrawal to be effected, or for the preparation of more organised resistance. When the New Model launched its assault on Maidstone in 1648 it found that the streets 'were barricadoed . . . and defended with Cannon'.[52] A defeated force sometimes set fire to houses to hinder pursuit, to deter those who were chasing it and to use the smoke as a screen to conceal its retreat. This tactic was used by the royalists fleeing from the battlefields of Langport and Cheriton. As the escaping cavalry rode through Langport they set fire to houses in the town and they had some success, for Cromwell admitted that the flames had hindered the pursuit.[53] To cover the retreat from Cheriton, a small party of soldiers was left in nearby Alresford, where they set a number of houses on fire, presumably hoping both to delay the parliamentarian forces and to keep the unfriendly citizens occupied.[54]

Preventive destruction was also carried out largely for defensive reasons and involved the demolition or slighting of buildings that could be, perhaps already had been, occupied by the enemy. The possession of a building or group that could hazard a garrison, together with the area under its control, was best prevented by rendering it unusable. This was often done in anticipation, but sometimes not until the inconveniences that it caused had been demonstrated. A hostile force could interrupt communications, hinder the gathering of intelligence, disrupt supplies and impose its own taxation and demands, depriving enemy garrisons of resources. Country houses and castles were eminently suited as bases for units engaged in such duties. Villages and small towns were used in the same way, although they were not as satisfactory because they provided less security. Buildings at least some distance from concentrations of population were more easily protected and fortified than those too close to groups of houses and they could be manned by fewer troops, an important consideration when the field armies were short of soldiers.

Such garrisons could be effective in gathering resources, denying them to the enemy, subduing the civilian population, controlling strategic points, and providing a defensive ring around important towns and cities. The royalists encircled Oxford with almost a score of garrisons, most of them in country houses and castles within fifteen miles of the city, but five of them more than twenty miles away. By 1645 Gloucester had a network of a dozen satellite garrisons at ten to twenty miles around it.[55] Clearly, such a cluster could dominate a substantial area. Even a single garrison could hold sway over a hinterland roughly twenty miles in radius; a day's ride for a patrol of horse. The extent of the area could be restricted by setting up a rival garrison close by, limiting the damage done by the opposite side. In the more intensely contested areas such garrisons could be very close indeed. The parliamentarians occupied Brill, only one-and-a-half miles from the royalists in Boarstall, and were afraid that if they withdrew some of their forces their quarters would be burnt. A parliamentarian attempt to establish a garrison at Apley House, three miles from Bridgnorth, in 1644 provoked a swift retaliation from the royalists who recaptured and subsequently demolished the house.[56] Garrisons could be deliberately placed in this way to constrict the enemy's activities. The pattern was further complicated by those garrisons that were not established by the senior commanders, but were set up by officers acting in a freelance capacity and operating more or less independently with troops which they had raised. In 1645 the parliamentarian Colonel Stephens was forced to surrender 'a garrison of his own making and choosing' between Hereford and Gloucester, where he had installed a force of thirty or forty men.[57]

The activities of such garrisons increased the problems facing the civilian population. In 1644 Lincolnshire was reported to be 'a ruinated country [where] noe man hath anny thing to call his owne nor asuer himself a quiett nights slep they ar[e] so surounded with garisons both of the kings & the parliaments what the one leavs the other takes'. The villagers of Preston Bissett near Buckingham were taxed and plundered by troops from ten or twelve garrisons, none more than fifteen miles away from them. Such intense activity also affected landlords. Bulstrode Whitelocke complained that he was receiving no revenue from his estates in south Oxfordshire because his rents were 'all devoured' by the garrisons in the area.[58] Indeed, although in military terms such small garrisons provided a satisfactory return on the manpower invested in them, their conduct often aroused resentment and hostility. This was certainly the case with Henry Bard's royalists based at Campden House in Gloucestershire, for he was admitted by

Clarendon to be a 'licentious governor' who 'exercised an illimited tyranny over the whole country'.[59] In some cases the antagonism led to the open defiance of the soldiers and even to attacks upon them. The governor of Berkeley Castle reported in 1643 that parties of armed civilians had attacked royalist patrols and killed some troopers.[60]

The difficulties caused by enemy garrisons operating in this way led to the destruction of many of their bases. These were captured but could not be held by the victorious force, either because it was unable to spare the men, or the place was too remote from other friendly garrisons to be held securely. The potential damage that could be done if they were reoccupied by a hostile force also had to be assessed. Greenlands House near Henley-on-Thames was captured from the royalists in the summer of 1644 and was then 'quite levelled . . . unto the Ground' by the parliamentarians because its position was such that its garrison was able to intercept barges carrying provisions and fuel along the Thames towards London.[61] Abandoned buildings were destroyed by the defenders as they withdrew, or by the troops of the other side, to prevent their reoccupation by the enemy. When the royalists removed their garrison from Stapleton Castle, Herefordshire, in 1645 they had little option, in military terms, but to set it on fire, for the house stood in a commanding position on a spur above the Lugg valley near Presteigne.[62] Satellite garrisons generally had to be abandoned if the head garrison was captured. When the royalists took Leicester in 1645 the parliamentarians withdrew their troops from seven smaller garrisons. Similarly, if a defensive ring was shortened, then the outer garrisons were destroyed, as, for example, were the bishop's palace at Cuddesdon and Godstow House at Wolvercote when the royalists at Oxford came under increasing pressure.[63] Other buildings were demolished or seriously damaged, not because they had been garrisoned but because there was a risk that they might be. Such destruction was carried out either in the face of a real threat or simply in anticipation that such a threat might arise in the future.

The identification of potential garrisons put many places at risk, for numerous houses, castles, churches and other buildings could be adapted relatively easily to accommodate a party of troops. Even a small town was not entirely free from the threat of destruction for this reason. As early as January 1643, the king sent an order to the Earl of Northampton to the effect that as soon as he was certain that the parliamentarians were moving to occupy Banbury he should 'speedily set it on fire and . . . burn it down'. Anthony Ashley Cooper suggested a similar solution to the problem posed by Wareham, writing that it was 'absolutely necessary to pluck down the town', because it could not be easily garrisoned by parliamentarian troops and the royalists would occupy it if it was left unmanned. The hostility of the inhabitants to the parliamentary cause and the fact that it was 'extremely mean built' were further arguments that he put forward for demolishing it, though apparently these did not carry sufficient conviction and his plan was not implemented.[64] Nevertheless, many commanders did destroy property which they felt posed a potential threat to their operations, even if no enemy force had occupied, or even approached, it.

The activities of parties of soldiers operating from garrisons created the potential for property destruction, particularly if the civilian population was

The plundering soldier was an image from the contemporary continental conflicts that many observers feared would become a feature of the Civil Wars. In this woodcut of 1642 a soldier carries looted goods rather than military equipment

recalcitrant or hostile. In addition to their collection of the regular payments of the assessments and contribution, troops also carried out raids in order to levy irregular payments, expressively known in continental warfare as *Brandtschatzung*, burning-money.[65] This kind of raid was backed by the implicit threat that soldiers would fire some buildings if they did not receive at least part of their demands. Such fines were most commonly imposed on villages, but they were also levied upon small towns, such as Droitwich in Worcestershire, which on one occasion paid £40 'for saving the town'.[66] Operations of this type did not normally lead to property destruction, because it was rare for the soldiers to be given a flat refusal, and in most cases the inhabitants successfully negotiated a reduction of the sum demanded. It was not always quite that simple, however, for the civilians faced the dilemma that, if they acceded to the demands of the soldiers of one side, they would provoke a visit from those of the other, anxious not to concede that the community lay outside their control. If that happened, then the population faced the prospect of paying double levies, one to the royalists and one to the parliamentarians. To avoid that, the inhabitants may have preferred to resist the soldiers, especially if the raiding party was a small one, despite the inherent risks of violence and the destruction of property. When the troops did not receive a satisfactory sum in response to their demands, or the civilians chose to defy them, then buildings could be deliberately set on fire as a punitive measure.[67] This can be classified as offensive destruction.

Some raiding was carried out to punish a rebellious area, or harass one which was under enemy control. The destruction of crops and buildings was one way in which the ability to support enemy garrisons and armies could be impaired. Prince Rupert sent his cavalry on a punitive expedition into Herefordshire in 1645 with the intention, in his words, that they should 'refresh after the Dutch fashion'.[68] When the troops had been given such instructions, then an operation of that kind was almost bound to involve some destruction of buildings. Royalist raids into western Somerset and north Devon, which were predominantly parliamentarian in sympathy, led to the destruction of twenty-seven houses in Ilfracombe in 1644 and the burning of parts of Bampton and Minehead by Goring's troopers in the following year.[69]

The contemporary military code permitted soldiers to burn empty buildings from which the occupants had fled so as to evade enlistment or payment of the demands that were being made upon them. This meant, of course, that the potential loss to the householder was far greater than the sums being levied, making it counter-productive to attempt to avoid payment in that way. Nevertheless, some chose to abscond and duly paid the price for their temerity. In November 1644 the royalists burnt down the house of a farmer at Stanton in Oxfordshire because he had fled to avoid enlistment.[70] Resistance was even more hazardous, for unless the civilians were organised and sufficiently well armed to fight off the soldiers then they risked death or imprisonment, the confiscation of their goods and the destruction of their property. The depredations of a detachment of royalist soldiers in Somerset in 1645 provoked an angry response from the villagers of Berrow, Lympsham and South Brent, which the troops countered by threatening that 'all the houses in the p[ar]ish of Berrow should be burnt to the ground'. When one Thomas Gilling tried to calm the situation he was told 'that his House was like to bee set on ffire'.[71] Nevertheless, there were occasions when parties of civilians did defy troops, either actively, by fighting them, or passively, by barricading themselves in the church. Soldiers could defeat passive resistance by smoking the villagers out of a church, or other building of refuge, or simply by setting it on fire, and by burning the houses until the villagers realised the error of their ways and submitted. The commander of a royalist force who was placed in just this position when the villagers of Swanbourne in Buckinghamshire retreated into the church reported to Prince Rupert that 'we fired the village, and at last forced them out of the church and took their arms'.[72] There was an even grimmer outcome to a similar incident at Barthomley near Nantwich on Christmas Eve 1643, when royalist soldiers, who had been fired on, smoked the villagers out of the church tower and, according to the report of one of the royalist officers, 'all the men were put to the sword to deterr any from the like insolence to face an armie with soe inconsiderable force'.[73] Active opposition was perhaps even more likely to lead to the destruction of property, as it did at Woburn in 1645, when a royalist force that had sustained several casualties fighting the inhabitants set fire to a number of houses.[74]

Fighting, either between opposing parties of soldiers or between civilians and troops, also created the conditions in which property could be destroyed, for it was accepted that if a soldier had received fire from a building then he was entitled to set it alight. Royalist troops were fired at from the windows and roofs in the suburbs of Bristol during their assault on the city in 1643, and the officer sent by Rupert to negotiate the terms of surrender spoke 'loud to the people of firing the town if they did not forbear shooting out of the windows'.[75] Not all attempts to take retribution in such circumstances were effective, but thatched buildings that were used as vantage points by gunmen were obviously at risk should an enemy soldier choose to exercise his rights in this way. A clash occurred at Sherborne in 1643 when a party of parliamentarian soldiers was passing through this predominantly royalist town. At one point a soldier was fired at from a window and 'in the heat of his blood shot up his pistoll into the thatch of a house . . . and all the house was presently on a light fire, it was in the very heart of the town too, therefore very dangerous'.[76]

Individual buildings could be hastily commandeered by soldiers requiring a refuge because they had been taken by surprise or had not had time to prepare a citadel. If the doors were barred and the windows were shuttered almost any reasonably substantial building could be successfully defended, at least for a while. Assailants could blow the door in by using a petard, but that could take time to prepare and might allow the enemy to reorganise and mount a counter-attack. It was quicker to use lighted straw, hay or brushwood to set the building on fire, forcing the defenders out. This method had the added advantage that the attackers did not have to enter the building and engage in the risky business of hand-to-hand fighting. In 1643 the royalists in Gainsborough were surprised by a parliamentarian force, but their commander, the Earl of Kingston, and some of his men managed to retreat into a house in the town, only surrendering when it was set on fire. In a similar action, royalists at Salisbury, having been driven through the town, established themselves in the George and the Angel inns, both of which were then set alight by the parliamentarian troops, compelling the defenders to yield.[77]

Punitive action taken after the capture of a place could include the destruction of property after the fighting had ended. When a surrender was formally agreed and the terms were approved by both sides, it was almost always one of the conditions that there should be no plunder or destruction. Although there were a few cases where it was alleged that the terms had not been strictly observed, normally a capitulation of that kind was an effective safeguard of the townsmen's property. An assault that produced a surrender without articles was potentially far more damaging, for it put the captured place at the mercy of its captors, who were fully entitled to sack it. There were, in fact, few instances where a victorious army did pillage a town in such circumstances, although the royalist victories at Liverpool and Bolton in 1643 were followed by the sack of those towns, and considerable loss of life.[78] Following the battle of Worcester in 1651, the city was plundered, 'all houses being ransacked from top to bottom, the very persons of men and women not excepted'.[79] There was always the danger that a blaze would break out as the soldiers went about in search of plunder, perhaps using the threat of fire to compel householders to reveal the whereabouts of their valuables. Early in the war a citizen of Oxford was confronted by a party of royalists who, under threat of blowing up the house, took away plate and rings valued at about £300.[80]

Destruction after an assault was sometimes more selective, however, with the properties of those known to be hostile, or to have been instrumental in the defence of the place, singled out for looting and perhaps burning. Such destruction was partly done to punish prominent supporters of the other side, but it also had a practical purpose, for much of the wealth of a seventeenth-century townsman was concentrated on his premises, in the value of the buildings and in the stock-in-trade and personal goods kept there, and to destroy the property effectively prevented the victim from giving further aid to the victors' opponents. After the capture of Cirencester by the royalists in 1643 the losses included 'the burning of some particular men's houses, which were purposely set on fire after the towne was wonne', and in the aftermath of the successful parliamentarian assault on Newcastle-upon-Tyne in the following year at least two houses were singled out and set on fire, one of them the home of Sir John Marley, the mayor, who was a prominent royalist.[81] There was a more directly military reason for the selective destruction of those properties which were being used to manufacture weapons for the enemy. Amongst the buildings deliberately set alight by the royalist troops after they had taken Birmingham was Robert Porter's blade mill, which was producing weapons for the parliamentary armies.[82]

Those places that had acquired the reputation of being strongly partisan ran the risk of receiving particularly heavy-handed treatment from hostile troops. Bolton's puritan population earned it the title of the 'Geneva of the North', for example, while its counterpart in southern England was Dorchester, which had undergone a godly reformation in the aftermath of a major fire in 1613.[83] In parliamentarian eyes Dorchester was 'as famous for piety and good affection' as nearby Blandford Forum was for 'its adversnesse to good'. Blandford was treated with consideration when the Earl of Essex's army passed through in June 1644, but its inhabitants strained their good fortune just too far a few months later when they detained one of his messengers and betrayed a party of parliamentarian troops, provoking a visit from another detachment, which plundered the town. Dorchester's defences were inadequately manned when a royalist force approached in 1643 and articles of surrender were quickly agreed, but another party of cavaliers arrived shortly afterwards and broke the terms, plundering the inhabitants and threatening to burn the town because of its allegiance. Where a community was regarded as being generally hostile, then such punitive destruction could involve considerable numbers of buildings.[84]

Setting buildings on fire was occasionally used as a tactic by a force attempting to capture a town or village, the intention being to drive the defenders out of the buildings, weakening the defences at that point. The blinding and choking effects of the smoke on the defending troops was a further reason for employing that stratagem, if the wind was blowing in a favourable direction. During the royalist assault on Manchester in 1642 the attackers succeeded in setting fire to a number of buildings near to the defences and the wind blew the smoke into the faces of the parliamentarian troops, although they held their positions. The use of the same ploy at Bolton six months later also failed. The royalists managed to capture some houses and set a number of them on fire, but the smoke did not force the defenders from their stations and the progress of the flames was stopped by the

MARLEBOROVVES MISERIES,
OR,
ENGLAND turned IRELAND,
BY

The $\begin{cases} \text{Lord } Digbey, \\ \text{and} \\ Daniel\ Oneale. \end{cases}$

READE and IVDGE,
This Being
A
Moſt Exact and a true Relation
OF THE

Beſieging $\}$ $\{$Pillaging, and
Plundering $\}$ $\{$Burning part of the ſaid Towne,

Written by *T. B. W. B. O. B. J.H.* who were not onely
Spectators, but alſo Sufferers in that moſt unchriſtian action.

Dedicated to all ENGLAND, and directed to the
City of *LONDON*, to ſhew the abuſe of the Subjects,
Liberty, and Priviledges of their owne goods.

Fœlix quem faciunt aliena pericula Cautum:

Jan: 13. 1642

Printed by one that Prints the Truth. 1643.

The capture and sack of Marlborough, Wiltshire, in December 1642 prompted the publication of this parliamentarian pamphlet, with its title drawing a parallel with the horrors of the war in Ireland

demolition of a house to create a fire-break. The royalists had greater success at Cirencester, where some of the defenders were 'almost smothered' by smoke from a blazing barn and the opportunity was taken to force an entry into the town close to that point.[85] At Alton in 1643 the parliamentarians attacking the town suffered a number of casualties because of the smoke from some buildings that had been deliberately set alight. Later in the same action the smoke from a burning thatched house 'so blinded' the defenders that they were driven from their positions. Buildings were set alight with similar intent during fighting at Marlborough and Birmingham, although in neither case was the amount of property destroyed very great.[86]

More extensive damage was done when the fighting was prolonged, if there were skirmishes between the garrison of a citadel and enemy forces occupying the nearby buildings. Such circumstances led to the destruction of parts of Banbury and Pontefract.[87] Where resistance continued after the defensive line had been breached, then deliberate destruction was almost bound to occur, as the attackers tried to press home their advantage by driving the defenders into a smaller and smaller area until they surrendered. In May 1645 the royalist army in Somerset managed to break through Taunton's perimeter defences and secure a foothold amongst the houses at the eastern end of the town. A surrender on terms could reasonably have been expected at that point, but resistance continued. Fighting virtually from house to house, the royalist troops made progress towards the market-place by setting fire to buildings ahead of their advance, driving the defenders away. It would presumably have served their purpose if the fires had taken hold and spread more widely, but that did not happen and, as a relief force drew near, they broke off their attack and withdrew, leaving much of the eastern part of the town in ruins.[88] The more prolonged the resistance in such circumstances, the more property was likely to be destroyed, for tactical burning of buildings in this way was an obvious method that could be used to expedite the difficult and potentially costly task of fighting at close quarters.

If an army failed to capture a place by assault or in a surprise attack and so was compelled to undertake a siege, then it almost always brought up artillery and began a bombardment. The purpose of a bombardment was either to effect a breach in the defences – which was followed by a summons to surrender and, if that was refused, an assault – or to reduce the morale of both the defenders and the civilians to the point where the governor's position became untenable and he sued for terms. The concentration of artillery fire at a particular spot in the fortifications in order to open a breach did not normally result in the destruction of property, although it was always likely that a few stray shots would miss the defences altogether and carry over into the buildings beyond. At the siege of Gloucester some shot which were too high 'flew quite over the town, or lighted at random'.[89] This experience might do something to unsettle civilian morale, but not to the extent that it became a problem to the soldiers. A general bombardment was not only liable to cause more destruction, especially if hot shot and mortar grenades were used, but also to distress the inhabitants to a greater degree. The New Model's bombardment of Bridgwater in 1645 started some fires and produced a surrender within a few hours, partly because the townsmen urged the governor to yield, although in that case the morale of the troops was itself very low.[90]

Sir Thomas Fairfaxes
ENTRING
BRIDGEWATER
By Storming; on Munday laſt.

In which Town he took from the Enemy ;

- 4. Collonels.
- 50. Captaines, Lieutenants, and other Officers.
- 500. priſoners, whereof ſome Papiſts.
- 60. Horſe.
- 1. Great piece of Ordnance, in the Royall Fort.
- The Royall Fort alſo taken.
- Mr. Harveys Houſe taken.

And a Liſt of all the particulars, and what loſſe was
on both ſides ; And the manner of the Fight :
And in what poſture the reſt remain in thoſe
Holds where they lye.

ALSO,

The Termes tendred by Sir *Hugh Cholmley*, for the
ſurrender of *Scarborough* Caſtle.

*Commanded to be printed, and publiſhed according
to Order.*

London, Printed by *B. Alſop*, and *I. Coe*. 1645.

*The capture of Bridgwater by the New Model Army in 1645 resulted in the destruction of
property during bombardments by both the defenders and the besiegers*

There were other occasions when artillery fire caused such dissension within a town that a capitulation quickly followed. The royalist bombardment of Rotherham in May 1643 set some houses on fire and that was given as one of the reasons for the surrender. The same tactic was successful at Gainsborough two months later. The besiegers' battery contained sixteen pieces of ordnance, including at least one mortar, and the grenades shot into the town set a number of buildings alight, causing the townsmen to threaten to surrender and to so pester the soldiers that, they claimed, they were unable to man the defences properly. The friction between the civilians and the garrison meant that the place could not be adequately defended and so it was surrendered on terms. A three-day cannonade at Tenby in the following year was also effective.[91] There is no evidence that the destruction in those towns was particularly extensive; rather, the victories were achieved by the demonstration that the besiegers had the potential to set fire to buildings inside the defences, thereby lowering the resolve of the defenders and alarming the townsmen. Such a display also gave the officers the justification to agree terms with the besiegers; to do so in such circumstances was not regarded as dishonourable, although to yield without compelling the besiegers to construct batteries and open fire was, in the military code of the time, quite reprehensible. If the besieged were not intimidated and were resolved to hold out, then the bombardment could become prolonged. This was potentially very destructive, although in practice there were, as we shall see, a number of problems for the besiegers to overcome and counter-measures which the defenders could take, both of which tended to limit the extent of the destruction.

In addition to these kinds of destruction deliberately carried out by the military, or which occurred during their operations, there was also the danger that accidental fires could cause considerable damage. The already substantial risks of such fires were intensified during the war years, especially in those towns that were fortified and garrisoned. It became increasingly difficult to contain the risks of fire in the conditions caused by the war, for many towns became overcrowded, their normal populations swollen by soldiers and their families, those made homeless by the destruction of suburban property, refugees from the countryside and the influx of various individuals seeking shelter and security within the defences. Although a Civil War garrison contained a high proportion of townsmen who did not require additional accommodation, the regular soldiers, their followers and supporting administration put considerable pressure on the existing housing. This was especially the case in the more strategically placed towns which became important military centres. Worcester appears to have suffered overcrowding for much of the war. In 1644 it was said to be 'abounding with people' and enumerations of soldiers and civilians taken in the spring of 1646 reveal that the population was then roughly 2,000 higher than the immediate pre-war figure.[92] A count taken at Coventry in 1644 shows a similar effect, with a population of 9,500, compared to a peacetime figure of perhaps 7,000. Similar counts at Oxford and Chester also show inflated numbers of inhabitants in towns where the housing stocks had been reduced by clearances for defensive reasons. In January 1644 a listing of inhabitants in Oxford showed an average of five such 'strangers' in each of seventy-four households in St Aldate's parish. Examples from Chester show even greater overcrowding there. In Grace Richardson's house in the Northgate Ward there were three members of the family, ten refugees from the suburbs and one soldier, and at Thomas Bennett's house there were three members of the family and fourteen men and women from the suburbs.[93] In such overcrowded conditions there was a greater likelihood of accidents as houses were subdivided and fires for heating and cooking were lit in rooms which were not equipped for the purpose. Furthermore, an influx of people caused a greater demand for food and drink and so an increase in activity by bakers, brewers, maltsters and other suppliers whose premises were potential fire risks, and who must have been tempted to keep larger stocks of corn and fuel than was advisable. Overcrowding and the diminished authority of the civilian authorities made it difficult to enforce the existing regulations guarding against accidental outbreaks of fire.

A military presence normally meant the establishment of magazines of match, gunpowder and other combustible materials. These added a new and potentially disastrous element to the existing fire risks. A permanent garrison also established powder mills near to a town. Both in their management of a magazine and in their quarters, it is likely that soldiers were more careless of fire precautions than were the civilians, who were protecting their own property, goods and lives by observing the regulations safeguarding against fire. When the Bell Inn at Henley-on-Thames was damaged by fire it was 'the Carelesnes of some Parlement soldiers quartered there' which was said to have caused the blaze.[94] Nor were things helped by the tendency for the fire-fighting equipment – ladders, buckets and hooks – to be neglected or appropriated. Many towns ceased to acquire such equipment during the war, partly because of the greatly increased pressure on civic finances, and partly because they were unable to trade with the London founders, who were the chief suppliers of leather buckets riveted with copper. Buckets with stitched seams were more widely available but were not as good or as durable. Gloucester's stock of buckets fell from 219 in 1640 to 32 in 1645, and Oxford did not buy any new buckets during the war years, although the corporation did attempt to maintain its existing stock in good order.[95]

A further problem was that water supplies were impaired during the Civil War, either through neglect at a time when the attentions and finances of civic governments were focused on other matters, or because of deliberate damage by an enemy force. They were obvious and vulnerable targets for a besieging army. One of the first steps taken by the royalists when they invested Gloucester in 1643 was to cut off the pipes running to the town from a nearby hill, and Waller's attack on Worcester in the same year caused some damage to the pipes carrying water to the cathedral close.[96] The parliamentarian forces besieging Chester used artillery fire to try to demolish the water tower near to the Dee Bridge, which supplied the town with water 'by the help of diverse leaden vaynes [pipes]'.[97] Other towns, such as Bath, also had their pre-war supplies reduced or severed.[98] The besiegers' chief objective was to cut off supplies of drinking water, forcing the besieged to use alternative sources that were less satisfactory and more difficult to obtain, increasing their discomfort and the risks of disease, but a side-effect of their actions was to reduce the amounts available for fighting fires.

Even after a siege was over, the problems and expense of restoring supplies were such that the work was not undertaken for some years. A part of Exeter's supply was interrupted when the pipes which conveyed it from outside the walls in Southernhay were 'cut and stolen away' and they were not replaced for at least ten years after the end of the final siege of the city.[99] In these circumstances, the risks of a minor fire getting out of control were much increased. There were five major town fires in England and Wales during the war years; two of them were in the East Anglian towns of Diss and Lowestoft, outside the war zone, but the most destructive was at Oxford, the royalist headquarters.[100] There were minor outbreaks in a number of other towns and near disasters at Stratford-upon-Avon, where the detonation of the magazine shattered the town hall, and at Lincoln, when a gunpowder explosion started a fire that burnt down a church and a number of houses. There was also an explosion at Norwich, during a riot at the outset of the second Civil War, when the magazine in the Committee House was detonated, perhaps by accident, causing the deaths of an estimated forty people and damage to two churches and many houses.[101] But although these accidents were destructive, it was direct military action that caused the greatest damage and it is necessary to consider how that destruction was effected, and also the factors which restricted it.

CHAPTER THREE

Methods and Limitations

This day came their Mortar piece which struck the poore Cittizens into an Ague fite of trembling and gazing at the strangeness thereof, not having seen the like before.

'The Siege of Lichfield . . .', British Library, Harleian MS 2043

Several methods were available to the soldiers when they decided that buildings should be removed. They were of differing efficiency, and it was usually the operational circumstances that determined which ones were chosen. It was not only technical considerations that governed the course of action adopted, however, for although the reasons for destroying property were, from the military point of view, strong and indeed often compelling ones, other factors had to be taken into account. An important consideration was the reaction of the civilian population, particularly that of the owners of property earmarked for destruction.

The defensive clearance of property in suburbs or close to a garrison was the easiest of such tasks. Buildings which were to be demolished could be removed at some leisure and the materials preserved for other uses. This was helped by the insubstantial nature of much suburban property, which typically consisted of simple wooden buildings constructed of boards or a basic timber frame with lath and plaster infilling.[1] Such structures could be removed with relative ease. The prefabricated nature of a timber-framed building allowed it to be taken apart piece by piece and the timbers stored, rebuilt on another site, or used in the construction of the fortifications. Some houses outside Leicester's south gate were dismantled and rebuilt elsewhere, for instance, and at Newark the town council ordered one citizen to take down his small tenement and 'to re-edifie [it] upon some part of the ground belonging to the Corporation'.[2] There was a similar policy at Stafford, where the parliamentarian committee allocated building sites within the defences to householders whose property had to be removed.[3] Many houses were apparently dismantled in such a way that they could be rebuilt later, even if they were not to be re-erected immediately. At Coventry the materials of houses and barns dismantled in the suburbs were sold by the corporation at prices which suggest that they could be re-used.[4] Joyce Jefferies sold her houses in the suburbs of Hereford when the area was being cleared of buildings and, even in the extremely unfavourable circumstances in which she was forced to sell, she received £71 15s. 0d. for three houses and some other timber. As one of the houses had cost her £25 when she had bought it in 1640, the prices which she obtained for buildings about to be dismantled were apparently not much less than she would have obtained in normal conditions.[5]

Such methods were adequate for the demolition of the majority of buildings, but not for the more substantial ones, particularly churches, chapels and almshouses, and houses built of brick and stone, such as those in the suburbs of Newcastle-upon-Tyne and Hull.[6] They were not easily demolished. If the nature of the ground permitted, the walls could be undermined, perhaps after the building had been fired in order to destroy the roof and weaken the structure. This was a relatively quick and effective way of carrying out the task, but was also rather wasteful. In fact, considerable care seems to have been taken in the demolition of some churches and chapels, with carpenters and masons employed to carry out the work. At Gloucester, the lead, timber, glass and fittings of St Owen's church were removed before the building was demolished.[7] Church bells were often appropriated by the military for use as gunmetal and were taken down before demolition began.[8] Not all of them met this fate, however. At least one of the bells from Spittal Boughton chapel near Chester was re-hung in St Mary's church within the town. Similarly, three bells from St Nicholas's in York were saved and given to the parish of St John, Ouse Bridge End, and its porch was later re-erected at St Margaret's.[9] The larger secular buildings were also dismantled with some care. The town hall at Bridgnorth stood outside the walls and when it was taken down the corporation managed to save the wooden roof shingles and store them in the church.[10]

The military were as concerned as were the householders and the governing bodies of towns to save the materials from demolished buildings. They required stone, timber and bricks for the construction of defences, storehouses and guardhouses; and earthworks had to be built with a timber framework and revetments, or a core of rubble. As supplies of timber and stone were likely to be disrupted, and the work had to be done quickly, demolished buildings were a useful source. At King's Lynn the 'Governour tooke away all the materials' of the corporation's houses that had been demolished, and Joyce Jefferies was glad to pay a small sum to save her timber when the royalist governor of Hereford instituted a search for materials with which to build defensive works.[11] Stone from some of the Dean and Chapter's properties in Carlisle and from a part of the nave of the cathedral were used by the parliamentarian soldiers to repair the town walls and build guardhouses.[12] Fuel was also needed by civilians and soldiers and, as well as magazines of food, arms and ammunition, the provision of a stock of fuel was an important part of a garrison's preparations for a siege. The governor of Bridgnorth appropriated the timber from demolished houses 'to serve the town for fuel'.[13] At Worcester, Henry Townshend noted with disgust that during the siege of 1646 outhouses were torn down by the soldiers, who sold the wood for fuel so that they could buy liquor. As a result of their depredations 'the most part of the suburbs of St Peters in Sidbury is defaced', and they had even begun to break up the gentlemen's coaches in their search for wood. The town had experienced a fuel crisis during the previous winter, when coal supplies along the Severn had been cut off, and the pulling down of extra-mural houses then was said to have been done partly to obtain fuel.[14] At the sieges of Liverpool and Reading the defenders were alleged to have pulled down houses for the same

Reading was captured by the Earl of Essex's army in April 1643, but reoccupied by the royalists later that year. The town was encircled by new earthwork defences supplemented by some detached works

reason, and during the siege of Carlisle the besieged mounted a sortie to bring in wood from houses outside the defences.[15] Even the thatch from the roofs was worth preserving, as it could be used for fodder. The garrisons of Taunton, Colchester and Carlisle ran so short of fodder during sieges that their horses were fed thatch, presumably after it had first been soaked in water.[16] A prudent governor would, therefore, try to preserve what he could of demolished buildings, partly because of the use which could be made of the materials and partly in order to appease the civilian population.

If the defenders did not have much time in which to destroy buildings beyond the fortifications, there was little they could do but to set them on fire. This could be effected fairly quickly and simply by using firebrands and burning match, or by firing hand-guns into thatched roofs or other materials that would easily burn. Problems arose in difficult conditions, if it was raining or there was no wind to spread the flames. The householders and soldiers may have already removed combustible items such as corn and hay stacks, leaving little that would readily burn. The suburbs of some towns were not set on fire until the last possible moment. At Carlisle the order to 'fire and pull down all the suburbs' was not given until the Scottish army had laid siege to the city and constructed its earthworks.[17] The royalists at Colchester in 1648 had not attempted to destroy the suburbs before they were driven inside the town and the burning of the extra-mural houses took several days to complete.[18] Such firing could be done by troops sallying out and occupying the buildings long enough for them to be set alight. The early stages of the siege of York in 1644 were punctuated by sorties as the defenders tried to destroy buildings close to the walls.[19] Soldiers were reluctant to take part in such hazardous operations, however. The infantry in the garrison at

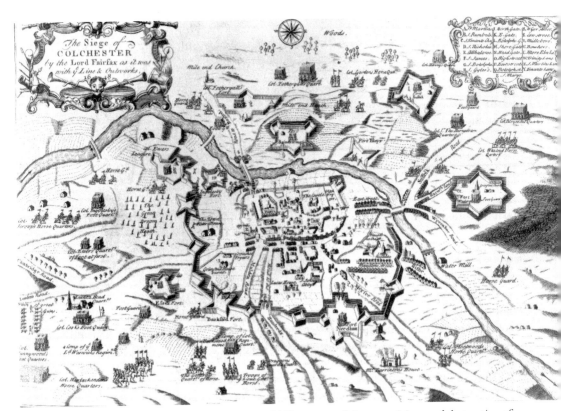

The parliamentarian siege of Colchester in 1648 was one of the most vicious and destructive of the Civil Wars

Leicester refused to make a sortie, which was eventually undertaken by some dismounted dragoons, who were able to clear the besieging royalists from houses outside the defences and then to burn the buildings down.[20] An alternative to a sally by a group of soldiers was an incursion by an individual incendiary, who, armed only with a tinderbox, could set buildings on fire if left undisturbed long enough to be able to kindle some flammable materials. A royalist soldier captured during the siege of York was carrying 'pitch, flax, and other materials . . . for the fiering of the suburbs', and at Chester some 'desperate fellows' – who were apparently townsmen, not soldiers – were sent into the suburbs at night to burn down houses. The rewards at Chester were £2 for each night's work and at Exeter in 1643 a man was paid £5 for setting fire to one of the besiegers' works, reflecting the dangers of the task.[21] There was certainly a fear of incendiaries in the Civil War and they could expect little mercy if caught; three suspected arsonists were lynched at Taunton in 1645.[22]

Fire was also the most common way in which country houses were rendered unusable to the enemy, although less drastic methods were used on some occasions. In 1645 Sir William Campion reported to Prince Rupert that Chilton House in Buckinghamshire was a potential parliamentarian garrison and he thought that it should be destroyed, indeed he wrote that 'my fancy this morning did much envite mee to set fyre to the house'. In fact, he desisted and asked for instructions, which were to pull down the outer walls and remove the doors 'the body of the House remaining whole'. Similarly, the parliamentarian commander who forced the surrender of the garrison in Besselsleigh near Abingdon, the house of William Lenthall, Speaker of the House of Commons, ordered that the walls and doors should be broken down as the minimum amount of damage that could be done to prevent the enemy from reoccupying it.[23] In many cases commanders did choose to burn a house, as the quickest and most certain way of achieving their objective. A blaze would destroy the roof, doors, windows and fittings, leaving little but a shell which could be restored for use as a garrison only with great difficulty. In the early stages of the Naseby campaign the royalists withdrew their troops from Campden House in Gloucestershire and set it on fire.[24] Their occupation of the house in the previous winter had prompted the parliamentarians from Warwick to destroy the Earl of Middlesex's house at Milcote near Stratford-upon-Avon, which was not occupied by either side. They set it alight in three or four places and waited until the flames had taken a firm hold before riding off.[25] Fire could also be used to dislodge a garrison during an assault on a house. This ploy was used with notably destructive effect when Sir Anthony Ashley Cooper's forces attacked Sir John Strangway's house at Abbotsbury in Dorset in 1644. They set the porch alight and, having forced the windows open, threw in burning furze faggots. The building caught fire and eventually the flames detonated the defenders' magazine. The house was completely wrecked by the fire and explosion.[26]

A hostile force attacking a town or village used similar methods. If it was in control of the buildings the firing could be done systematically and care taken to destroy particular structures if desired, rather than setting them alight at random. Not all such attempts at burning were successful, however. The soldiers who tried to burn down a house at Prescot, Lancashire, were disappointed, for 'the walls being of stone, and the roof well shot over within, they could fasten no fire upon the house, though they severall times essayed so to doe'. Those attempting to start fires at Woburn had more success, pushing firebrands into corn and hay ricks and thatched roofs.[27] Fire-pikes could also be used for the purpose. A fire-pike was a typical short pike of the period with a wad of flammable material fixed near to its head.[28] A soldier with a fire-pike succeeded in setting a house and some nearby corn and hay ricks on fire during the royalist attack on Cirencester in 1643. Fire-pikes were also effective at the capture of Bristol later that year.[29] Another method of firing a building at close quarters was by discharging a gun into combustible materials within or close to it, or at a thatched roof. When the royalists temporarily held much of Nottingham in 1644 they attempted to burn buildings by firing guns at thatched roofs and throwing burning coals into the hay in stables.[30] A particularly destructive fire resulted from the chance discharge of a musket against a thatched house at Beaminster in 1644 during a brawl between sections of Prince Maurice's army quartered there.[31]

Artillery played a significant part in sieges and assaults and was an important weapon for a force which was unable to get close enough to buildings to set them on fire by other methods. The smaller field pieces, firing shot weighing only a few pounds, were too light to be effective against buildings, but the larger guns were used to demolish or damage brick or stone structures and to batter masonry walls or earthworks. Stone buildings were particularly vulnerable to such fire. A parliamentarian battery sited in Gosport ruined the nave and tower of St Thomas's church in Portsmouth within two days in 1642, two churches in Scarborough were badly damaged by artillery bombardments, and Lichfield cathedral also sustained heavy damage as a result of battering with round shot.[32] Country houses were equally vulnerable to cannon fire. The royalists surrendered Greenlands House near Henley-on-Thames when it was no longer tenable, 'the whole structure being beaten down by the cannon'.[33] Unheated round shot was less suitable for destroying the majority of ordinary houses and other comparatively insubstantial buildings, and commanders probably regarded the use of heavy artillery in this way as a waste of powder and ammunition. At the outset of the Civil War Lord Strange's troops bombarded Manchester, but although the cannon fire 'did make holes in divers houses, and battered downe a piece of a chimney . . . [it] did little harme'.[34] There were similar cannonades at Reading in 1643 and Tenby in the following year, but it is not clear that they caused a great deal of damage.[35] Houses near to the centre of Worcester were damaged by cannon balls during the siege of 1646, when the target of the parliamentarian gunners seems to have been St Martin's church rather than the houses, and the intention may have been to lower civilian morale rather than to destroy property.[36]

Artillery fire could be used to demolish or badly damage houses, but the task was done more efficiently by using heated shot or other projectiles to set them on fire, creating a fire-storm which would spread and destroy property more quickly, perhaps more completely, and more economically than a bombardment with unheated shot. The damage done by red-hot shot was not related to the weight of the shot fired, and so the smaller calibre pieces could be used for the purpose. A furnace was set up close to the battery and when the ball was hot enough it was transferred to the cannon by using tongs or pincers. The gun was then discharged as quickly as possible. Care had to be taken that the ball did not come into contact with the charge – they were kept apart by a wooden tampion and perhaps a moist wad as well – and that no loose gunpowder remained in the barrel of the gun before the hot ball was inserted.[37] A hot cannon ball which lodged in thatch or amongst stacks of hay, corn or fuel was likely to start a fire, although there was probably a greater chance that it would fall harmlessly where there was nothing to ignite. Another of the limitations of heated shot was that it did not explode, and so the fire only began at the spot where the ball lodged, making it easier for defenders to put out the flames before they spread. The chances of success were greater if the attempt was made at night, when the defenders' task was more difficult, although the dangers of handling heated shot in an artillery battery were also greater in the dark. The royalists fired heated shot into Gloucester during the siege of 1643 and made quite an impression on the besieged, who saw them 'flying in the ayre like a starre shooting', but they did little damage and no serious fires were started.[38] The royalist besiegers of Hull tried the same tactic, but they had only one furnace and when it was broken a number of days passed without any heated shot being fired into the town. There, too, the attempts to set fire to the buildings by using this method did not succeed.[39] During the siege of Lyme Regis red-hot pieces of anchors and bars of iron, as well as round shot, were fired, and 'Slugs of hot iron' were used at Bridgwater when the royalists in the town set fire to the district of Eastover.[40]

The same technique was applied to small shot fired from muskets. Many more musket balls could be heated at one time than in the case of artillery shot, and the number of muskets available was also comparatively high, so that a greater rate of fire could be achieved than with artillery. One problem was that the limited range of muskets meant that the furnace had to be set up quite near to the enemy's lines. Another was that because of the small size of the ball it may not have retained enough heat during its flight to ignite anything when it reached its target. The premature discharge of the gunpowder was prevented by using a wad or, as in the attack on Bridgwater in 1645, wrapping the red-hot bullets in leather.[41] Heated musket balls were used on a number of other occasions. During the struggle for the control of Weymouth in 1645 royalist troops fired from their muskets 'small Iron Sluggs heated in a Forge, which . . . set fire on a Thatcht-House'. The parliamentarians retaliated in kind and several houses were destroyed. At Lichfield in 1646 Brereton's troops successfully fired a house and a hay rick by shooting hot slugs from their muskets.[42]

Some of the limitations of heated shot discharged from cannon and muskets were overcome by the use of mortars firing explosive grenades. Because of the high trajectory fire of a mortar, its projectile could be delivered over the tallest defences into the buildings beyond. A further advantage was that its exploding grenade affected a larger area than did a cannon ball. Indeed, a grenade exploding amongst densely packed buildings of timber and thatch had the potential to do considerable damage. Moreover, a mortar was as effective at a long range as at a

The mortar was probably the most potent siege weapon of the period. This example, known as 'Roaring Meg', was cast for the parliamentarian forces and now stands, on a modern bed, at Hereford

short one, for the damage which it caused was the result of an explosion, and was not dependent upon the force of the projectile hitting its target, as was round shot. A grenade consisted of a metal sphere, filled with gunpowder or other explosive mixture and ignited by a fuse. Ideally the fuse was set so that the grenade exploded more or less on impact, but this required fine judgement and in practice it did not always occur. The fuse of a grenade that landed in a street during the siege of Gloucester was extinguished by a woman who threw a pail of water on to it, for example, and there were other instances of grenades being made harmless.[43] The preparation of a grenade and the firing of a mortar were justifiably regarded as more dangerous employments than the operation of a battery of long guns and, perhaps for that reason, mortars were generally operated by their own crews, directed by specialists. In the Oxford army the mortars were supervised by the Master Fireworker, who also had charge of the manufacture of the other incendiary devices.[44]

Mortars had come into common use in continental warfare in the late sixteenth century and were highly praised by writers on military affairs, especially for their effectiveness in siege warfare.[45] Most Civil War armies included mortars amongst their artillery, although only in small numbers. The Oxford magazine contained four mortars and thirty other artillery pieces in May 1643, the Earl of Essex's army had only one mortar in its train for most of that year's campaign, and Fairfax's force which set out from London in 1645 also had only one mortar.[46]

A great and bloudy

FIGHT

AT

COLCHESTER,

AND

The ſtorming of the Town by the Lord Generals Forces, with the manner how they were repulſed and beaten off, and forced to retreat from the Walls, and a great and terrible blow given at the ſaid ſtorm, by Granadoes and Gunpowder. Likewiſe their hanging out the Flag of Defiance, and their ſallying out upon Tueſday laſt, all the chief Officers ingaging in the ſaid Fight, and Sir *Charles Lucas* giving the firſt onſet in the Van, with the number killed and taken, and Sir *Charles Lucas* his Declaration.

London Printed for *G. Beal*, and are to be ſold in the Old Bayley, and neer Temple Bar, 1648.

This illustration from a pamphlet describing the siege of Colchester in 1648 graphically conveys the contemporary impression of the destructive power of a mortar grenade

Mortars were used at many sieges and in almost all cases the intention seems to have been to destroy property within the defences. Brereton sent a warning summons to that effect to the garrison of Chester before his troops began a mortar bombardment. The grenades did do considerable damage and destroyed some buildings, although no major fires were started.[47] Amongst the buildings in Newark destroyed by mortar grenades were those of Charles Piggot, whose house was 'blowne upp with a grenado and all his goods burnt and broken', and the house of Alderman Hercules Clay, which was 'entirely destroyed'.[48] Elsewhere, at Rotherham, Gainsborough, Bridgwater, Bridgnorth, Newcastle-upon-Tyne and in the first siege of Exeter, grenades were successfully used to set buildings on fire, sometimes in conjunction with other methods.[49] They were particularly successful when fired into a comparatively confined space. At the sieges of the castles in Devizes and Winchester in 1645 it was mortar grenades which did most to induce the garrisons to surrender, and at the siege of Lathom House it was 'The morter-peece . . . that troubled us all . . . the stoutest souldiers had noe hearts for granadoes'.[50] Towards the end of the siege of Chester, when both the citizens and soldiers 'began to be very impatient and mutinous', the parliamentarian mortar bombardment was effective in producing dissension, Byron later writing that 'Every Granadoe that was shot now, caused a mutiny'.[51] Indeed, grenades seemed to have a greater impact on defenders' morale than any of the other methods used by besiegers.

Another projectile suitable for setting fire to buildings at a distance was the fire-arrow. A bag containing a flammable mixture was tied around the shaft of an arrow near to its tip, or that part of the arrow was wrapped in a sheet soaked in tar or pitch, and the arrow was then fired from a bow or a musket. A short musket had to be used, so that the flammable part of the arrow projected from the muzzle, and the feathers were removed from the shaft so that it would fit into the barrel, in which case it was more properly referred to as a fire-dart.[52] Fire-arrows and darts had a number of advantages: they were cheap to make and easy to prepare for firing, required very little gunpowder, and when they were fired from a longbow a high rate of fire could be maintained. There are comparatively few examples of their use during the Civil War, but where they were employed some success seems to have been achieved. The royalists within Chester fired burning arrows into thatched houses in the suburbs and succeeded in setting a number of them on fire.[53] They were also used at the siege of Lyme Regis and a part of the town was set alight by that means on one occasion.[54]

Wildfire was a further incendiary device of considerable potential. It was a similar substance to Greek-fire – a liquid or semi-liquid petroleum-based composition containing sulphur, with resins added as thickeners. A late-sixteenth-century arsonist who planned to set fire to Dieppe was armed with a ball of wildfire which included aqua vitae (brandy or whisky), saltpetre, camphor and brimstone.[55] If it was held in a projectile thrown by hand then a clay or, less probably, a glass container that would break upon impact was used. Malthus noted that incendiary devices in canvas were suitable for setting a town on fire only if the buildings were thatched, because they were not of such 'violent execution' as brass ones.[56] At Modbury in 1643 the balls of wildfire which set a number of houses alight were fired from cannons and so must have been contained in metal cases.[57] Wildfire in some form was used to burn down buildings at Wokingham and in the suburbs of Chichester. The royalist besiegers of Gloucester sent for four cartloads of wildfire from Oxford for use in their attempts to set parts of the town on fire.[58] It may be that the 'fire balls' referred to on other occasions when buildings were burnt down were projectiles containing similar substances.[59] Wildfire may have been used to fill mortar and hand grenades, although a gunpowder based mixture was safer, and probably easier to prepare, and so was more commonly used. Because it could not easily be quenched with water, the fire precautions issued in London in 1643 included the advice that wildfire could be extinguished by using milk, urine, sand, earth or dirt.[60] The defenders of Colchester used wet cloths dipped in milk and vinegar to smother hand grenades thrown into the town.[61] Hand grenades, which were incendiary clay pots, were widely employed in the Civil War: the royalist magazine at Oxford contained over 800 of them in May 1643.[62] Like fire-pikes, their main use seems to have been against enemy troops rather than to fire buildings, although they were also suitable for that purpose.[63]

Other ways of disseminating fire were employed where circumstances permitted. Ships could be used in port and riverside towns, for example. During fighting in Weymouth the parliamentarians sent fireships across the harbour to set fire to the vessels on the royalist side. The flames spread amongst the combustible quayside stores and from them to buildings in the town, destroying a number of houses. A similar ploy was attempted by the Scottish army assaulting Newcastle in 1644.[64]

Nevertheless, despite the range of methods available for setting fire to buildings from a distance, there were relatively few occasions when considerable numbers were set alight. Often the firing of a few houses and the threat of further destruction achieved the object of the operation and led to a surrender without the need to set fire to more buildings. This was apparently the case at Rotherham and Gainsborough during the Earl of Newcastle's summer campaign in 1643.[65] There were some instances, however, where the intentions of the besieging forces were to set a town on fire and yet they failed to do so. This occurred at Newark, Nantwich, Hull, Chester and Gloucester. At most of these towns some buildings were 'much battered' and a few were destroyed, but there was no fire-storm and the destruction was limited.

Unfavourable weather conditions may have been one of the reasons for the lack of success in some cases. The bombardments of Nantwich, Newark and Chester took place during the winter, when the timber and thatch of the buildings were probably too damp to catch fire easily. The siege of Hull occurred in the early autumn, however, and that at Gloucester during a dry summer spell of almost four weeks in which there was only one wet day.[66] The conditions could make attempts at firing difficult, but this can only be a partial explanation of the inability of besiegers to set towns alight.

Another reason was that the risks of fire had been reduced by the measures taken by the civil authorities in normal, peacetime, conditions. Among the towns which were subjected to prolonged sieges, Worcester had imposed a ban on thatched roofs in 1467, Oxford in 1582 and Reading in its charter of 1638.[67] Such regulations may have been enforced only intermittently and with varying degrees of success, but it seems that sufficient was done to reduce, if not totally eliminate, thatching. A ban on thatched roofs within the walls at Exeter seems to have been effective, with buildings in that part of the city covered with small stone slates.[68]

Precautions to reduce the risk of an outbreak of fire and to limit its spread if there was an accident were backed up by the provision of equipment and directions designed to produce a prompt and orderly response in an emergency. In dangerous conditions extra night-watchmen were deployed to keep a look-out for fires, so that they could be tackled as quickly as possible. Buckets were kept in accessible places and the provision of a supply of water close to hand was ensured by requiring inhabitants to place tubs of water outside their houses. At Norwich there was a by-law that, on the sounding of the alarm bell, carriers and brewers should get their carts and horses ready to carry water to the fire.[69] The senior members of the corporation and the parish officers were expected to direct the efforts of the fire-fighters, and try to prevent the panic and chaos which threatened if a fire began to get out of hand, tempting the inhabitants to abandon the struggle and make off to secure their own possessions.

Such arrangements and precautions were continued and augmented during the war years. The blockade of the ports of the north-east coast prevented coal from the region reaching London and the towns of eastern England, and alternative fuels had to be used. The inhabitants of Aldeburgh in Suffolk burned 'flagg and heath', and in September 1643 the corporation made an order that the ashes should not be dumped anywhere except in the sea, because of the risk of fire. At Chester in 1644 an order was made that the inhabitants were to be allowed only three loads of gorse on their premises and that the remainder should be moved to three designated sites.[70] The steps taken by the civilian authorities were reinforced by the military, particularly when a siege was imminent. The directives which Lord Fairfax issued before the siege of Hull in 1643 were typical. They stipulated that combustible matter such as flax, hemp, pitch, tar and gunpowder should be stored in cellars or, where none were available, in the lowest room in a building. Vessels of water were to be kept outside every house, to be immediately at hand in case of fire, and householders were made responsible for watching their own property for the fall of heated shot. These measures proved successful and were no doubt helped by the predominance of fire-resistant building materials in the town.[71] The steps taken by Lord Byron in a less favourable urban environment at Chester, where timber buildings predominated, were similar. Surplus stocks of fuel were destroyed before the beginning of the siege, all householders were required to keep tubs of water outside their doors, and raw hides were provided to smother wildfire. Sentries were posted to spot where projectiles fell and only those assigned to put out a fire were to gather at the scene, to minimise the confusion and to ensure that fire-fighters were available to tackle any other blaze that might begin.[72] These precautions, too, were sufficient to prevent a general conflagration, despite the destruction of individual buildings. At Lyme an order was made during the siege of 1644 that all thatched buildings should be unroofed, to reduce the risk of fire, although it was apparently not fully

Lord Byron had gained military experience in the Low Countries before the Civil War. Initially prominent as a cavalry commander, he was royalist governor of Chester during the siege of 1645–6

observed.[73] Such counter-measures and the careful siting of magazines did much to lessen the effectiveness of attempts to set towns on fire.

The besiegers faced logistical problems of their own. Some arose because of the restricted range of artillery. The range of the heavier calibre guns allowed a battery to be sited some distance away from a town or garrison, giving gunners a choice of site.[74] Even so, it was often placed quite near to the defences, sometimes no more than a pistol shot from them. The two culverins placed against St Mary's church at Colchester in 1648 were initially sited a musket shot away, but were inaccurate at that range and so were moved sixty yards closer, to within pistol shot, and from that distance they were able to knock down the church steeple. This put the artillerymen at risk and two members of the gun crews were killed and a number of others were wounded in the course of that bombardment.[75] The location of mortars also caused problems, for although they were effective at 1,000 yards or more, their accuracy was uncertain at such a range and they were commonly placed relatively close to their target. At the attack on Cirencester La Roche set up a mortar 150 paces from the defences and at that distance its fire seems to have been effective. At the siege of Lathom House the mortar was placed 'about halfe musket shott' from the house.[76] It was not always possible to get so close. Most of the grenades fired during the siege of Hull fell short of the town, suggesting that the mortars were operating at or near to maximum range, perhaps because the defenders had flooded the low-lying land around their perimeter.[77] Where batteries could be placed close to fortifications the gunners were exposed to the fire of marksmen from within the defences. Although they could be protected by blinds, this must have made their task both difficult and dangerous, as the example from Colchester indicates. The royalists had three or four 'principal cannoneers' killed in one day by marksmen firing from the defences at the siege of Gloucester, and during the siege of Sherborne Castle in 1645 the New Model lost several gunners in the same way.[78]

There were other practical considerations that restricted the rate of fire of artillery batteries. These included the special care that had to be taken when firing grenades and heated shot, the need to allow the piece to cool after each discharge, and shortages of ammunition and gunpowder. There was also the problem of the availability of ordnance. At first the armies were equipped with relatively small numbers of cannon, but as the war progressed more and more pieces were produced or acquired. Even so, mortars were in short supply for much of the conflict. The New Model was able to deploy six against Raglan Castle in 1646, although that was at the very end of the first Civil War, when the artillery could be concentrated against the few remaining objectives.[79] Moreover, the New Model was the principal parliamentarian army in the field, so that it could both command the resources which it needed and retain captured royalist ordnance. The less important units on both sides had a lower priority when trying to obtain the use of artillery pieces suitable for siege work. There was also the problem of moving the heavier pieces, particularly over muddy roads in wet weather. When the royalists abandoned the siege of Plymouth in January 1646 they were obliged to abandon their artillery because the weather was so bad that they could not move it.[80]

Bombardments during Civil War sieges were of fairly low intensity. The greatest rates of fire were achieved when a besieging force attempted to breach the defences prior to demanding a surrender and, if the demand were refused, mounting an assault. In the first five days of the bombardment of Pontefract Castle in January 1645 the six guns in the besiegers' battery discharged 1,364 shot against the defences. This was an unusually intensive bombardment and when it was realised that the breach made was too small to assault, or to produce a surrender, the rate of fire fell sharply. Over the next thirty-eight days only a further forty-two rounds were fired. The overall rate of discharge from the beginning of the bombardment until the end of the first siege of the castle averaged five and a half shot per cannon per day. During the first and the greater part of the second sieges the defenders replied with an average of fewer than four rounds per day from an unspecified number of cannon.[81]

It has been estimated that during the siege of Gloucester 441 round shot were fired by the royalists' six largest guns, a daily rate of fire of less than three rounds per gun. This is supported by the reports of the defenders, who thought that they had been subjected to between 300 and 400 shot in the course of the siege. The greatest effort was directed against one part of the defences, which received 150 shot, most of them in a single day. The number of heated shot is not known, although on one particularly busy night more than twenty were fired into the town, aimed at destroying property rather than creating a breach. The defenders also gave a figure of more than twenty mortar grenades fired during the siege,

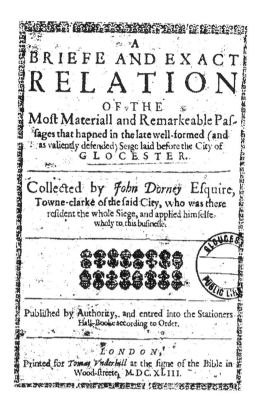

A
BRIEFE AND EXACT
RELATION
OF THE
Moſt Materiall and Remarkeable Paſ-
ſages that hapned in the late well-formed (and
as valiently defended) Seige laid before the City of
GLOCESTER.

Collected by *John Dorney* Eſquire,
Towne-clarke of the ſaid City, who was there
reſident the whole Siege, and applied himſelfe
wholy to this buſineſſe.

Publiſhed by Authority, and entred into the Stationers
Hall-Booke according to Order.

LONDON,
Printed for *Tomas Underhill* at the ſigne of the Bible in
Wood-ſtreete, M.DC.XLIII.

There are eye-witness accounts of many of the sieges during the Civil War. This narrative of the siege of Gloucester was written by John Dorney, the Town Clerk

with six discharged in one twenty-four hour period and 'several' on another night.[82] One of the two mortars in the besiegers' battery cracked early in the siege and a replacement had to be sent from Oxford, causing a delay which may have reduced the number of grenades fired. Even if the defenders' figure of twenty slightly underestimated the number actually discharged, the overall rate of fire would still have been no more than one grenade per day. The royalists were not short of grenades, and their standard issue was roughly thirty to each mortar. At least fifty were issued from the Oxford ordnance stores for use at Gloucester and others had presumably been brought with the artillery train from Bristol, but fifty-three were returned to the stores at the end of the campaign.[83]

There were similar rates of fire at other sieges. In the first eight days of the parliamentarian mortar bombardment of Chester sixty-two grenades were fired into the town, before the supply was apparently exhausted and stone balls were used instead. Although the average was only eight grenades per day, this phase was regarded by the besieged as an intense bombardment. Nevertheless, the parliamentarian commander, Sir William Brereton, complained that shortages of grenades and powder had impaired the effectiveness of the mortar barrage.[84] The mortar placed against Lathom House fired thirty-two stone balls and four grenades in the twenty-four days in which it was operational.[85] At Nantwich, eighty 'fire-balls' were fired into the town over a period of about four weeks at a rate of roughly three per day.[86] During the siege of York in 1644 the

Sir William Brereton was commander of the parliamentarian forces in Cheshire, whose main objective was the capture of the royalist fortress of Chester. This was eventually achieved in February 1646, but only after many of its buildings had been destroyed

parliamentarian batteries 'shot well-nigh forty Fiery Bullets out of their Morter-pieces', which represented an average of approximately one every two days.[87] To take a final example, Henry Townshend noted the numbers of shot fired by the parliamentarian besiegers into Worcester in 1646 and his figures show that over a period of fifteen days the average was roughly ten per day. He made no reference to grenades or heated shot.[88]

One reason for the low rates of fire may have been a shortage of expert gunners. In February 1645 it was said that good gunners were hard to come by. Sir William Waller had attempted to attract gunners to his service by offering a 'great advance and certain pay', but he had no success and was compelled to use gunners' mates in their place.[89] The firing of a mortar required even greater expertise than the operation of long guns, chiefly because of the difficulty of accurately judging the required trajectory and range. In the early stages of the siege of Lichfield cathedral close in 1643 the grenades were intended to set fire to the prebends' houses, but 'either they were too wide or too short and some fell into . . . the Mill Pool'.[90] The mortar which the parliamentarians placed against Belvoir Castle in 1646 was successfully employed by a Mr Garner to force a surrender, but he was apparently unavailable when the same piece was transferred to the siege of Newark, where it was so ineffective that its bombardment was suspended because 'the fire-man cannot find the ground'.[91] It was inadvisable to waste the grenades, for they were sometimes in short supply and they were also relatively expensive. The extra cost involved in casting a hollow sphere rather than a solid ball meant that they were much more costly than round shot: one of the New Model Army's suppliers charged £42 per ton for grenades and £12 for cannon-balls.[92] Such considerations made artillery officers cautious in using their supplies of grenades, especially if they were not even landing on the targets.

*Sir William Waller, who had
experience of European warfare, was
one of the most successful of the
parliamentarian senior commanders
during the early years of the Civil
War*

The rates of fire, especially the low numbers of mortar grenades discharged, go some way towards explaining why artillery was not a particularly effective means of destroying property. They suggest that the balance of advantage lay with the defenders, who could usually deal with the consequences of each projectile separately, putting out a fire that had been started before having to tackle the next one. Their efforts could be impeded if small arms and artillery fire was directed at a spot where a fire had begun, keeping the fire-fighters away until the flames had taken hold, as was done at Nantwich, Weymouth and Bridgnorth.[93] But in most cases it was possible to restrict the damage caused by a fire and to prevent a fire-storm. Indeed, contemporary writers recognised that, unless the buildings were thatched, even grenades were unlikely to be effective in starting fires.[94]

It is clear from this discussion that the extent of destruction was dictated by the circumstances in which it was carried out. By burning and demolition, a force completely in control for a sufficient time was able to destroy those buildings that were earmarked for removal. If the soldiers were harassed, or had only a limited time to effect their purpose, then they could not be thorough and the destruction was likely to be only partial. A force besieging or assaulting a garrison or fortified town was also faced with a number of problems when attempting to destroy buildings, particularly where the defenders succeeded in keeping their assailants' lines and batteries some distance away. Despite the array of methods available, the inefficiency of those methods, technical constraints, and counter-measures taken by the defenders, restricted the attackers' ability to set buildings alight.

Other considerations also governed the amount of destruction. Limitations were imposed upon garrison commanders who wished to carry out defensive destruction by the knowledge that they would thereby deprive their own troops of a useful resource. Quartering the soldiers in the remaining housing could cause such overcrowding that it would damage morale, as well as placing a further strain upon the relations between the garrison and the civilian population. Suburbs outside the defences were especially useful to the garrisoned towns which imposed a curfew, for they provided quarters for those troops or civilian suppliers who arrived after the gates had been closed. The inhabitants of Westport close to Malmesbury complained that they had 'suffered and sustained more than ordinary losses' for that reason, being forced to lodge 'abundance of soldiers' who had reached the town too late to be admitted until the following morning.[95]

There was also the need to consider the reactions of the civilian population. To clear away property in advance of an attack was to risk alienating the community concerned, particularly in the early stages of the war, before such practices had become relatively common and their necessity generally accepted. There was civilian opposition for a number of reasons. Those householders who were displaced would lose their homes and perhaps their belongings, while landlords would lose their property and the capital which it represented. With little hope of adequate compensation, these were likely to be serious losses. The community as a whole would be deprived of the functions carried on within the destroyed buildings and there was always the fear that serious and perhaps long-term economic problems might ensue. The migration of the displaced citizens, the loss of their skills and the possibility that the country people would prefer to use other markets, could all affect the prosperity of the town. The threat of economic decline raised in turn the prospect that the buildings might not be replaced. Moreover, an immediate and considerable problem of accommodation was created when housing was removed, for although some of the homeless may have gone elsewhere, many would have sought shelter with relatives and friends within the defences, or have quickly built temporary dwellings there. Such hastily constructed buildings, made of whatever materials were readily available, added considerably to the risks of fire. More seriously, the influx of people who were all but destitute created tremendous problems of poor relief at a time when civic finances were already strained by the increased costs of war and military taxation. Yet something had to be done to assuage the complaints of those who had a common, and tangible, cause to resent the authorities, and to deflect possible breakdowns in public order.

Civilian unrest could quickly be aroused. The proposed demolition of one of the suburbs of Chester created such strong rumours that the others were also to be destroyed that the authorities, fearing the possible outbreak of popular disturbances, issued a proclamation stating that this was not the intention.[96] Colonel John Hutchinson's plan to demolish a number of houses was the cause of one of the many quarrels between him and the parliamentarian committee at Nottingham.[97] A governor's authority was such that he could overrule the civilian government and suppress popular discontent if he wished, but as many garrisons contained significant proportions of local citizen-soldiers, attempts to act too resolutely may only have served to expose the practical weaknesses of his position. Byron at Chester regarded many members of the city's regiment as 'suspected persons' – he noted that a third of them had had to flee from their property in the suburbs – and bemoaned the fact that the citizens' obedience was given more to the mayor than to him as governor.[98] Governors would have to feel that they were in complete control of their garrison before they issued unpopular orders for the large-scale destruction of property and many may have thought it prudent not to force such an issue. It was important that the civilians be aware of the need for such destruction, so that they would not only acquiesce in what was done, but would continue to give their assistance to the military thereafter. During a siege or assault a commander required the active help of the population, not just its passive neutrality. The problem was well known to military writers, such as Monluc, who recognised that to take such a step prematurely was 'to create so many enemies in our entrails, the poor citizen losing all patience to see his house pulled down before his eyes'.[99] A governor had to identify the correct moment at which to suggest demolition, so as not to alienate the population, or have such superior strength that he did not need to be influenced by the possibility of a hostile response.

The problem of civilian opposition also had to be considered in the case of country houses. In some circumstances the local population actually favoured destruction, if the garrison had been especially oppressive, for example. It was 'the country people' who were blamed for the fire that destroyed Shelford House in Nottinghamshire immediately after its capture, intending to prevent its parliamentarian captors from continuing to maintain it as a garrison, the royalist one having 'sorely infested' them. Another motive for destruction was the loot available in the confusion which followed the capture and destruction of a country house. When Milcote was burned some of the contents which had been carried out of the house before it was set alight were stolen before they could be secured, so that 'betwixt the soldiers and other bad people a great deal thereof was lost of that'.[100] Yet a garrison also offered a degree of protection to an area, despite the levies which it imposed upon it, a benefit that the locals must have been aware of. The preventive destruction of houses which had not contained garrisons was likely to provoke discontent if not actual resistance because of the impact which the destruction of a country house, the hub of an estate, made upon the local economy. Where there was opposition to destruction, the rural population was less able to orchestrate effective resistance than townsmen, given the problems of assembling quickly enough and in large enough numbers to deter the soldiers from setting a house on fire. Even so, they were occasionally effective and could not always be ignored. The royalist commander Charles Lloyd admitted that when his troops had set about making a West Country house untenable as a garrison they had been able to render it uninhabitable – presumably by wrecking the doors and windows – and drain the moat, but had not set it on fire, 'because it would have incensed the Countrey'.[101]

There was also the problem of those who, because of their standing and influence, were able to save their property even when there was a general clearance. The otherwise thorough preparations at Bridgwater were marred by

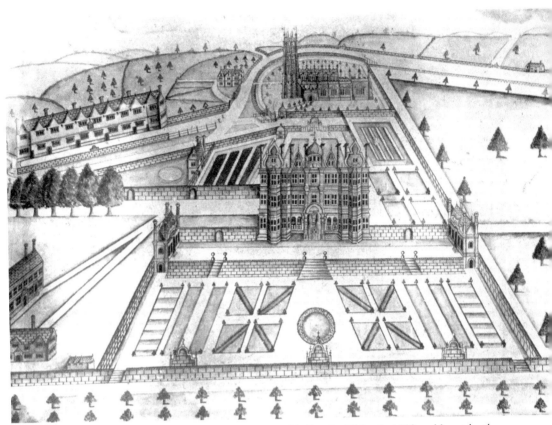

Campden House in Gloucestershire was built by Sir Baptist Hickes in 1613 and burnt by the royalists in 1645. This is a reconstruction drawn by William Hughes c. 1750

the fact that Henry Harvey, the lord of the manor, would not allow the soldiers to demolish his house outside the defences, and it was captured and used as the site of a battery when the New Model attacked the town in 1645. Harvey later had the gall to claim that damage worth £200 had been done to the house by the defenders' fire.[102] Such considerations could also apply to a whole neighbourhood, if its inhabitants had such sway that they were able to get their properties treated as an exception. The inhabitants of the Trinity district of Exeter were predominantly pro-parliamentarian and the area was included within the defences when the parliamentarians fortified the city early in the war, despite the long line that was required, but it was excluded and demolished when the royalists overhauled the fortifications in 1645.[103] The prevarication which resulted from such factors explains why property which should have been destroyed if purely military considerations had been applied was not removed until a besieging force appeared and even, in some cases, until after a siege had been successfully resisted.

On the other side of the fortifications, commanders of besieging forces also faced something of a dilemma, in choosing whether or not to employ a

A fragment of wall and the two flanking pavilions are all that remains of Campden House

bombardment to set fire to the buildings inside the defences. Some were reluctant to use such a tactic, for, although it did produce quick results on occasion, they preferred to undertake a siege so as to take the town intact rather than capture it after it had been substantially damaged. The extent of the destruction caused by a fire could not be predicted and a blaze begun in the circumstances of a siege might spread and burn down much of the place, despite the steps taken by the defenders to counter it. This would destroy accommodation, provisions and other resources, as well as reducing the amount of taxation that could be levied, and perhaps alienating the population to the extent that subsequent garrisoning would be particularly difficult. It was counter-productive to impoverish a place before capturing it. Brereton thought that it would be possible for his army besieging Chester to set the city on fire using mortar grenades, but that ruining it would defeat his object, which was to capture it intact.[104] Sir Walter Raleigh had pointed out that 'that Commaunder is more given to anger than regardfull of profit, who upon the uncertain hope of destroying a Towne, forsakes the assurance of a good composition'.[105] The number of bombardments using grenades, heated shot and the various incendiary devices available may have been limited for this reason and not solely because of the technical problems.

A certain reluctance to carry out destruction born of fear of retribution can also be detected. The orders governing the conduct of the armies that were issued by both sides in the autumn of 1642 prohibited, in similar terms, the burning of buildings, with the death penalty prescribed as the punishment for offenders.[106] These were designed to prevent the wanton destruction of property by the common soldiers and they may have been reasonably well enforced. Most destruction was carried out on the orders of the commanders and senior officers, or with their authority, but even they showed a certain apprehension in some cases. Where they were faced with the prospect of destroying the country house of a powerful supporter of their own side then they were wise to seek authority from their superiors before they carried out the task: it would not have been prudent to appear to have acted too hastily or unnecessarily. There was also the prospect of legal reprisals. There certainly was a backlash by civilians against the military after the war, with attempts to seek compensation through the courts, particularly for the taking of goods and quarter without payment. The destruction of property also featured in such cases. Sir Allen Apsley, the royalist governor of Barnstaple, was sued for compensation for a house in the town which had been demolished as part of the defensive preparations there, and Sir John Boys was arrested following the surrender of Donnington Castle and held 'until he gave satisfaction for the Damage to the Neighbour Inhabitants' whose buildings had been burnt down on his orders.[107] How far such moves were anticipated during the conflict is uncertain, but the more experienced and perceptive commanders may have been aware that they were possible, even likely, when the war came to an end.

Parliamentarian soldiers who found themselves defendants in civil actions brought against them for offences which they were alleged to have committed could appeal to the Committee of Indemnity, established in 1647, claiming that they had acted out of military necessity. There was no such redress for the royalists, although some commanders negotiated immunity for themselves and their subordinates in the articles of surrender. Apsley should have been protected by the clause in the Barnstaple articles which specified 'That no knights, gentlemen, clergymen, officers, citizens, or soldiers, or other persons comprised within these Articles, shall be questioned or held accountable for any past act by them done or by their procurement relating to the unhappy differences betwixt his Majesty and the Parliament'.[108] But this did not prevent him from being harassed, because the articles were contracted between the opposing commanders and were given little or no credence by the civilians whose property had been destroyed. Those governors who were sued had to make contact with the commander with whom they had concluded the articles and secure his assistance in getting the case against them cancelled, which inevitably took time and expense. This was an issue of some importance in the years following the war, for it was incumbent on both parties to articles of surrender to see that the terms were observed, and it tended to their dishonour if they were not. The army pressed Parliament for some process to protect commanders who were 'sued or molested' contrary to such articles and the response was the Act of Articles of 1649, which created a commission empowered to take action in such cases. The Act was valid only for a year, however, and was not renewed until 1652.[109]

Some cases referred to higher authority produced directives that buildings should not be destroyed. The example of Prince Rupert's order to Sir William Campion not to destroy Chilton House has already been mentioned (p. 45). Similar instructions were issued by the Committee of Both Kingdoms, which in a number of instances directed local committees not to burn particular houses. In

November 1644 it responded to the Sussex committee's request as to whether a number of houses, including Cowdray, should be garrisoned or demolished with the instruction that they should be left intact, at least for the time being. It also took the initiative in some cases, writing in January 1645 to the committee at Derby that it understood that there was an intention to demolish Chatsworth House and Hardwick Hall and commanding that they should not be demolished or defaced, except 'upon the greatest reason and necessity' and then only on its direct order. A similar order was made in the case of Burghley House, where it directed that as little damage as possible be done to the building while it was being fortified.[110] Such instructions may have been made because of an awareness of the detrimental economic effects of destruction upon an area. The personal impoverishment of allies was another consideration. The House of Lords responded to the appeal of George Lord Berkeley by ordering that Berkeley Castle should not be demolished because its destruction would add to his financial losses and be 'an irreperable mischief and prejudice to his posterity in the future'.[111]

There was a conscious attempt to limit the damage caused by the war, particularly on the parliamentarian side towards the end of the conflict. In April 1646 the Committee of Both Kingdoms countermanded the Shropshire committee's intention to burn High Ercall House to prevent its future use as a garrison, pointing out that slighting the works and draining the moat were sufficient safeguards. It added a more general remark, that it did not 'think it fit that all houses whose situation or strength render them capable of being made garrisons should be pulled down. There would be then too many sad marks left of the calamity of this war.'[112]

There were, therefore, both practical and cultural considerations to set alongside the technical ones as restraints upon the apparently very strong military rationale for the destruction of property. The soldiers' desire for security had to be considered in the light of other factors, and it was the balance between them which determined the extent of the destruction. Much depended upon the judgement and experience of the military commander, the strength of his position, the resources available to him, his relations with the civilian population, and the effectiveness of the opposition which he faced.

CHAPTER FOUR

The Extent of Destruction

> . . . miserable it is to see the multitudes of Inhabitants and their Children flocking in the streets of the bordering Townes and Villages and have not a house to putt their heads therein, whereby to exercise their Calling.
>
> *House of Lords Record Office, Main Papers, 23 Sept. 1648*

Contemporaries were struck by the dramatic effects of wartime destruction. John Taylor, the water poet, passed through Faringdon in 1649, describing it as 'a good handsome market town turned into ashes and rubbage'. During his journeys in Wales three years later he came to Pembroke, which had sustained a long siege in the second Civil War, where he found 'some houses down, some standing, and many without inhabitants'. George Newton, a puritan minister of Taunton, used more graphic language to describe that town when he delivered the sermon on the first anniversary of the raising of the siege of 1645, inviting his congregation to 'looke about her and tell her heapes of rubbish, her consumed houses, a multitude of which are raked in their owne ashes. Here a poore forsaken Chimney, and there a little fragment of a Wall.' Newton had spent the war years in the comparative seclusion of St Albans and must have been shocked to see the extent of the damage when he returned to Taunton. A third witness to the impact of destruction was Joshua Sprigge, who had been a member of Viscount Saye and Sele's household at Broughton Castle near Banbury before the outbreak of the Civil War. His reactions were similar to Newton's when he went back to the area and found that at Banbury there was 'scarce the one half standing to gaze on the ruins of the other'.[1]

These four towns had all suffered particularly badly, but over much of England and Wales people were aware of property destruction and their correspondence provides evidence for the extent of the damage. Among the more formal sources are the petitions for assistance that were directed to both the Justices of the Peace and the government at Westminster, in which the victims pleaded for relief from taxation and some contribution towards the costs of rebuilding. The number of petitions was such that in January 1648 a Committee of the House of Commons was established 'to examine and consider how, and in what Manner, such

Churches, Towns, or Houses, as have been burnt, demolished or spoiled since these Wars, may be repaired'. It came to be referred to more simply and expressively as the 'Committee for Burning'.[2] The petitioners employed the language characteristic of appeals for help during the period and understandably tended to stress, sometimes in fairly melodramatic terms, the extent of their losses and the dire consequences which they faced if they did not receive some aid. There was a check upon their claims, however, for peace brought the re-establishment of the normal system of relief after a fire, with qualified assessors reporting the scale of the damage to the Justices. The ruins at Faringdon were surveyed by five masons, three carpenters, two glaziers, two blacksmiths, two slaters, a plumber and a joiner, and those at Leighton Buzzard by the Bedfordshire Justices themselves, assisted by two carpenters and a mason. Coventry supported its claim by pointing out that the assessment of its losses had been made by 'severall persons of qualitie skillfull in Architecture and Lands'.[3]

Surveys were also taken to establish the value of particular estates, especially those of royalist delinquents, and of charitable, crown and church lands, and they indicate the amount of destruction, as do the property descriptions in deeds and leases of other land which changed hands in the years following the war. Other material refers to destruction in a more incidental manner, without mentioning its cause. For example, entries in the burial register for Chepstow note that one or more houses there collapsed in January 1645, killing four people, including a soldier.[4] The works of the eighteenth- and nineteenth-century antiquarians also present problems of interpretation, for their references to destruction, although not necessarily false or misleading, may be difficult to substantiate. There is, therefore, a range of material that can be used in conjunction with the testimony of eyewitnesses and the reports in the newsbooks and pamphlets of the 1640s when assessing the extent of the destruction of the war years.

The evidence indicates that at least 150 towns and 50 villages sustained some destruction of property during the Civil War. Both figures under-represent the true number, which for towns may be somewhat higher, but not markedly so, and for villages is perhaps much greater, possibly over 100, although this is harder to estimate because of the comparative difficulty of verifying reports of destruction for small communities. A degree of imprecision is unavoidable, for it may not be possible to corroborate contemporary accounts, particularly those partisan ones which alleged destruction by the enemy. Not only was there a propagandist value in stressing the destruction caused by the other side, but there was also a tendency for the first reports of an incident to exaggerate the scale of destruction. Such exaggeration based on first impressions was also typical of accidental fires in peacetime, when it was not unusual for a fire initially reported as a major conflagration to be later found to have caused comparatively little damage.

A further difficulty in estimating the scale of the damage for some categories of buildings is a terminological one, for contemporary usages of the words 'destroyed' and 'demolished' were not precise. Indeed, some buildings referred to in those terms show considerable survival of pre-seventeenth-century elements. The petition requesting assistance towards the rebuilding of High Ercall church in Shropshire described the building as 'demolished and pul'd downe to the ground', yet much of the medieval fabric survives and the petitioners set the sum needed at the rather low figure of £800, suggesting repair rather than complete rebuilding.[5] This is not a problem so far as the bulk of houses and other structures are concerned, for most of those which were damaged were rendered irreparable, but does make it difficult to estimate the numbers of the more substantial buildings demolished, particularly churches and country houses. An assessment of the losses of country houses suggests that between 150 and 200 were destroyed, although this may be an under-estimate, and many more were damaged in some way.[6]

Because of these difficulties, a figure for the total number of houses destroyed cannot be aggregated from information for all of the affected communities, but has to be estimated from those for which relatively reliable evidence exists. Reworking the data from a sample of twenty-seven towns and seven villages into an estimate for all communities which lost buildings suggests that 10,000 houses were destroyed in cities and towns and 1,000 in villages. Applying the average number of occupants per house in the early modern period to this estimate, including country houses, of 11,200 houses destroyed implies that approximately 55,000 people were made homeless. They constituted little more than one per cent of the total population. But the sample shows that there was far more destruction in the cities and towns than in the countryside, and by excluding rural communities and London, which contained a half of the urban population but experienced little of the damage, the estimate indicates that at least one in ten of those living in provincial cities and towns saw their houses destroyed in the Civil War.[7]

Although the total numbers cannot be precise because of the nature and, in some cases, the sparsity of the evidence, they do give a true sense of the balance of the scale of destruction between the different types of settlement, for it is clear that more towns than villages were damaged. Indeed, roughly one in four towns within the war zone sustained some loss of property, while the proportion of villages affected was very small. Moreover, some of the villages that did sustain damage suffered because of their proximity to fortified towns. That was the case at Stoborough, close to Wareham, and in a number of villages around Bristol.[8] On the whole, villages were less likely to be destroyed, partly because it was unusual for them to be garrisoned; soldiers may have billeted in them, but generally they did not seek to defend them. The damage that they did suffer was carried out in raids, or because there were garrisons in houses or castles within or close to them, such as Raglan and Brampton Bryan.[9] Only a few occupied positions of such strategic importance that they had to be destroyed, although that did apply in the case of Beachley, at the confluence of the Wye and the Severn, which was demolished by parliamentarian troops from Gloucester in 1644, following two sharp skirmishes with royalist forces attempting to fortify it.[10]

There was also a greater probability that a small market town would emerge from the war years physically intact than one of the larger towns and cities. In the much fought over county of Shropshire, the four largest towns all had buildings destroyed, but only three of the other fourteen seem to have suffered in the same way. Many of the smaller towns were indefensible, useful to the troops for

Brampton Bryan Castle in Herefordshire, the home of the Harley family, was damaged during two sieges, before its parliamentarian garrison eventually surrendered in March 1644. It was then slighted

billeting and for the revenue which they yielded, but of little or no use as permanent bases. On the other hand, many of the larger and middle sized towns had existing fortifications which could be brought up to date relatively easily, and they occupied sites that had a defensive value and had originally been settled for that reason. They were also in economically, and therefore strategically, advantageous locations; the focus of communications, ports, or bridging points on the major rivers. This pattern was a reversal of that of accidental fires. The larger and more important towns were less prone to suffer conflagrations than the smaller ones, probably because of the effective application of building regulations and other precautions aimed at reducing the incidence of fires. The authorities in the smaller towns, especially those which were unincorporated, found it difficult to enforce the necessary restrictions. The Civil War caused extensive destruction in such towns as Exeter, Newcastle-upon-Tyne, York, Leicester, Hereford, Gloucester, Worcester and Carlisle, all of which had escaped major fire damage during the sixteenth and early seventeenth centuries.

Location was another factor determining the incidence of destruction. East Anglia and the South East represented the core areas of parliamentarian control during the first Civil War. They were not invaded by the royalists and so the places within them did not have to resist a hostile force or prepare for a siege. King's Lynn marked the limit of military activity to the north-west of this area and it suffered from some destruction of property as a consequence of the siege of 1643.[11] Cambridge was close enough to the area threatened by royalist operations to be at least partly fortified and sixteen houses there were destroyed when the castle's defences were renovated.[12] There was some destruction at London when its fortifications were constructed and, to the south, Arundel marked the easternmost limit of royalist incursions, sustaining some damage when the castle was besieged and recaptured by parliamentarian troops in 1644.[13] Generally, places east of a line drawn between these four towns did not suffer loss of property for military reasons during the first Civil War, with the exception of some comparatively minor destruction in the fortified ports, such as Great Yarmouth. This pattern was modified somewhat by the events of the second Civil War because of the campaign in Kent, including the defence of Maidstone by the royalists, and the siege of Colchester, where 186 householders were burned out.[14]

Over much of the remainder of England and Wales communities did suffer physical damage, for most areas were subjected to some military activity. The intensity of the conflict varied, however. While some regions, especially the Midlands, were repeatedly fought over and so suffered considerable losses, others were not heavily contested and so escaped with relatively little destruction. There were areas within the war zone that were disputed territory for only a part of the conflict. Much of northern England was pacified as a result of the campaigns of 1644, with only a few royalist garrisons remaining to be subdued in the following year. But with the decline in the royalists' fortunes following the defeats of the king's armies in 1644 and 1645, those regions that had been largely under their control were invaded and the defended towns within them sustained sieges or assaults.

There was a chronological as well as a geographical pattern to the destruction, with an increasing incidence as the war progressed. This was partly a reflection of the widening of the war and the greater number of places that were fortified or otherwise affected. It was also a consequence of the intensification of the conflict, the greater numbers of men under arms, an improvement in the supply of artillery pieces and their ammunition, the increasing dominance and power of the military, and the greater authority gained by professional officers with previous experience of war. Destruction began in the summer of 1642, but there had been little extensive damage by the end of that year. It was in 1643 that the pattern of military operations was largely established and the fortification of many towns was first undertaken. During that year there were destructive sieges at Gloucester, Exeter, Reading, Hull, Bristol and King's Lynn, and the precautionary demolition of buildings at a number of other towns, including Coventry, Chester and Shrewsbury. Also in 1643, raids and assaults resulted in the loss of property at Birmingham, Cirencester, Gainsborough, Lancaster, Swanbourne and elsewhere. Nevertheless, had the war ended at the close of that year it would not have caused a considerable amount of damage. It was from that point onwards, and especially in the last two years of the first Civil War, that the greatest destruction was inflicted. Suburban clearances were completed at many towns in this phase of the conflict, during which York, Newcastle-upon-Tyne, Carlisle, Exeter, Oxford, Hereford and Worcester, amongst the larger towns,

Dauentry

Brimidghani

The moſt Illuſtrious and High borne PRINCE RUPERT,
PRINCE ELECTOR, Second Son to FREDERICK
KING of BOHEMIA, GENERALL of the HORSE
of His MAJESTIES ARMY, KNIGHT of the Noble
Order of the GARTER.

Prince Rupert was the bogeyman of the parliamentarian propagandists. Here his equestrian portrait, a characteristic form of the Civil War, is pointedly set against a background of Birmingham in flames

suffered their greatest losses of property. It also saw many sieges, including the particularly destructive ones at Pontefract, Banbury and Lyme Regis, as well as the burning of Taunton, Axminster, Bridgwater, Bridgnorth and Faringdon.

The length of the first Civil War limited the extent of the destruction, however, for had the royalists somehow been able to revive their fortunes and continue the conflict beyond 1646 – thereby prolonging the campaigns, increasing the numbers of sieges and extending the search for revenue – the amounts of property destroyed would surely have been greater. The second Civil War, in 1648, was marked by intensive but localised campaigns, with particularly destructive sieges at Colchester, Scarborough and Pembroke, and at Pontefract, where the royalist garrison of the castle did not surrender until 21 March 1649. But again, the failure of the royalists to widen the war or sustain their efforts restricted the amount of destruction.

Inevitably, the severity of the destruction varied, with some towns and districts escaping relatively lightly, while others within the same region suffered comparatively heavy damage. The area around Lyme Regis was intensively fought over and experienced considerable losses of property. The town itself was subjected to a royalist siege in the spring of 1644. During the royalist army's preparations a fire was accidentally started by troops quartered in nearby Beaminster. The blaze spread and by the time it had been quenched 144 houses had been burnt down,[15] more than in any fire in England since that in Wymondham in 1615, although the conflagration in Oxford a few months later was to be even more destructive. This desolation of the town removed a useful resource and was an inauspicious beginning to the royalists' operation against Lyme, which they had expected to be a brief one. The successful resistance of the garrison in a siege lasting eight weeks resulted in the destruction of many houses, including most of those outside the defences, which the parliamentarians had cleared in anticipation of an attack. The town was subjected to bombardments and raids by the besiegers and several fires were started; one of them destroyed twenty houses and another gutted three more. By the time that the royalists had abandoned the siege 'there was scarce a house in the whole Towne that was not battered, and scarce a roome into which, shot had not beene made'.[16]

In addition to the damage at Lyme itself, both sides were busy during the subsequent months destroying houses in the vicinity to prevent them being garrisoned. In January 1645 it was reported that 'All the great houses' around the town had been destroyed, with the exception of Lord Arundel's at Chideock Castle, and that was slighted during the following summer.[17] There was a burst of preventive destruction by the parliamentarians in November 1644, when they feared a renewed threat to Lyme, during which Abbotsbury House was destroyed.[18] They also mounted two raids on Axminster, which had recently been reoccupied by the royalists. Unable to drive the defenders from the church, the raiding parties set the houses on fire and virtually all of the town was burnt down 'unless it were some few houses'. It was later reported that 200 houses had been destroyed. This action was justified on the grounds that the royalist garrison there was a threat to both Lyme and Taunton and obstructed communications between these, the only two parliamentarian garrisons in the area.[19]

Another market town that suffered such extensive destruction was Faringdon in Berkshire, where Faringdon House, on the edge of the town, was one of the ring of defensive garrisons around Oxford. In April 1646, anticipating a siege, its garrison destroyed almost the whole of the town.[20] An attempt to capture the house in a surprise attack in the previous year had failed, but it is likely that the experience gained by the defenders on that occasion, when the town itself had been occupied by the enemy, was an important factor as they made ready for a siege. The church stood within the defensive perimeter and so it was not taken down, although it did sustain substantial damage during the siege. At one point the parliamentarian artillery fire was directed at the steeple, where the royalists had posted marksmen, and as it seemed likely that it would fall into the moat the garrison undermined it in such a way that it collapsed within the defences. On another occasion a mortar grenade scored a direct hit on one of the transepts, inflicting such damage that it was subsequently demolished.[21] The loss was certified as 'the whole Towne almost pulled down, demolished & wilfully consumed by fire' and a detailed assessment of the scale of the damage gave a figure of 1,210 'bays of building' destroyed and reported that 236 families had been made homeless, suggesting that approximately 200 houses had been destroyed.[22]

Other towns in the defensive ring around Oxford to suffer destruction included Abingdon, Wallingford – where two churches close to the castle were pulled down – and Woodstock.[23] Some country houses were also destroyed and a number of villages were damaged.[24] Buildings in Swanbourne and Chinnor were burned down in royalist raids in 1643,[25] but the greatest damage in the area was caused as Oxford itself came under increasing threat towards the end of the war, when its satellite garrisons were attacked. In June 1645 the futile attempt by the New Model to capture Boarstall House was immediately followed by the destruction of the village and the church. Although there had evidently been some earlier destruction, it is curious that the experienced governor, Sir William Campion, did not clear the buildings before, rather than after, the siege.[26] The same error was not committed five months later when a parliamentarian force under Colonel Dalbier approached Donnington Castle, for the governor there, Sir John Boys, promptly destroyed the nearby village of roughly thirty houses, to prevent the besiegers from quartering in it.[27]

The most concentrated destruction in the region came not from military action, however, but in an accidental fire in Oxford in October 1644. It began near the North Gate and cut a swathe through the town, running southwards to the Thames and destroying approximately 300 houses, twice the scale of the damage suffered at Beaminster. This major disaster was one of the worst blazes in a provincial town in the seventeenth century, but because of the circumstances in which it occurred it attracted comparatively little sympathy and attention.[28]

There was also some clearance of buildings for defensive purposes around Oxford. In 1643 a large fort was constructed in St Clement's on the east side of Magdalen Bridge, displacing seventeen households. Those who were made homeless were given careful consideration; some were assigned accommodation elsewhere in the town and others were allotted land on which to build new

The earthworks beyond the moated enclosure at Boarstall in Buckinghamshire mark the site of the village which was destroyed in June 1645. The house, a royalist garrison, stood within the moat and has since been demolished. The church was rebuilt in 1663; it stands to the side of the moat

houses.[29] This sympathetic treatment may indicate the royalists' desire not to alienate the population in the comparatively early stages of their occupation. It contrasts with their attitude in the autumn of 1644, when they received a petition from the citizens outlining their grievances and mentioning the distress caused by the fire. It was received with scant sympathy and those presenting it were thrown in gaol.[30] Nor is there evidence that provision was made for those displaced in the next major phase of defensive destruction at Oxford, which was more extensive. This was prompted by the approach of the New Model in the spring of 1645, when the defenders were reported to have burnt the remaining suburbs beyond the lines. This siege was unsuccessful and seems not to have been vigorously pursued, but the king's defeat at Naseby shortly afterwards made a more determined attempt a distinct possibility and so the clearance was carried out over a wider area. It included the destruction of Marston and North Hinksey, both well over a mile from the city.[31] The stage by stage demolition at Oxford was characteristic of defensive destruction during the war.

Some towns were not approached by an enemy force and so only preliminary destruction was carried out and there was no need to follow it up by more extensive clearances. This was the case at Southampton, where some buildings, including the houses on the site of the former chantry of St Mary, were destroyed, but as the town was not besieged there was no need for a complete removal of the extra-mural properties.[32] Its neighbours were not so fortunate. There was extensive damage at Winchester, both in the suburbs and within the city, and Portsmouth was bombarded by a parliamentarian battery in 1642.[33] The smaller Hampshire towns also sustained losses of property. A royalist raid on Gosport resulted in the burning of twenty-five houses there, and a number of

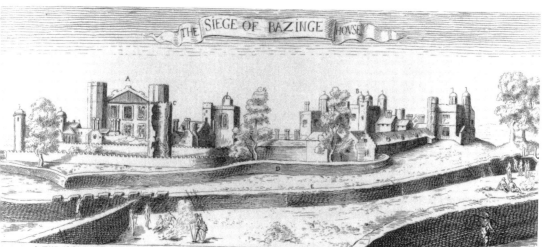

A. THE OLDE HOVSE. B. THE NEW. C. THE TOWER THAT IS HALFE BATTERED DOVNE. D. THE KINGES BREAST WORKS. E. THE PARLIAMENTS BREAST WORKS.

This view of Basing House in Hampshire during the Civil War shows the damage inflicted by the parliamentarian batteries. Almost total destruction followed the capture of the house in October 1645

Although the earthworks of Basing House remain impressive features, little survives of the Marquis of Winchester's medieval castle and sixteenth-century mansion, defended by the royalists until stormed by the New Model Army in October 1645. Much of the nearby village was also destroyed

houses were set on fire during the parliamentarian capture of Alton in 1643 and at Alresford in the following year.[34] Basing suffered extensive damage during the sieges of Basing House, with both the besiegers and the defenders setting buildings on fire at various times. In 1645 the House itself was destroyed, partly by bombardment and partly by a blaze which began following its capture by Cromwell's troops.[35] Basing's chief rival garrison, to the east, was at Farnham and there was some destruction in the neighbourhood as well as in the town itself. Some of the losses in the town may have been the result of defensive demolition in the vicinity of the castle, but others occurred in the fires started during a royalist raid. John Evelyn described Farnham in 1654 as having 'newly ben fir'd, during the Warrs'.[36] To the north, in the Thames valley, was Reading, which neither side was able to hold for long; the citizens lamented that the town was 'the frontyer to them both'. It was enclosed within earthwork defences and property outside the fortifications was cleared. There was further damage during the siege by the Earl of Essex's army in 1643 when the bombardment 'beat down many houses' and the steeple of one of the churches.[37]

In Sussex the damage was limited because the royalists failed to penetrate further east than Arundel. There were thirty-eight claimants for compensation for property destroyed in that town, their losses being valued at £3,772.[38] Even more damage was inflicted upon Chichester, an early casualty of the war, which was bombarded by Waller's artillery for two weeks before the governor, Sir Edward Ford, surrendered the city in early January 1643. The suburbs and the two extra-mural churches were destroyed, partly by the royalists before and during the siege, and partly by the parliamentarians completing the task after they had captured the city, in order to secure their prize.[39]

The extent of such defensive clearances largely depended upon the perception of the scale of the potential threat and the determination of those in charge to make the defences as secure as possible. This was reflected in the contrasting reactions at Coventry and Gloucester to the danger posed by the successful royalist campaign in the summer of 1643, which included the unexpectedly swift capture of Bristol on 26 July.

Coventry had endured a brief, though crucial, siege in August 1642, when the king's demand to be admitted had been refused and his army had been successfully resisted until relief arrived. That experience and the city's commitment to the parliamentarian cause may have influenced the reaction to the prospect of another siege a year later.[40] On 15 August 1643 the Common Council decided to act on the recommendation of the city's parliamentarian committee that, because of the danger of a siege, houses in the suburbs should be pulled down, all the hedges and trees around the city removed, and the ditches filled in. To hasten the completion of the task it ordered that all the shops should close, except on market days, so that the citizens could 'wholly imploy themselves about the work'.[41] Many of the city's wartime losses must have occurred during this period. They were later reported to be four houses, a barn, a mill, a malthouse and a further 580 'bays of building', suggesting that approximately 100 houses were destroyed. A survey revealed that ninety individual owners, fifty-two tenants, the city corporation, Holy Trinity parish and seven guild companies had suffered losses. The valuation was £3,484 17s. 10d. for the buildings and other unspecified losses, presumably including goods.[42]

Gloucester is fifty miles closer to Bristol than Coventry and was an obvious target for the royalists, anxious to secure its bridge over the Severn and so open direct communications between Oxford and their recruiting grounds in South Wales. Like Coventry, it contained a dominant puritan element, and it, too, had already been threatened by royalist forces. Prince Rupert had summoned the town to surrender in the previous February and it had been approached by an army moving in from the west a few weeks later. These incidents may have led to a consideration of the ability of its defences to withstand a siege, and indeed some of the housing in the suburbs had been destroyed and the church of St Owen taken down by the summer of 1643. Moreover, the possibility that the remainder of the extra-mural property would have to be cleared had been recognised a month before the fall of Bristol, when a committee had been appointed to allocate accommodation to those who would be made homeless. It is therefore all the more surprising that most of the suburbs were not set on fire until the evening of the day that the royalist army appeared before the town and the king demanded its surrender.[43] This delay cannot plausibly be attributed to a major error of judgement by Edward Massey, the governor, for he was one of the more able Civil War commanders and must have been aware of the danger of leaving the suburbs standing as an enemy army approached. It might have reflected his comparative weakness when dealing with the civic magistrates and the divided opinions within the corporation's ruling élite about the advisability of resisting the king's army. Perhaps it was thought that to destroy the suburbs before it was absolutely necessary to do so would be regarded by the royalists as an act of defiance and provoke a military response which the civic leaders wished to avoid. The question of destruction was faced only at the very last minute, when it could no longer be put off. The reactions of the chroniclers of the ensuing siege reflect the contrasting attitudes of the two sides to the burning of the remaining houses. The royalist opinion expressed by Clarendon was that the loss of the suburbs would cause unrest and strengthen the hand of those citizens who favoured coming to terms with the besiegers, while John Corbet's view from within the town was that the conflagration 'did secure and more strongly engage us, and which the enemy

Edward Massey was the parliamentarian governor of Gloucester during the siege of 1643, when the garrison resisted the king's forces for four weeks until relieved by the Earl of Essex's army

beheld as the act of desperate rebells; for those dreadfull sights doe seeme to heighten and bloud the minds of men'.[44] In fact, the pro-royalist elements were relatively weak and did not influence the course of the siege, and Gloucester resisted until relief arrived almost four weeks later, bringing the royalist army's run of successes to an end.

An investigation made in 1646 evaluated 'all the losses sustained by firing and pulling down of Houses in the Suburbs' and listed 241 houses, but did not quantify the 'many barnes, stables, out houses, gardens, orchards, which were also destroyed'. The value of the property destroyed was £22,240, a figure of £4,500 was given for the goods which had been lost, and £2,000 was added for damage caused by the deliberate flooding of the meadows near to the town. The total of £28,740 did not include a sum for the loss of St Owen's church.[45]

The contrast between the two cities is striking. Not only was Coventry's financial loss a relatively modest one, scarcely one-eighth of Gloucester's, but the proportion of houses destroyed there was also much less than at Gloucester, for the number removed at Coventry was only 40 per cent of those cleared away at Gloucester, yet Coventry was much the larger of the two, perhaps half as big again as Gloucester. These two cases indicate the differing scale of defensive destruction suffered by a town which sustained a siege and one which prepared for an investment but was spared the experience.

Gloucester's ordeal of being defended in a major siege which involved the removal of virtually all property outside the defences was shared by many of the cities and towns in the Severn valley, the West Country, Wales and the Marches. Exeter, Hereford and Worcester had the common experience of being attacked in 1643 and sustaining major sieges in the later stages of the war. At all three cities the bulk of the extra-mural property was cleared away and, by analogy, the losses cannot have been less than at Gloucester: at the larger cities of Exeter and Worcester they may have been considerably more. The removal of Exeter's suburbs was spread over more than three years, culminating in the royalist preparations for a siege in the autumn and winter of 1645–6. By the time that the garrison yielded to the New Model in April 1646 buildings had been cleared from outside the defences in the Southernhay, Holloway, St Sidwell's, St David's and St Thomas's districts.[46] The losses included the Magdalen and Wynard's almshouses, which between them had accommodated twenty-four of the eighty-nine almspeople provided for in the city.[47] Hereford was briefly held by parliamentarian forces in the spring of 1643, but was in royalist hands for most of the first Civil War. It resisted a month-long siege by the Scottish army in August 1645, but was taken in a cleverly executed surprise attack in the following December. Much of the destruction occurred because of the siege in 1645. Sir Henry Slingsby had quartered there in the early part of the war and when he returned with the royalist army that raised the siege he set out to visit the house where he had lodged, but 'found it pull'd down, & ye Gentlewoman yt had liv'd in it dead upon grief to see ye ruins of her house'. As well as the suburban housing, the two extra-mural churches of St Owen's and St Martin's were also destroyed.[48] At Worcester property was destroyed on all sides of the city, including the suburb of St Clement's across the Severn. The losses caused by the 'Burning of the suburbs, hospitals, &c &c' were valued at £100,000. This was apparently an estimate, not the result of a detailed survey, and the figure is suspect because it is both high and 'round'. Nevertheless, it is possible that as many as 400 houses, one-fifth of the city's total, were destroyed.[49]

Bristol suffered the unfortunate experience of twice being taken by assault. The extensive defences protected many of its suburbs. Even so, there was considerable destruction, caused by the clearance of the property outside the perimeter on the south side of the city, some demolition around the castle, and in the fires started during the parliamentarian assault in 1645.[50] There was also an accidental fire in 1643, which burnt down four or five houses 'of great eminency', and another, more serious, one in 1647, when twenty-four houses on the bridge were destroyed. The fire in 1647 was especially damaging because the houses destroyed belonged to some of the wealthiest of the citizens and it came at a time when money was needed to replace the wartime losses.[51] Villages around the city also suffered badly during the defensive clearances carried out by the garrison. The inhabitants of Bedminster claimed that not only had their parish church been gutted, but that 'a great number of their houses were . . . likewise burned to the ground'. The losses there were valued by 'able workmen' at £5,470.[52]

The smaller towns in the Marches and the West Country that were fortified also suffered considerably. The suburbs at Shrewsbury were cleared in 1643 on the orders of Lord Capel and a large fort was built at Frankwell, on the west side of the Severn.[53] At Oswestry, which was captured by the parliamentarians in 1644, St Oswald's church and 'many houses that were without the wall' were pulled down, and at the parliamentarian garrison of Wem 'all houses and buildings outside the towne were burned'.[54] Some of the suburbs of Ludlow were saved by the arrival of the parliamentarian force which captured the town in 1646, before the defenders could destroy them, but some property there had already been destroyed.[55] In the West Country, Bridgwater was well defended and it not only lost its suburbs, but also those buildings burnt during the New Model's attack in 1645, including virtually all of those in the district of Eastover.[56] The whole loss during the Civil War was put at 120 houses, and as the parish had contained roughly 400 houses at the beginning of the war, the estimate that a third of Bridgwater had been destroyed was approximately correct.[57] A similar number of houses was reported to have been destroyed when the royalist garrison of Tiverton Castle cleared away property in the town in anticipation of a siege in 1645, but the figure was given in parliamentarian sources and there was no post-war survey to support it.[58] Nor can the numbers of houses lost at Barnstaple, Dartmouth, Malmesbury, Devizes, Poole and other defended towns in the region be determined. The explosion of the royalists' magazine in Great Torrington during the successful attack by the New Model in February 1646 wrecked the church and many of the houses, doing so much damage that the town was described as 'a meere desolation, and ugly as the face of War', although it is not clear that any buildings were actually destroyed.[59]

The garrisoned towns in north and mid-Wales were damaged, particularly towards the end of the first Civil War, when they were threatened with sieges following the parliamentarian successes in subduing most of Cheshire and

Shropshire. Property outside the town walls at Carnarvon and Denbigh was destroyed, a part of Bangor was burnt by its defenders, and 'many fair houses' in Aberystwyth were ruined.[60] In addition to the deliberate destruction by the military, there was an accidental fire in Wrexham in 1643 that burnt down 143 houses, which was said to represent one-quarter of the town. It was the worst fire in the principality during the seventeenth century.[61]

The larger towns in South Wales also suffered losses of property. The damage at Pembroke was particularly extensive because of its role as a key parliamentarian garrison in the first Civil War and the lengthy siege of the castle in 1648. Destruction caused when the royalists under Gerrard attacked the town in 1645 was carried out by both the defenders and the assailants, and three years later Cromwell's forces used artillery to set fire to houses within the fortifications. The damage inflicted during those sieges was not limited to the town itself, for houses in the nearby village of Monkton were also destroyed. Again, the number of properties demolished and burnt was not assessed.[62]

The extensive losses in two small towns in the Welsh borders were appraised, however. Bridgnorth's position commanding a bridge over the Severn gave it considerable strategic importance and the royalists made suitably thorough efforts to secure it, removing the extra-mural buildings and fitting up the castle as a citadel.[63] Following the capture of the town the garrison withdrew into the castle and started fires which burnt for two days and did extensive damage in the High Town.[64] The appeal for assistance stated that 300 families were affected by the destruction and valued the losses at £60,000, figures which probably incorporated allowances for the earlier demolitions outside the town walls, as well as the effects of the fire.[65] The losses of two individuals help to put these claims into perspective. One had thirty-five houses and barns destroyed, valued at about £3,000 and producing an annual rent of £15, and the other had lost seventy-four houses, which had brought him an annual income of £200 before the war and were valued at £12,000.[66] Many of the buildings gutted were in the main street, which contained some of the finest houses in the town. The valuation, which included personal possessions, may therefore have been a realistic one; it was only £3,000 greater than that for Faringdon, where rather fewer houses were destroyed.

There was a similar situation at Holt, where the castle commanded the bridge over the River Dee and was fortified, although the town itself was not defensible. The result was that much property there was destroyed, especially during the parliamentarian investment of the castle in 1646. The garrison was accused of destroying much of the town and a petition presented after the Restoration put the loss at 103 houses.[67] The village of Farndon, on the opposite side of the Dee, also fared badly. It suffered some damage when Brereton's troops forced the river crossing in November 1643, and again when the garrison at Holt carried out preventive destruction of buildings in February 1645, following the withdrawal of the parliamentarian force which had been placed there to restrict its movements.[68]

The Midlands saw much fighting and several sieges during the first Civil War, but some of its towns escaped relatively lightly, while others were badly damaged. Although Coventry escaped a prolonged siege and so suffered only limited

Lord Brooke was parliamentarian commander-in-chief for Warwickshire, Staffordshire, Leicestershire and Derbyshire. He was killed by a marksman in March 1643 while directing the siege of Lichfield Close

destruction, its neighbours had mixed fortunes. Some property at Northampton was destroyed for defensive reasons and there was a contingency plan to clear away the suburb of Cotton End if a siege seemed likely, but the threat did not materialise.[69] Warwick was less fortunate in that respect. The castle was besieged as early as August 1642, having already been fortified by Lord Brooke, and some buildings in the town were demolished when the earthwork fortifications were constructed.[70]

Leicester suffered much more badly, for although suburban property there was destroyed, the task was only partially completed, and the buildings that were left contributed to the weakness of the defences when the royalists appeared before the town in 1645. An urgent warning had been sent by the Committee of Both Kingdoms a few weeks before, pointing out that the defences were inadequate. Some buildings were burnt down at the eleventh hour, when the royalists had already invested the town, and at an even later stage in the proceedings than at Gloucester. The defects in the defences were apparent to the king and his officers, who chose to mount an assault rather than a siege. Their judgement proved to be correct, for the town was captured, and then, for its pains, it was 'miserably sackt without regard to Church or Hospital'. It was later alleged that houses that were useful to the royalists had been standing intact at the time of the attack, many of them within pistol shot of the defences, despite the earlier warning.[71] If awards for

Leicester was stormed by the royalist army in May 1645 and was recaptured in the following month, having sustained considerable damage in the two operations. Prince Rupert is shown sending a summons to the garrison before the assault

prevarication had been made during the Civil War, Leicester would have been a very strong contender for first prize.[72] The town's later misfortunes were not so clearly of its own making. Only sixteen days after its capture by the royalists the New Model appeared before it, fresh from its victory at Naseby, and when its summons to surrender was rejected it mounted a siege and began to bombard the town. The governor quickly surrendered on terms, but the hand-over was so badly conducted that not only did members of the garrison leave their posts prematurely to carry out some further plundering, but they were joined by some stragglers from the New Model, as well as the prisoners who had been released and who 'finding the Garrison a Plundering they fell a Plundering too'.[73] The citizens subsequently claimed that more than 120 of their houses had been destroyed and 'much ground digged up and spoyled'.[74]

In the West Midlands, Dudley Castle contained a royalist garrison, which did not attempt to fortify the town, but cleared away St Edmund's church and other buildings close to the castle's outer wall. When a parliamentarian force approached, the soldiers set fire to a number of houses. Despite these measures, Colonel Leveson, the governor, surrendered the castle soon afterwards. He was escorted away from the castle by a troop of parliamentarian horse for his own safety, as he had aroused hostility by his activities in controlling the area and then

The most spectacular damage inflicted on St Chad's cathedral at Lichfield was the demolition of the central spire. Restoration of the fabric, including the rebuilding of the spire, was carried out in the 1660s. The above view, by William Smith, was published in 1588, and that below, drawn by William Dugdale after the Civil Wars, shows the extent of the destruction

incensed the inhabitants by surrendering without resisting a siege, so that the buildings had been destroyed unnecessarily.[75] Lichfield cathedral close was fitted up as a citadel, but the town was regarded as indefensible. Sieges of the close in 1643 and 1646 caused destruction both there and in the town. The cathedral was damaged by artillery fire and some buildings in the close were destroyed, while the royalist defenders burnt down property outside their perimeter, including Beacon Street, on the west side of the close, where fifty-two houses belonging to the Vicars' Choral were destroyed.[76] Birmingham was even more vulnerable, being not only unsuitable for defence but also lacking a building or group which could be fortified. Its inhabitants were, therefore, extremely rash to oppose the passage of Prince Rupert's army in 1643. The royalists destroyed some buildings both during their successful assault and later, as they withdrew to continue their march. Some reports stated that 'near a hundred dwellings' had been burnt down, others put the number at eighty.[77]

There was also destruction at the smaller Midland garrisons. The parliamentarian governor of Edgbaston House, 'Tinker' Fox, allegedly 'pulld downe the church to make the workes'. The building was later said to have been 'totally Demolished', although it seems that it was a case of severe damage rather than destruction. Other buildings near the house were burnt.[78] Hawkesley House and Beoley House to the south of Edgbaston, Stoke House in Warwickshire, and Astley House near Coventry were among the garrisoned houses that were destroyed.[79] The house and church at Rushall formed a group which was fortified by the royalists and during the successful parliamentarian assault in 1644 the church was badly damaged by artillery fire from a battery that included the 'Stafford Greate Piece'. The losses in Leicestershire included the burning of the manor house at Coleorton, a parliamentarian garrison near to the royalist-held castle at Ashby de la Zouch.[80]

The towns in the North Midlands experienced similarly contrasting fortunes. Derby was garrisoned and precautionary demolition caused the removal of buildings outside the defences, but because it was not assaulted the extent of such destruction was limited.[81] Nottingham Castle served as a citadel and was successfully defended by its parliamentarian garrison, but the town was captured on one occasion, despite its earthwork fortifications. The experience gained resulted in the clearance of some property within the town, including St Nicholas's church, which had been shown to be a potential threat to the castle.[82] Stafford was also fortified, initially by the royalists, and later by the parliamentarians, who captured it in 1643. The property in the suburbs was cleared away, particularly that in the long Foregate Street, and at the Grey Friars, on its north side. Much of the destruction was ordered following its capture, but there is no indication of the numbers of houses or the proportion of the buildings in the town that were destroyed.[83] Nor are figures available for Burton-upon-Trent, which may have suffered quite severely, for it was taken by assault by the royalists in 1643, and Sir Arthur Capel wrote that 'a greate parte of the towne' was burnt during the fighting. St Modwen's church was damaged at that time, when some gunpowder stored in it was accidentally ignited, 'which blew up the roof and burst all the windows'.[84]

In the East Midlands, both Newark and Lincoln suffered considerable damage. Newark's position close to the point where the Great North Road crossed the Trent gave it considerable strategic importance. It was garrisoned by the royalists in 1642 and did not surrender until May 1646, by which time it was protected by extensive earthwork defences. It sustained an assault in February 1643 and two major sieges, one in 1644 and the second from November 1645 until its capitulation. The first assault illustrated the danger posed by the houses outside the defences and soon afterwards the governor, Sir John Henderson, ordered them to be burned, together with the Countess of Exeter's house known as the Spittal. The ruined walls of the Spittal were not demolished, however, and in the siege of 1644 the parliamentarians 'built them up' and made entrenchments there; only after that siege was raised were they cleared away. In addition to defensive

The siege of Newark in 1645–6 by the Scottish and English armies was one of the longest sieges of the first Civil War. By then the defences were fully developed and the besiegers constructed their own elaborate earthworks

destruction, the town also suffered some loss of property in the bombardments during the two sieges. The parliamentarian press reported in 1646 that there were 'thatcht houses and ricks of Hay and Corn' within the town and that 'divers houses [were] burnt and battered' by their artillery. It was later estimated that one-sixth of the town had been destroyed, and some of the villages around it were also damaged.[85]

At Lincoln, houses outside the defences on all sides of the town were destroyed, as were some within them, including those burnt down in the fire which began accidentally on 3 May 1644 and also gutted St Swithun's church. Among the other churches destroyed or severely damaged were St Nicholas's, Newport, and St Peter's in Eastgate – both of which were demolished because they stood too close to the defences – St Martin's, St Benedict's, St Michael's-on-the-Mount and St Mary Magdalene. St Botolph's was so badly damaged that it collapsed in 1646. The city clearly suffered very badly, although its historian has concluded that the extent of the damage cannot be calculated.[86]

Among the smaller garrisons in the region which were damaged were Gainsborough, where a fire broke out when it was captured by the Earl of Newcastle's army in 1643, and the houses at Wiveton, Shelford and Torksey, all of which were destroyed after they were captured.[87] The village of Belvoir was cleared away because of its proximity to the castle, which was itself slighted in 1649. To the south, Crowland lay on the frontier of territory controlled by the royalists and that held by the Eastern Association, and the town was occupied by both sides at different times, sustaining a siege by the parliamentarians in 1644. Some buildings there were demolished for defensive reasons. At Rockingham the damage done when the church, houses and other buildings were removed on the orders of Sir John Norwich, the governor of the castle, was valued at £2,000.[88]

The same pattern can be recognised across much of northern England. There were extensive suburban clearances at most of the larger towns, notably Newcastle-upon-Tyne, Carlisle, York and Chester. At Newcastle the numbers of houses destroyed were variously and erratically estimated at 'several hundred', 500 and almost a thousand.[89] There was further destruction in some of the neighbouring communities: in 1644 the royalists reported that they had set fire to Newburn, for example.[90] The extent of the devastation at Carlisle is also uncertain, although the suburbs were burnt down before and during the siege of 1644–5, and other damage involved the demolition of a part of the cathedral nave and some of the canons' houses. The surrender was followed by a severe and prolonged outbreak of plague and in 1647 the city was reported to be a 'modell of miserie and desolation'.[91] The impact of the Civil War upon York included the destruction of the suburbs, with 'all the houses in some streets being burnt and broken downe to the ground'. In 1642 the suburbs had contained one-sixth of the houses in the city, which can be interpreted as approximately 400 houses.[92] At Chester the losses included virtually all of the suburbs, the nearby villages of Boughton and Christleton, half a dozen mansions outside, but close to, the city and a number of houses within it that were destroyed by the parliamentarian bombardment in 1645–6. More than 1,600 people were reported to have been displaced, suggesting that between 300 and 350 houses were destroyed. The figure given for the value of the 'damages sustained by Demolitions' was £200,000, but that was surely an exaggeration, especially as a valuation of nine houses and twelve outbuildings destroyed at Boughton totalled a little under £600 for both structures and goods.[93]

Destruction elsewhere was caused by the clearance of suburban property – at Hull, Manchester and Liverpool, for example – while Liverpool and Bolton both suffered badly when they were taken by assault. Liverpool was described as having been 'in a great Part destroyed and burnt'.[94] The operations around Hull and York produced damage at the towns in the area, such as Tadcaster – where houses were burnt down during an assault in December 1642 – and Selby. Beverley's defences were renovated and the body of St Nicholas's church was demolished, and Bridlington was subjected to a naval bombardment by parliamentarian ships following the landing of the queen there in 1643.[95] The raiding between the garrisons in the West Riding led to destruction in the towns and some of the villages. At Heptonstall fourteen houses and barns were burnt by a party from the royalist garrison at Halifax that was anxious to displace an enemy force that had based itself there.[96] More extensive damage was caused in a larger operation of the same kind at Lancaster, where the royalists succeeded in capturing the town, but could not force the surrender of the castle. They were compelled to withdraw and, as they did so, they deliberately started fires which destroyed ninety houses and almost as many other buildings. The Earl of Derby reported to Prince Rupert that as his summons had been rejected he had 'made bold to burn the greatest part of the town'.[97]

Scarborough and Pontefract suffered in a similar way to Lancaster, but over much longer periods; indeed they were among the worst affected towns in the north, so far as intensity of destruction was concerned. In both cases their castles were besieged in both the first Civil War and in 1648, by forces occupying the respective towns. In such circumstances it was almost inevitable that considerable damage would be done. At Scarborough it was St Mary's, the wealthiest quarter of the town, which suffered most badly and the church there was ruined. But the whole town was affected to some extent, with all four of the mills demolished and St Thomas's church 'quite ruined, and battered down'.[98]

At Pontefract the castle was held by its royalist garrison during two sieges which began in December 1644 and lasted for seven months, with an interval of only three weeks between them. In the second Civil War there was a further siege, in which the castle was defended for twenty weeks. The castle stood between two sections of the town, and All Saints' church and vicarage, with much of the housing, lay between the castle and the lines of circumvallation. Once the parliamentarians had taken control of the town in 1644, the garrison attempted to burn property near to the castle and was said to have destroyed 100 houses within two weeks of the beginning of the siege. Thereafter, the two sieges of 1644–5 were punctuated by the destruction of buildings, mostly by the defenders, in sallies or with projectiles, but some of the damage was attributed to the besiegers. The body of the church was ruined, as were the town hall, courthouse, town bakehouse and a windmill. The siege of 1648 probably led to further destruction and certainly interrupted the process of recovery. Because of the position of the

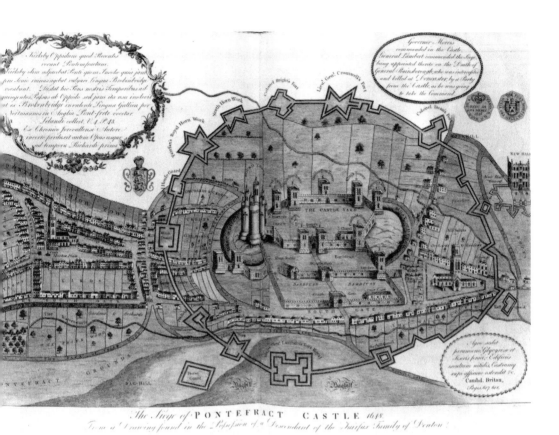

The Siege of PONTEFRACT CASTLE *1648.*
From a Drawing found in the Possession of a Descendant of the Fairfax family of Denton.

Pontefract Castle was besieged twice in 1644–5 and again in 1648–9. The plan shows that part of the town lay between the castle and the besiegers' works. Not surprisingly, many buildings were destroyed during these operations

castle relative to the town, and the duration of the military operations, there was severe damage, with the total loss put at roughly 200 houses and the value at £40,000. This was a classic case of a garrisoned citadel within a town which was itself indefensible resulting in heavy defensive destruction over a prolonged period.[99]

The circumstances at Scarborough and Pontefract readily fit into the general scheme of Civil War destruction, but two further examples, one from the north of England and the other from the south, show that the pattern was far from simple or predictable. The small village of North Scale on Walney Island off Furness in north-west Lancashire was away from the main areas of warfare, was not fortified and did not contain a building which could serve as a citadel, yet it was almost totally destroyed in 1644. Following Prince Rupert's defeat at Marston Moor a part of his force under Sir John Mayney marched into Furness to oust a detachment of parliamentarians which had begun to levy taxation, and so restore royalist control there. Mayney's men were victorious in a clash near Dalton and aimed to follow up their success by attacking some parliamentarian troops that had withdrawn to North Scale, but they were driven off, Mayney being ignominiously tumbled from his horse during the encounter. They returned on the following day, found the village abandoned and set the houses on fire, except for one belonging to a known royalist supporter and another that was built of stone.[100] The second example is Bath, a walled town in a strategically important position controlling passage along the Avon valley, that was garrisoned for most of the first Civil War, changed hands twice, and yet emerged intact. It was occupied by the parliamentarians, abandoned by them following Waller's defeat at Roundway Down in 1643, was then garrisoned by the royalists, and was surrendered, to everyone's surprise, to a party of Fairfax's horse and dragoons in 1645 after little more than a brisk exchange of small arms fire. The garrison's lack of resolution in 1645 was partly due to its own low morale, the growing hostility of the inhabitants, news of the outcome of the siege of Bridgwater a week earlier, and perhaps to a realisation that the high ground around the town made it indefensible if artillery were to be sited there. Even so, the failure of both sides in turn to strengthen the defences by demolishing the suburbs is not readily explicable.[101]

Although there were some anomalous cases, such as North Scale and Bath, they did little to distort the general pattern, which contrasted with that of peacetime destruction. As mentioned earlier, it was the larger cities and towns that suffered most badly during the war years, reversing the pattern of accidental fires. It was reversed in another way, for communities in those parts of the country where large-scale fires were largely absent, because of the availability of fire-resistant building materials, were nevertheless sufferers when military logic was applied. Furthermore, the degree of damage caused in the wartime destructions was generally greater than it was during peacetime fires. A number of chance factors influenced the extent of the losses in a blaze that had begun by accident: the time of day or night at which it broke out, how soon it was discovered, the speed and efficiency with which it was tackled, the presence of combustible materials in the vicinity of the fire, the strength and direction of the wind, the warmth and dryness of the weather over the preceding days or weeks, all affected the scale of the damage that was done. These did not apply in the majority of Civil War cases, in which the destruction was deliberate and purposeful, and so was more complete than in accidental fires. Some buildings usually survived the flames in an area that was generally burned down, even in a major fire. In a district that was cleared for military reasons, however, the destruction was often complete.

The destruction in the Civil War was also far more concentrated in time than that caused by accidental fires. There were eighteen fires that destroyed more than 100 houses in provincial towns during the seventeenth century, excluding the years of civil war, but during the six years of conflict in the 1640s at least twenty-three, and perhaps as many as thirty, towns lost property on that scale. Similarly, although there were occasional destructive fires in villages and country houses in peacetime, the comparatively dispersed nature of buildings in country settlements, even nucleated ones, made multiple house fires relatively rare events.

Although there was no strong correlation between the weather and fires, some association has been identified for such warm and dry periods as the mid-1660s and the late 1680s, when there was some grouping of serious outbreaks of fire.[102] Clearly, the deliberate firing and demolition of property was not dependent on the prevailing weather, which was only likely to have an important effect during those artillery bombardments that were designed to start fires. It was because of the concentration of destruction in a relatively short period that this one aspect of the war made such an impact. Accidental fires were not concentrated in time, but occurred at irregular intervals, and so generally attracted sympathetic attention and donations to help the victims. During the Civil Wars, with so many communities affected by similar disasters and the other adverse effects of the conflict, the assistance that was forthcoming was likely to be less and its benefits more diffused than that following peacetime fires.

A related factor was that in almost a half of the cities and towns which lost more than 100 houses during the Civil Wars, it was the relatively highly valued town-centre properties which were destroyed. The low values of average losses per house, including goods, of £80 at Gloucester and approximately £30 at Coventry, compared with figures of perhaps £200 at Pontefract and £250 at Faringdon, point up the contrast between suburban premises and those in the centres of towns. This was important in respect of the consequences of the losses and the speed of restoration, for a community where the better-off citizens were affected because of the destruction of their houses and stock was much more badly impoverished than one where they had suffered little, even though the suburbs may have been destroyed. This was only a difference of degree, however, for whether it was the houses of the wealthier inhabitants or those of the poorer suburban dwellers that were destroyed, for most communities affected by this aspect of the war the destruction itself and the other deleterious effects of the conflict could only serve to exacerbate the considerable problems of recovery.

CHAPTER FIVE

Recovery and Rebuilding

Faringdon . . . begins to bud and spring out again, for here and there a pretty
house peeps up: so that it will in short time be rebuilt, and Phoenix like (out
of its own cinders) be revived and renewed. . . .

John Taylor, Wandering to see the Wonders of the West, *1649*

Amongst the tasks facing the communities and owners whose property had been
destroyed were the provision of alternative accommodation and the replacement
of the buildings lost. The destruction had been most concentrated in the cities
and towns which had experienced the other deleterious features of the war,
including sieges, high mortality, the influx of refugees, quartering, taxation and
occasional levies. A place captured and sacked was in a far worse position than
one which had been surrendered on terms, but the citizens of the latter faced
payment of the fine customarily levied by the victorious army in lieu of
plundering, and it was also common for the captors to take forced loans from the
leading townsmen, particularly those sympathetic to the other side. Taxation and
fines depleted the resources of the individuals upon whom they were imposed,
but because a garrison spent a part of the sums levied within the town, on
quarters and provisions, they produced a redistribution of money within the local
economy and not a complete loss to it. That part remitted to the field armies or
the central treasuries, on the other hand, was an absolute loss, as were crops burnt
or trampled, grain and livestock taken away, and household and trade goods
plundered.

The effects of the financial losses are difficult to assess. Much depended on the
number of times a town changed hands or endured a siege and on the behaviour
of the troops garrisoning it or passing through. There was a clear preference for
locally raised units to serve as a garrison. The unsavoury reputation of Lord
Goring's royalist horse was such that the corporation at Exeter voted Sir John
Berkley, the governor, the large sum of £100 in acknowledgment of his success in
keeping them out of the city in 1645.[1] As well as the direct economic effects of the
war, there were the indirect ones, such as the impact of plague. An epidemic not
only produced high mortality but also drove away those inhabitants who were able
to live elsewhere until conditions improved, and they were generally the wealthier
citizens. The interdiction of trade routes and the disruption of business caused by
the embargoes placed by both sides on commerce with areas in the hands of their
opponents also had an impact, particularly upon communities that relied heavily

upon a single industry, such as the West Country clothing towns. Worcester complained bitterly about the adverse effects that the royalist embargo on trade with areas under parliamentary control was having on its textile industry.[2] Local conditions were also likely to cause problems, for towns grumbled that the presence of a military garrison deterred country people from frequenting their markets. Moreover, soldiers were alleged to forestall the markets by meeting the suppliers some way out of town and buying their produce. There were possible benefits, such as orders for goods for the armies, to set against the detrimental factors. Northampton profited from the contracts placed by the parliamentary forces for footwear, but it was also fortunate because it remained in parliamentarian hands throughout the conflict.[3] It was those places that did not change hands which could benefit most from such opportunities, and they generally escaped relatively lightly in terms of demolition of property. The destruction of buildings and their contents in itself represented a major loss of capital and communities which had sustained such losses were, by implication, those which had suffered relatively badly in the war.

It was against this background that resources for reconstruction had to be found. The capacity of individuals to rebuild was impaired by their losses during the war, not least the destruction of their property. Such difficulties justified a collective appeal for assistance, and in normal conditions a community affected by a fire or other disaster received fairly prompt gifts of money and provisions from the surrounding area and nearby towns. Other financial help could be obtained by procuring a brief, issued by the Lord Chancellor, which authorised charitable collections within a specified region. The defects of the brief system were that it was slow to bring in money, was expensive to operate, was open to corruption, and was dependent on the willingness and ability of individuals to contribute.

After the widespread destruction and economic disruption of the Civil War, this was an even less effective method of raising money than at other times. High taxation continued after the war and the late 1640s were also a period of high food prices. Many places needed assistance of some kind, or faced problems of poor relief, and the general economic situation, together with the impoverishment of communities and individuals who would normally have made donations, reduced the amounts which were collected. Parliament was reluctant to issue briefs during the war years, fearing that they might be used to raise money for the king. Yet it did authorise collections for towns which had suffered particularly badly or had attracted especial attention. In 1645 permission was given for one to be made for Taunton, which had endured a siege and an especially destructive assault, and early in the following year another was authorised to assist the victims of a destructive royalist raid on Woburn. In 1648 a brief was issued for money to be raised throughout England and Wales for the inhabitants of Faringdon.[4] All three places had suffered well-publicised destruction at the hands of the royalists and may have been regarded as special cases because of the damage which they had sustained. Also in 1648, collections were authorised for those whose property had been burnt in the fire at Wrexham five years earlier, and towards the repair of Great Torrington church, badly damaged when the magazine stored within it had exploded in 1646.[5] Despite Parliament's willingness to approve collections in these cases, the sums raised by these appeals may not, in the circumstances, have been very great.

Those places which were regarded as having been pro-royalist, or had been occupied by the king's forces for most of the first Civil War, received scant sympathy at a time when Parliament was unable to provide satisfactory assistance for communities loyal to its own cause. Oxford had to wait until after the Restoration before a collection to assist the victims of the fire of 1644 was authorised; the brief was issued in 1661.[6] Nevertheless, a few places did manage to obtain help under both regimes. A brief for Bridgnorth was issued in 1648 and another in 1661.[7] The earlier one was presumably granted on the basis that the destruction had been carried out by the royalists and the later one because the town had suffered for its loyalty to the king's cause, being captured only after an assault. It must also have been in the town's favour that its leading citizens were persistent in pursuing their appeal, submitting their petition to the House of Commons in September 1646, complaining seven months later that their claim 'hath bin buried in obscuriety', and finally obtaining the grant of a brief in January 1648. Oswestry also managed to obtain two briefs for collections towards the cost of rebuilding St Oswald's church: the first was issued in 1657 and the second in 1676.[8]

As the normal system of relief was inadequate for raising funds on the scale required, other methods of providing assistance had to be found. Both before the

The ruined nave of All Saints' church, Pontefract, is a legacy of the damage caused during the three sieges of the castle

end of the first Civil War and within a short time after it Parliament received petitions from many other communities that had suffered destruction of property, including Gloucester, Leicester, Coventry, Liverpool, Leighton Buzzard, Beaminster and Pontefract. It was because of the number of appeals and an awareness of the scale of the problem that the Committee for Burning was established (p. 65), but it was unable to find a solution, and the question of relief was still being considered in 1653.[9]

Unable to provide direct financial aid, Parliament authorised other methods of raising funds. Forfeited estates in Ireland were drawn upon to supply compensation for Gloucester and Liverpool, which were each allocated land worth £10,000.[10] Despite repeated efforts, neither town seems to have obtained any income from these grants until 1658, and little real benefit even then.[11] This source of assistance seems to have been regarded as a failure, for no other similar grants were made.

Some places were permitted to collect funds or take materials from the estates of royalist delinquents. This was done in the cases of Swanbourne and King's Lynn in 1643, and of Lancaster in 1645.[12] It subsequently became a fairly common way of providing assistance. In some instances the grant consisted of timber for building. Liverpool was allocated 500 tons of timber from the lands of the Earl of Derby and six other local royalists, specifically for the purpose of rebuilding. This was found to be inadequate compensation and £10,000 was later granted to the town from the estates of several royalists who were alleged to have been with the army which captured the town.[13] In 1646 Banbury was awarded timber and boards valued at £400 from the estate of Richard Powell at Forest Hill, twenty-two miles away, and 'so far remote and distant' that it was later realised 'that the Charge and Expence of Carriage will near amount to the Value of the Timber'. The town was, therefore, permitted to sell Powell's timber *in situ* and buy some closer to Banbury. Lyme Regis was given 2,000 oak trees from Lord Paulet's woods and much of the rents and profits of his sequestered lands.[14]

Although grants from the estates of royalists seemed to offer a solution to the problem of obtaining aid, many difficulties arose from such awards. It was not always possible to pin down those concerned. The inhabitants of Faringdon complained that some of the royalist commanders responsible for burning the town were 'fledd & not to be found' and that the others had compounded for their estates within the six months provided for in the articles of surrender of Oxford, which included Faringdon, and so could not be mulcted further. Similarly, when Sir Hamon Lestrange and a number of other leading royalists who had defended King's Lynn against the parliamentarians were summoned to pay compensation for the town's almshouses destroyed during the siege, he complained that he had already paid more than the value of the property, and that the terms of the articles of surrender exempted him from liabilities of that kind.[15] In other cases there was difficulty in obtaining the value of the grant. It was several years after Beaminster had been allocated £2,000 from the estates of the local royalist George Penny before the whole of the sum was received, partly as timber and partly in cash.[16] Only a half of the £10,000 initially given to Taunton from various delinquents' estates could actually be raised and so a further £2,000 was allotted to the town from another source.[17] Disputes arose there about the fairness of the distribution of the compensation. There were complaints of a similar nature at Coventry, where the treasurer entrusted with the relief funds, who had received £2,000 from the estates of a number of Midland royalists, was accused of not paying the money to those who had been made homeless.[18] Doubts must have arisen about the allocation of the funds at Bridgnorth, for a committee was appointed to check the accounts and ensure that the money was 'proportionably divided' among the victims, but as it was not established until December 1653 – almost six years after the brief had been issued – it may have come too late to check any misappropriation of the receipts.[19] There must have been many such cases, which were also characteristic of the distribution of relief after collections taken in the aftermath of peacetime fires.

The amount of assistance that reached the victims was reduced not only because some of the fingers through which it passed were stickier than they should have been, but also because civic needs took precedence. Some councils regarded the reconstruction of their public buildings as a priority and drew upon the relief funds to pay for the cost of new town halls, gaols and churches. They were particularly anxious to rebuild their town halls, for they were the seats of borough government, the repositories of civic goods – such as the regalia, muniments, arms, armour and fire-fighting equipment – and symbols of borough status. Such buildings did not come cheap. The costs of the town halls erected in

Much of Bridgnorth was destroyed during the Civil War. The new town hall, in the centre of the High Street, was built in 1652

four towns in the first half of the seventeenth century ranged from *c.*£260 to *c.*£600. Such expense was commonly far more than the annual civic revenues,[20] and in the period immediately after the Civil War those revenues fell short of their usual levels because rental income from destroyed and damaged properties was reduced or lost. Councillors therefore turned to the money received as compensation to finance such rebuilding, before passing on the residue to those who had sustained private losses. Bridgnorth's replacement for its town hall was built in 1652. The timber-framed hall, which is traditionally said to have been a barn brought from Much Wenlock, stands on an open-arched piazza of stonework straddling the High Street, in a much more prominent position than that occupied by its predecessor, which stood outside the walls. Banbury was even quicker off the mark, rebuilding its gaol in 1646.[21]

The collective petitions were only a part of a whole mass of appeals for assistance, for there were also numerous pleas from individual owners and tenants directed to the city and borough councils, justices of the peace, county committees, army commanders, the Houses of Parliament, and the various committees at Westminster. The petitioners were recompensed in a number of ways: perhaps given the freedom of the borough without paying a fine, a lease on favourable terms, or a place in an almshouse. Such cash payments as were authorised tended to be small. One householder whose house in Devizes had been burnt down was given £5, for example.[22] The parliamentarian committee at Coventry took a sympathetic view of the petition of John Frem because of his 'great age' and 'extraordinary poverty' and awarded him 5s. to compensate him for his house, which had been pulled down, and most of his goods, which he had been unable to save after they were thrown into the street because he was too poor to hire any carriage for them.[23] Andrew Hall, a tanner of Colchester, was treated rather more generously, being allowed an annual pension of £4 as a recompense for his houses burnt down in 1648, but this was not granted him until 1659.[24] Those who incurred greater losses and were prepared to pursue their claims to a higher level could do better. In 1647 the House of Commons allotted five Leeds clothiers £300 to divide between them, but they had attended on the House for nine months before obtaining the grant.[25] The search for reparation could certainly be a long and wearisome business and involve considerable expense. During the siege of Cockermouth in Cumberland in 1648 two merchants there sustained losses, including the demolition of houses, which were valued at almost £2,000. Cromwell's arrival at Carlisle raised the siege, and when they approached him about the possibility of compensation he advised them to apply to him in London. By the time that they made the journey he had gone to Ireland, and in 1654, with their creditors pressing, and having failed to obtain help from elsewhere, they tried another direct petition to him.[26] With so many appeals for assistance for losses of various kinds caused by the war, and the difficulties of raising funds, it is hardly surprising that financial help was difficult to come by.

Of more practical use were the materials from dismantled fortifications. With the end of hostilities the maintenance of town walls and other defences was again neglected and many were allowed to deteriorate, a continuation of the process which had been interrupted by the Civil War. By 1651 Gloucester's fortifications were said to be very ruinous and they had to be hastily restored as the Scottish army marched southwards.[27] The walls and citadels of many of those towns which were not garrisoned by the army during the post-war period were demolished or slighted on the orders of Parliament, providing materials and money which could be used to help in rebuilding. The sites of the fortifications were themselves used for new houses in some places. The outer wards of Denbigh Castle were built upon, and by 1673 the large fort to the north of Bristol had been 'converted into houses and pleasant gardens'.[28] Some of the stone and timber from demolished buildings that had been incorporated into defensive works could be re-used. When the castle and other fortifications at Devizes were dismantled, timber, other materials and the frames of wooden houses taken from the townsmen earlier were set aside so that they could be reclaimed.[29] Banbury corporation petitioned for the demolition of the castle there and this was duly approved, with 'the Materials . . . bestowed upon the Town of Banbury, to assist them in the Repair of the Ruins made . . . in the late War'. In 1647 Hereford's guildhall was repaired with stones taken from the castle and ten years later stones from a sconce and a wall near to the castle at Bridgwater were given to the town for rebuilding the almshouses there.[30] In some instances the materials were sold and the receipts used towards the costs of reconstruction. When Pontefract Castle was demolished the sale of the stone and lead salvaged brought in £1,779 17s. 4d. and from this £1,000 was allotted to the town to repair the church and rebuild the minister's house. A further £120 9s. 9d. was later solicited to pay for the rebuilding of the Moot Hall. Not all demolitions were as profitable. When the costs of dismantling Wallingford Castle were deducted from the proceeds of the sales of the materials only £66 12s. 3d. remained, and the disgarrisoning and demolition of Montgomery Castle cost £5 3s. more than the value of the materials recovered.[31] Items retrieved from buildings that had been demolished earlier were also sold. Money received from the sale of the bells of St Pancras church at Chichester, which had been pulled down, was used to help those who had been made homeless in that parish.[32] An even more drastic step was taken at Worcester, where in 1648 the 'Leaden Steeple', a bell tower close to the cathedral, was taken down and the materials sold. It was anticipated that £1,200 would be raised, but, after the costs of the demolition had been paid, the receipts were only £560. From the proceeds, £113 3s. 1d. was allocated to rebuild Inglethorpe's almshouses, which had been demolished during the war, and £180 towards the repair of three churches in the county, with the balance devoted to the re-endowment of charities.[33]

Because the cost of reconstructing public buildings took precedence over the needs of individual property owners, the expense of rebuilding houses had to be found from the resources of the landlords and their tenants. The losses caused by confiscation or destruction of goods, fines, taxation and reduced rental income had weakened the ability of many owners to rebuild. There was also the economic impact of the destruction of the buildings themselves. Indeed, the demolition of their houses was the most costly single loss experienced by the majority of those who suffered such a calamity, greater than sums taken in taxation and plunder, and likely to be exceeded in value only by the large-scale confiscation of trade goods. The destruction of implements such as ploughs, harrows, farm vehicles, looms and other working tools may have caused only temporary difficulties, for they were not expensive items and could be replaced in time, but the destruction of stocks of wool, cloth, grain, hay, cheese and other produce represented a more serious setback. The burning of barns and store buildings in the months immediately after harvest was potentially very damaging for a community, destroying both food stocks and seed corn, and a blow from which it was likely to take some time to recover.

The costs of erecting new buildings varied greatly, from perhaps £10, or even less, for the smallest peasant or suburban houses, to £40 for a timber-framed farmhouse, £60 for a stone one, £60–£80 for the average town house, several hundred pounds for gentry houses, and a few thousand pounds for the squirearchy's country mansions. The typical expenditure on a good sized country house in the early seventeenth century was £3,000 to £4,000 – the costs for country houses rose appreciably during the 1630s – while the aristocracy's 'prodigy houses' could absorb tens of thousands of pounds.[34] There was a wide range of costs within each category. For example, Trentham Hall in Staffordshire was built in the 1630s for Sir Richard Leveson for slightly over £6,000, but in 1669 the comparatively modest Ryston Hall in Norfolk, designed by Sir Roger Pratt, cost £2,800.[35] Similarly, the estimate given after the Civil War for rebuilding a house in Taunton, described as the owner's 'principal mansion house', was £600, while the expenditure on country manor houses could be less, and Deanham Hall, Northumberland, was built for £250 in 1669.[36] The more modest town houses generally cost under £100 to erect. The owner of three destroyed tenements at Holt was told that it would cost £250 to rebuild them and at Exeter £40 was allowed for the construction of 'a little tenement'.[37] Much depended on the amount of materials that had been salvaged or was readily available.

Some problems in rebuilding property held by lease may have arisen over doubts about where the responsibility lay. Clearly, the lessee of a destroyed building would be reluctant, and perhaps unable, to continue to pay the whole of the rent and would not undertake the cost of reconstruction without being offered favourable terms to do so. Few leases contained a clause which covered this kind of destruction, but in an important judgement in the case of Paradine versus Jane, heard in 1646, it was ruled that the lessor was entitled to receive the full rent in such circumstances. The basis of this decision was that 'as the Lessee is to have the advantage of casual profits, so he must run the hazard of casual losses, and not lay the whole burthen of them upon his Lessor'.[38] Some tenants were successfully sued by their landlords for failing to maintain the property in good repair, as stipulated in the covenants of their leases, and for arrears of rent. The case of Miles Brand illustrates some of the problems that could arise. Before the war he had taken a lease of a mill and some land at Whitechapel, at an annual rent of £16. He had repaired the mill and built a number of tenements, but because of the construction of a fort and other earthworks on the site the houses had been demolished and the mill 'made uselesse', causing him losses which he estimated at £400. This did not deter his landlord from bringing an action against him for the unpaid rent, although Brand had not only lost the benefit of the premises and his investment in the new buildings, but was paying rent to the Committee for Compounding to satisfy a quit rent due to the Earl of Cleveland, a royalist delinquent.[39]

In addition to the problems which arose regarding the payment of rent, the implication of the judgement made in 1646 was that the onus of rebuilding lay with the tenants, not the landlords. Although this clarified the legal position, there were practical difficulties to overcome. In particular, it was hard to force a lessee, who had probably lost much personal wealth when the property was destroyed, to pay the costs of rebuilding. Many tenants may have absconded rather than allow themselves to be sued by their landlords. In 1650 it was reported that not all of the tenants who held leases of demolished property in the parish of St Bartholomew at Chichester were known, and a rental could not be found.[40] Indeed, the loss or destruction of documents made it difficult for landlords to enforce the terms of tenancy agreements or bring legal actions against their tenants. The leases and deeds of Bridgnorth corporation's properties were destroyed in the corporation's chest, which was burnt when the town was fired.[41] In practice, the rent of most properties was lost until new buildings were erected. The solution of many corporate landlords was to grant a new lease containing a covenant which stipulated that the lessee should rebuild the property within a specified time and to a certain standard, for they wished to have a new building that was at least as large and well built as that which had been destroyed. In the 1660s the Dean and Chapter of Lincoln granted leases of the sites of demolished buildings in the city, each tenant covenanting to erect a property 'full as longe and broad as the old ruines of a former house thereon built doe extend and make dimension' and, in the case of the Greyhound inn in Eastgate, 'in as large and ample manner as the said Tenement or Inn was formerly builded'.[42] In 1652 Coventry corporation granted the site of a demolished tenement to one William Ward on the condition that he build a 'good and sufficient house' of three bays within one year, when he would be given a new lease at the same rent. The corporation's other leases also stipulated the number of bays to be erected, and that was the requirement of other lessors.[43] An alternative was to specify the amount of money to be spent on new buildings. Exeter corporation issued seventy-seven leases of this kind, mostly during the 1650s, of sites of its property destroyed in the Civil War. The average minimum amount which the tenants were to spend was £65, but the range was considerable, from £10 for each of two tenements, which must have been very small, to £300 on the Black Horse, outside the South Gate. The time allowed the tenants to complete the new buildings varied from one to four years.[44] The governors of St Oswald's hospital at Worcester granted a number of similar leases of plots of ground in the northern suburbs of the city. The tenants who complied with the covenants to rebuild commonly had their terms extended by the grant of a new lease, without a fine.[45] This seems to have been a successful, if slow, method of encouraging lessees to put up new buildings of a certain standard.

Even when the legal position was sorted out and prospective tenants were available, a further problem that was likely to be encountered was identifying and setting out the boundaries of the plots. This had to be done as accurately as possible to avoid future wrangles. In 1647 Exeter corporation appointed a committee to survey the sites of its suburban property which had been destroyed, in order to be able to secure its ownership of them and prevent the 'wrongs and suites of others'.[46] This indicates the kind of difficulties that were anticipated; it is also a testimony to the thoroughness with which the land had been cleared. The longer the delay before a survey was carried out to discover and mark the boundaries between plots, the more difficult the task became. After the Restoration, the Bishop of Worcester's steward reported that he had been unable to collect rents and re-establish ownership of suburban properties around the city because he did not know 'the very ground where each house stood'.[47]

Some delays in rebuilding were caused by the earthwork defences, for the sites which they occupied had to be levelled and cleared before new building could begin. Those places which retained a garrison after the end of the Civil Wars had to keep their defences in being, even if in a somewhat neglected state, with the owners of the ground unable to begin even the task of clearance. Liverpool petitioned for the removal of its defences throughout the late 1640s, but they had not been cleared by the end of 1650.[48] Even where the fortifications were no longer required, the sheer scale of the task of removing them was a problem, especially as the civil authorities or individual owners did not have the power of compulsion to enlist the forced labour which the military had been able to use when the works were constructed. One solution was to make some allowance to the tenants of the ground occupied by the works if they would demolish them.

The earthwork fortifications were not removed at many towns until the 1650s. This account, in the corporation records, is for the clearance of part of the defences at Gloucester in 1653

Some of the corporation of Colchester's tenants were granted reductions of rent in return for clearing the earthworks on their land.[49]

Building activity had fallen to a very low level indeed during the Civil War, not only in the regions which were fought over, but also in those which had escaped the military campaigns. Some buildings were erected in 1643, but few were put up in 1644–6, producing an unusually deep and long slump in the building cycle.[50] Landlords complained of being unable to collect their rents, and the taxation levied from them must have been a further disincentive to building. They also had to make some allowance in their rents for taxes which their tenants had to pay. One owner in Covent Garden complained that he had 'not made any considerable rent of his house' during the war years. Similar grievances were expressed by landowners throughout East Anglia and the South East, who felt that they were little better off than their counterparts in the regions directly affected by the war 'saving that our houses are not burnt downe'.[51] In such circumstances, with both income and confidence at a low ebb, no quick revival could be expected.

The economic, legal and practical problems experienced by owners meant that at many places there were delays before rebuilding could begin. Meanwhile, those displaced by the destruction of housing had to find accommodation wherever they could. Some probably shared with friends or relatives whose property was still intact, but others were forced to find shelter in whatever vacant buildings were available. In the circumstances, any building was likely to be adapted as a dwelling. The inhabitants of Faringdon lodged in 'outhouses, barnes & other desolate places' nearby. One family at Gloucester was allocated a pigeon house in which to live, and given permission to build a chimney for it. A widow made homeless when her tenement at York was demolished was allowed to make her home in a stable without paying rent.[52] The church's properties could be used for accommodation. A year after the final surrender of Exeter the buildings in the cathedral close were inhabited by 'poore people . . . whose howses were burnt downe in the severall seiges'. Some of them had apparently established themselves there on a more or less permanent basis and paid rent for the properties which they had occupied. The corporation later bought the deanery and divided it into sixty tenements for 'the baser sort of people'.[53] Canons' houses in the precincts of Chichester cathedral were occupied by refugees from the suburbs and the stables of the bishop's house in the close at Gloucester contained 'poore people put in by the Maior of the Citty'.[54] If there was overcrowding in the town where the property had been destroyed, then it could be relieved by migration, perhaps initially over fairly short distances. Refugees from Taunton settled in Hestercombe House, three miles to the north, and they had not moved out by April 1649, having defied an order of 1646 that they should leave. Similarly, many of those made homeless by the destruction of property at Bridgwater were sent to the village of Wembdon, a mile away, where they were accommodated 'sometimes in one place thereof sometimes in another'. They were still there in 1649 and the authorities at Bridgwater, unwilling to increase their own problems of poor relief, were reluctant to allow them to return.[55] Migration of that kind could become a lasting transfer of population, but only shifted the problem of insufficient accommodation to another community.

In some places reconstruction began fairly soon after the buildings had been cleared and the immediate military emergency had passed. Part of Handbridge suburb on the south side of the Dee at Chester was 'too hastily & unadvisedly' rebuilt during the war and the new structures had to be demolished when the city was threatened by a parliamentarian force in the spring of 1645.[56] Within three weeks of the end of the siege of Gloucester an order was made for some land to be surveyed with a view to building new tenements there. Leases were subsequently granted of ground near to the site of the former castle and construction of a new street of houses was begun before the end of 1646.[57] As well as new building of this kind, there may have been attempts to repair housing which had been only partly destroyed and to salvage materials that could be re-used in some way. Indeed, one of the first tasks must have been to clear the streets and discover what could be retrieved from the debris. Some people were rather too enthusiastic in that respect, collecting items from sites which were not their own. In 1649 Derek Lakins found himself indicted on a charge of theft for taking a rapper and hinges from the ruins of Alderman Thomas Talcot's house at Colchester and later selling them.[58] The pilfering of such small items may have been common, but it was not as easy to make off with the more substantial building materials and some must have been recovered for future use.

A common solution to the problem of accommodation was to build rather insubstantial structures from whatever materials were available. As conditions returned to normal, many of those displaced moved back into the suburbs or places close by and lived, at least initially, in hastily built cottages or houses. Several people were reported for building cottages on the waste and commons in the Foregate at Stafford, one of the suburbs destroyed in the war.[59] Such structures were presumably intended to be temporary, but often they remained in use for many years and, with some improvements perhaps, became permanent habitations. This created problems for the civic authorities, who were reluctant to see such shanty communities grow up on the edge of their town, and in some cases orders were made that houses erected without permission should be demolished. At Worcester, some of those made homeless by the destruction of the suburbs 'did erect many cottages upon the waste' nearby. This caused difficulties of poor relief for the parishes in which the cottages had been built, and so in 1661 it was decided that the buildings should be pulled down whenever the occupants either left or died and that any new inhabitants should be removed. This may not have been a very practical proposal, and whatever steps were actually taken did not solve the problem, which was still the cause of complaints at the end of the century.[60]

The replacement of houses destroyed in the war with substantial structures was apparently a slow process. There was a revival in building activity in 1647, but it was short-lived and was succeeded by a further slump.[61] In some towns rebuilding did not begin on any scale until a few years had passed. When John Taylor was at Faringdon in June 1649 he noted that rebuilding there was in its early stages. It had taken three years since the town was burnt for the recovery to get properly under way. Reconstruction was apparently completed by the time that Baskerville visited it more than thirty years later and described it as 'now pretty well built'.[62] There was an even slower start at Wrexham, where most of

An early nineteenth-century drawing of the ruins of Harlech Castle, a royalist stronghold until its surrender in March 1647

the houses burnt down in 1643 had not been rebuilt by the spring of 1648.[63] Several other Welsh towns were slow to recover, as Taylor's journal of his tour through the principality in 1652 indicates. He noted that Flint, Bangor, Harlech, Aberystwyth and Pembroke all showed signs of the impact of the war. He wrote of Flint that 'War hath made it miserable . . . the Town is so spoiled' and portrayed it as 'a pitiful discription of a Shire Town', and Harlech he found 'all spoild, and almost [un]inhabitable'.[64] Nor was there a speedier recovery at Colchester, where the losses sustained in 1648 were still all too apparent to Evelyn eight years later, when he described it as 'a faire Towne but now wretchedly demolished by the late Siege; especially the suburbs all burnt & then repairing'.[65]

An indication of the condition of a number of other towns is illustrated by surveys taken in 1649–50 of the confiscated property of the crown and the church. Some of the buildings which the surveyors included had survived the conflict intact, and so the figures drawn from the surveys reflect the proportion of a district in ruins, rather than that which had been reconstructed. They show that at Lincoln two tenements had been rebuilt by the end of 1649, and another three were then under construction, but that twenty-one other buildings were still in ruins.[66] There was a similar proportion of vacant house plots at Worcester, with eighteen out of twenty-five still empty, and rather lower percentages at Chester and Chichester, where roughly a half of the sites were unoccupied.[67] On the other hand, an impression of busy activity at Denbigh emerges from the survey of an area of seven acres of Crown land close to the castle, where it was reported in 1650 that houses had recently been built and there were 'moore and moore daylie building'. There is also evidence of some rebuilding at Lichfield by 1649. A slightly later survey indicates that in 1653 ten out of forty-three house sites at Banbury were vacant, although there had been considerable building activity there in the late 1640s and early 1650s.[68] It may be that such surveys are not entirely representative of all properties destroyed, for tenurial uncertainties could have contributed to delays in reconstruction. Nevertheless, their evidence strengthens the impression that there was much rebuilding still to be done in the affected districts three or four years after the end of the first Civil War, and that in some places it was only just beginning.

Other evidence suggests that the 1650s and 1660s saw much of the reconstruction. The descriptions of properties granted on lease give an indication of the building chronology. In those cases where the lessees who had fulfilled covenants to put up buildings were rewarded with new leases that effectively extended their terms, the period during which the structures were erected can be dated with some accuracy. The numbers of cases before the civic courts that relate to activity by building workers and disputes over landownership and boundaries provide other, albeit less precise, evidence.

At Chester, the effects of the final siege, the post-war recession and a very serious epidemic in 1647 combined to delay the recovery of the city. Comparatively little rebuilding had been carried out there before 1650, but the pace of activity quickened thereafter and in the mid-1650s much building work was taking place.[69] Not all of the new houses were on the sites of those destroyed in the Civil War. St Olave's Lane, for example, which was within the walls, was built up for the first time during this period.[70] Some leases stipulated the materials to be used in rebuilding, and there is evidence of considerable activity by brickmakers.[71] The public buildings, as well as houses, were reconstructed. A new house of correction was built between 1655 and 1657, and the tower of St John's church was extensively repaired at much the same date.[72] The chronology at Exeter was broadly similar, with little new building during the late 1640s, followed by considerable activity during the following decade. St Thomas's church on the west side of the Exe, burnt down in early 1646, was rebuilt by 1657, following an appeal in quarter sessions in 1654 to raise £1,400 for the purpose.[73] The city's economy recovered quickly after the end of the first Civil War, judging from its trade, particularly in textiles, but the revival was soon halted and the late 1640s and the 1650s were not a prosperous period. This may have affected the speed of reconstruction, and some plots which had been built upon before the conflict were still empty in the 1680s.[74] It is arguable that Oxford's wartime experiences, however grim, had been less economically damaging than those of either Chester or Exeter. Even so, rebuilding after the fire of 1644 continued well into the 1650s, with a new Butcher Row and a group of six tenements close by not being constructed until 1655–7.[75]

The high mortality of the war years and the demographic stagnation that followed may have reduced the demand for new housing and so contributed to the delays in reconstruction. There may also have been an effect from the supply side of the equation, with places where considerable destruction had taken place being unable to provide housing, or the resources to erect it, quickly enough to retain

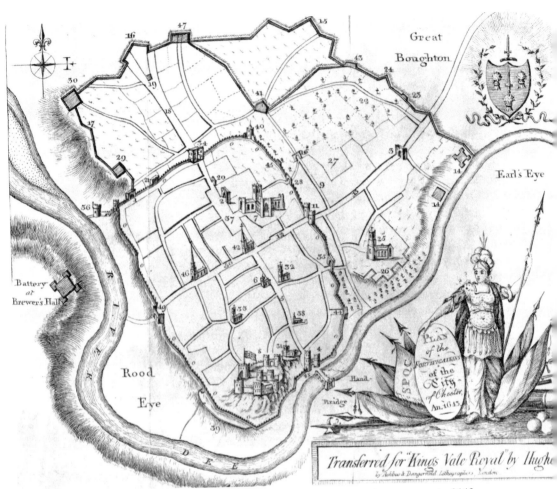

The royalist fortifications at Chester are shown here at their maximum extent, in 1643

the inhabitants left without accommodation, or to attract potential residents. Those communities which were hardest hit by property destruction – leading to a loss of population through migration – and general economic and demographic disruption certainly had a slow rate of recovery. Roughly one half of St Nicholas's ward at Worcester lay outside the walls and so was destroyed during the war. Between 1641 and 1678 five enumerations were made of the city and the figures for St Nicholas's, expressed as a percentage of the aggregate for five other wards, clearly show the decline and recovery of the ward. Its share fell from twenty per cent in 1641, to nine per cent in 1646, and then rose to fifteen per cent in 1662, reaching its 1641 value only in 1670, and slightly exceeding it at twenty-three per cent in 1678. These figures are confirmed by the numbers of baptismal and burial entries in the registers for St Nicholas's parish, which was virtually coincident with the ward. There were 80–100 registrations per annum during the 1620s and 1630s, excluding plague years, a figure which fell to just under fifty during the period 1645–9, and scarcely rose above that level before 1660. Not until the 1660s did the number of registrations begin to rise appreciably and only in the 1670s did they reach their pre-war level.[76] The slow return to normality in this district took thirty years or more, and, as at Exeter, there were some vacant house plots in 1680.[77] The sack of Worcester following the battle in 1651 – when the losses of 266 citizens who were regarded as 'well-affected' to parliament were put at £18,708 19s. 7d.[78] – checked the city's post-war recovery, and was a contributory cause of the slow rebuilding of the suburbs.

Similar patterns can be detected at Scarborough, which suffered destruction throughout the town, and Stafford, where the demolition was mainly in the suburbs. Scarborough's population fell from an estimated 2,870 inhabitants in 1640 to fewer than 1,584 in 1660, and was still only 2,380 by c.1680.[79] Stafford also experienced a sharp decline. It had 1,550 inhabitants in 1622 and registration data suggest that this figure rose to almost 1,700 in the 1630s, before falling to fewer than 1,400 during the 1650s and 1660s, with an estimate of 1,350 for 1666. The population level of the 1620s was only achieved during the 1670s.[80]

At York and Gloucester the impact of the Civil War lasted even longer, with large parts of the suburbs not rebuilt before the early eighteenth century. Both cities complained of stagnant economies after the end of the war, although in neither place were the effects of the conflict and the destruction of property the fundamental causes of their problems. Their previously important textile industries had declined during the late sixteenth and early seventeenth centuries and both places had turned to other sources of employment, including services for the county gentry. York had remained the leading centre in the north of England and the home of the two busy agencies of the Council in the North and the Ecclesiastical Commission for the Province of York. Their abolition dealt a heavy blow to the city's prosperity and the corporation petitioned repeatedly for the re-establishment of the Council in the North, abolished in 1641.[81] At Gloucester the growth of metal working had not been enough to compensate for the decline in textiles and capping. In the mid-1620s it experienced an economic and demographic crisis that was aggravated by growing disputes with the county justices regarding the taxation of the two hundreds of the county administered by the city, known as the Inshire, which alienated the gentry. It had not fully recovered from the crisis of the 1620s before the outbreak of the Civil War.[82]

There was some reconstruction at York in the late 1640s, and by 1649 there were 'diverse convenient houses' outside the Walmgate, where the horse fair and market were revived, having been suspended because of the wartime destruction of the houses and the 'unfitt' state of the street.[83] The process then seems to have come more or less to a halt, however, and c.1660 Sir Thomas Widdrington wrote that there were 'hardly left any footsteps' of the suburbs which had been destroyed in the war.[84] Rebuilding had not progressed very far by 1680, when the 'three or four fine streets' of the pre-war suburbs had been replaced only by 'some few straggling houses here and there built of late to let us see that in time there may be hopes that she [the city] may againe recover her selfe'. It is also evident from surviving houses that there was little building activity outside the walls in the second half of the seventeenth century.[85] Recovery was still not complete by the 1730s, when the 'long course of houses out of Walmgate' that appears on Speed's plan of 1611 was still not rebuilt, and even by the 1760s the city's population was still only at its pre-Civil War level of approximately twelve thousand.[86]

In 1646 John Dorney, the town clerk, described Gloucester as 'a garment without skirts' and in Ogilby's *Britannia* of 1675 it was described as 'not fully recover'd of its late Calamities'.[87] A comparison of Speed's plan of 1611 with Kip's perspective view published in 1712 shows that the suburbs were much less extensive at the later date. This is confirmed by the leases of vacant house sites that were granted throughout the late seventeenth century. By the early eighteenth century only a few houses had been built outside the South Gate, the Alvin Gate and the Outer North Gate, where 174 houses had stood before the siege. St Owen's church was not rebuilt and in 1648 its site was levelled so that it could be used for drying cloth. Several house plots to the east of the town were also left vacant.[88] The city's population was just over 5,000 in 1640, but only 4,756 in 1696.[89]

A further aspect of urban reconstruction in the period following the Civil War was that many of the buildings erected were of low quality. Few places took the opportunity to impose minimum building standards. York corporation's order that all new buildings should be of brick was unusual anywhere before the regulations governing reconstruction after the Great Fire of London were issued, and the costs of using this still relatively expensive material may have been one of the reasons for the very slow recovery of the suburbs.[90] Prohibitions of thatched roofs in towns were much more common, but they were not widely adopted to reduce fire risks amongst the properties rebuilt after the Civil War. Exeter corporation did not take the opportunity to extend its injunction against thatching within the walls to property in the suburbs, and the distinction between tiled and slated buildings inside the city and thatched ones in the extra-mural districts still existed in the early eighteenth century.[91] There and elsewhere the civic government may have been concerned primarily that the suburbs were rebuilt and preferred not to risk discouraging potential builders by introducing regulations which may have added to the costs. Nor were the authorities in the smaller towns willing or able to regulate the standards of the new buildings, even where the need to reduce the fire hazards must have been apparent. Houses of cob and thatch were noted at Axminster in the late 1660s, when the town had recovered its pre-war size.[92]

Lack of controls, pressure upon surviving accommodation, and shortages of capital and materials tended to produce smaller, inferior, dwellings to those which were being constructed before the Civil War. Indeed, relatively simple house types which had been superseded reappeared after the war. The single-storey medieval house was steadily being replaced in the midland towns during the sixteenth and early seventeenth centuries, but was again being built in such towns as Coventry and Derby during the 1640s. At Lancaster, too, the process which had seen a move towards stone buildings was interrupted by the reconstruction necessitated by the destruction of so many houses in 1643. The numbers of timber-and-thatch houses still present in the streets in the centre of the town in 1684 indicates that the buildings hastily erected after the war had not been replaced a generation later.[93]

The pattern in the countryside seems to have been broadly similar, with a sluggish start to rebuilding, followed by increasing activity in the 1650s and

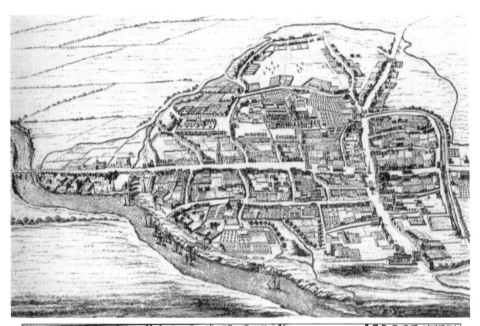

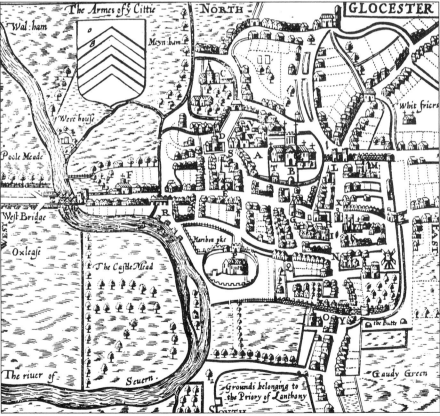

Kip's view of Gloucester from the south in 1712 (above) shows that the suburbs and St Owen's church shown on Speed's plan (below), drawn a century earlier, and destroyed in the Civil War had not been replaced

1660s. Many of the villages which had been destroyed were rebuilt, such as Donnington, North Scale and Beachley. Some recovered only very slowly and others incompletely, however. In 1643 Swanbourne, Buckinghamshire, was granted timber to help with rebuilding and the fact that it was able to obtain a brief for the same purpose in 1651 suggests that it had not fully recovered by then. The process was even more sluggish at Stoborough in Dorset, which contained only forty houses in the mid-eighteenth century, although one hundred families were said to have been displaced when it was destroyed.[94]

Much of the onus fell upon the individual landlords or lords of the manor, who may have been unable to provide a great deal of assistance in the immediate aftermath of the conflict. Other sources of help were obtained, but not always with much effect. In 1648 the inhabitants of Brampton Bryan were assigned £2,000 from the estates of delinquent royalists in Montgomeryshire, but it is not clear how much of this was received. The rebuilding of the church of St Barnabas was completed in 1656, largely at the expense of Sir Robert Harley, despite his losses because of the war, which he put at £12,990. The church incorporates some earlier work, indicating that it had not been totally destroyed, although the building clearly underwent a reconstruction rather than extensive repairs. Harley himself was unable to embark upon the rebuilding of the castle, the destruction of which he valued at £5,500, and he died in 1656 in rented accommodation in

The church of St Barnabas at Brampton Bryan, Herefordshire, was ruined during the Civil War and rebuilt in 1656, incorporating parts of the earlier building

Ludlow. The village itself had not fully recovered when the church was rebuilt.[95]

Other church reconstructions in the Welsh Marches during the post-war years included that at Bishop's Castle *c.*1648 and the nave of Loppington church *c.*1656. In a number of cases the building was replaced in stages. There were two examples in Shropshire, where the nave of St John the Baptist at Stokesay was reconstructed in 1654 and the tower and chancel roof in 1664, and the nave of Shrawardine church was erected in 1649, but the chancel not until 1722.[96] These delays suggest difficulties in financing the rebuildings. That certainly was the cause of a long delay at Edgbaston, Warwickshire, and justified the issue of two briefs. Work begun using receipts from the brief issued in 1658 had to be abandoned when £430 of the estimated cost of £800 had been spent, and it was not completed until money was raised from the second brief, authorised in 1684.[97]

Some of the church rebuildings incorporated surviving earlier work, such as the first three storeys of the tower of St Chad's at Farndon, Cheshire, which date from the mid-fourteenth century, although the remainder of the fabric was constructed in 1658. Similarly, the lower parts of the tower at Compton Wynyates in Warwickshire were repairable, but the body of the church was rebuilt *c.*1665, although it still lacked such basic fittings as a pulpit, reading desk and seats in

The church at Compton Wynyates, Warwickshire, which dates from c. 1665, replaced the earlier building ruined during the Civil War. The nearby mansion was garrisoned by both sides in turn

1684.[98] In other instances there was a total reconstruction. At Taynton, Gloucestershire, the opportunity was taken to move the church to a more convenient position. The new building was erected shortly after the end of the wars by the lord of the manor, the parliamentarian soldier and M.P. Thomas Pury the younger. The earlier church and the rectory had been destroyed in 1643 by the royalist governor of Taynton House. They had been inconveniently placed for the majority of the parishioners, and so a plot of glebe land some distance away was adopted for a new churchyard, and the replacement church was built there, where it was much more accessible to the inhabitants. The necessary Ordinance was obtained in 1648, and the new church was probably built shortly afterwards. The church at Woolsthorpe in Lincolnshire, ruined in the Civil War, was also abandoned because it was too far from the village and services were held in a more conveniently sited chapel, which may have been built soon after the end of the war as a replacement. A new church was eventually erected in 1846.[99]

The construction of a new church represented something of a return to normality, although it did not necessarily follow that the village which its predecessor had served would also be rebuilt. At Benthall in Shropshire the church was rebuilt in 1667, when the dedication to St Brice was changed to that to St Bartholomew, but the village was never replaced on its former site to the

The church at Taynton in Gloucestershire was destroyed by the garrison of the nearby house and the present building was erected on a new site in or soon after 1648. The chancel was added in 1894

north of the hall.[100] The church completed at Boarstall, Buckinghamshire, in 1663 was a smaller and simpler structure than the one which had been destroyed in the Civil War. A larger building was not needed, for the village that had been cleared away in June 1645 was not rebuilt and its site became a pasture field. In the late seventeenth century the parish contained dispersed farms and cottages, and a small group centred on the manor house and church. Lady Denham, who owned the manor and paid for the church, was evidently content with the new arrangements, which increased the area of pasture and incidentally gave the manor house greater privacy. It is possible that this change was already in the offing as a part of the process which saw the clearance of woodland and the enclosure of the open fields there following the disafforestation of the royal forest of Bernwood in 1633. Lady Denham may have had plans to remove the houses and convert the arable to pasture which were accelerated by the opportunity provided by the wartime destruction of the village, but in the event it was the action of the garrison of the house which actually caused the desertion of the site.[101] The same was true at Belvoir in Leicestershire, where the ground occupied by the former village, destroyed in November 1644, was later incorporated into the park of Belvoir Castle, built by the Earl of Rutland to replace the fortress slighted after the Civil War.[102]

Country house building took some time to resume. In Gloucestershire, there was some building activity at Forthampton Court in 1643 and then nothing was done until work began at Sneyd Park and at William Leigh's new house at Adelstrop Park, both around 1650. There was an even slower start to the recovery in Warwickshire, with very little construction until the late 1650s and a significant pickup only after the Restoration, followed by something of a boom which peaked in the last two decades of the century. In Northamptonshire, too, there was scarcely any new building of country houses during the Civil War and Interregnum.[103]

The owners who were faced with rebuilding or repairing a house had first to overcome the problems caused by their own losses incurred during the conflict, as well as restoring their rent rolls and getting in what arrears they could. House building in the seventeenth century was commonly financed out of current revenues and so it was necessary to restore them to an acceptable level before embarking on a programme of building. Those whose tenants had sustained significant losses, or had left, were likely to find the process of recovery a difficult one, although it was helped somewhat by the high agricultural prices of the late 1640s. Royalist owners also had to pay composition fines for their delinquency, with the added uncertainty for many of them of the precise terms under which they were to be assessed, and so the size of the sum which they had to find. Compensation for houses destroyed or severely damaged could be obtained by determined owners prepared to face a lengthy process. John Cartwright, a parliamentarian, pursued a claim for £10,000 against the Earl of Northampton for the burning of Aynhoe Park in 1645, but Cartwright died in 1676 and payment was not received until 1680.[104]

The contrasting fortunes of two owners in Wiltshire whose houses had been burnt by the royalists in 1645 is illustrated in John Evelyn's record of his tour through the county in 1654. He found that Sir John Glanville 'lived but in the Gate-house' at Broad Hinton, as he was unable to replace his 'very faire dwelling house', but that Sir Edward Baynton had abandoned his ruined house at Bromham and built a new one on another site at Spye Park.[105] Other new country houses were built in the West Country during the 1650s, including Highnam Court in Gloucestershire, dated to 1658, which replaced the building seriously damaged during the campaigns around Gloucester in 1643.[106] But it was not until after the Restoration that building activity really revived. This coincided with a renewed interest in house building, reflected in the publication of an increasing number of books on the subject, which may indicate changing architectural taste among the gentry, as well as the need to repair the ravages of the Civil War. A characteristic figure was the parliamentarian Edward Peyto, whose library contained a number of works on architecture, who was the first Warwickshire landowner to build a country house in the county after the Civil War, constructing Chesterton House, probably to the designs of John Stone, between 1657 and 1662.[107]

Among the most notable houses of the late seventeenth century which replaced Civil War losses was Kingston Lacy, designed by Sir Roger Pratt for Sir Ralph

Highnam Court, Gloucestershire, was built in 1658 to replace an earlier mansion on the site that was wrecked in 1643

The Bankes family's residence at Corfe Castle, Dorset, was damaged during the Civil War and slighted after it. It was replaced by a new house at Kingston Lacy, built in 1663–5. The south front is shown here

Bankes and built in 1663–5 to succeed the irreparably damaged dwelling at Corfe Castle.[108] Other families chose to abandon damaged, and unfashionable, houses constructed within medieval castles in favour of new or remodelled ones. Henry Somerset, grandson of the first Marquis of Worcester, recovered possession of Raglan before the end of the Interregnum, but chose to build a new mansion at Badminton rather than repair the Elizabethan house in the castle, and the Hastings family preferred Donington Park to Ashby de la Zouch.[109] Wardour Castle in Wiltshire had been fashioned into a fine house by Robert Smythson in the 1570s, but it was severely damaged during two sieges. Its owner, and assailant during the second siege, was the third Lord Arundell, who lost his estates in 1652 because of his delinquency, but regained them after the Restoration. He made no attempt to repair the damage to the castle, preferring to erect the much smaller Wardour House and other buildings just outside the wall of the bailey, in the 1680s. Not until the New Castle was built in 1769–76 was there a proper replacement for the building damaged in the Civil War, which came to serve as a picturesque ruin in the park.[110] Amongst the other houses more or less abandoned by their owners was the

Spencers' manor house at Wormleighton, Warwickshire, the remnants of which became a farmhouse, with the Spencers concentrating their attention on Althorp, which they remodelled in the late 1660s.[111] Some properties were neglected until acquired by new owners who were able to undertake the costs of restoration. Wootton Lodge in Staffordshire was badly damaged in a siege by parliamentarian forces in 1643 and stood derelict until it was bought and restored by the Wheeler family at the very end of the century. There was an even longer delay before the reconstruction of Sudeley Castle began, for it was not put in hand until after William and John Dent acquired the estate in 1837.[112]

One category which was generally not reconstructed until after 1660 consisted of the properties of the cathedral authorities. Although some lay purchasers did undertake repairs and restoration, others found it preferable to dismantle the damaged buildings and sell the materials rather than pay for reconstruction. The demolition of the deanery and the houses of nine prebendaries at Winchester apparently took place after 1649, for example.[113] The building of replacements began in the 1660s, but the very high expenses on repairs and restoration faced by the cathedral chapters in those years may have caused some further delays. The houses in Winchester Close which replaced those destroyed were completed by 1664, having absorbed roughly a third of the chapter's income during the first three years after its reinstatement.[114] Rebuilding of the four vicars' houses at Lincoln began in June 1664 and was finished by the October of the following year, at a cost of £400, most of which was raised from gifts and loans. Not all such

Sudeley Castle near Winchcombe in Gloucestershire was damaged during two parliamentarian attacks, in 1643 and 1644, and was slighted in 1649. Much of the fabric was eventually rebuilt, but the ruins of the fifteenth-century banqueting hall remain

buildings were replaced; two of the canonical houses at Wells which had been 'utterly ruined' were never reconstructed.[115]

The bishops also had to reconstruct their destroyed or ruined property. The Archbishop of York's palace at Bishopthorpe had been described as 'much ruinated and unrepairable' shortly after the end of the Civil War. It was restored, partly by its lay purchaser and partly by the expenditure of £3,000 upon it during the 1660s, but the archiepiscopal palaces at Southwell and Cawood were demolished. Much of the work needed to restore Farnham Castle was carried out in 1663–6, and by 1668 John Cosin, the first Restoration Bishop of Durham, had laid out £17,000 rebuilding his castles at Durham and Bishop Auckland, and his house at Darlington.[116] The reinstatement of palaces continued throughout the late seventeenth century, with Hartlebury Castle, which had been left in a ruinous condition at the end of the war, largely rebuilt during the episcopate of James Fleetwood (1675–83), and those at Cuddesdon, Lichfield and Eccleshall built in 1679, 1687 and 1695 respectively. In terms of scale and costs, episcopal palaces were equivalent to substantial gentry houses. The new one at Lichfield cost £3,972, George Morley, Bishop of Winchester from 1662 until 1684, spent £10,640 on Farnham and £2,200 on a new palace at Wolvesey, designed by Wren and begun in 1684. The expense of restoration partly explains why some palaces were not replaced. Some bishops chose to restore one or more of their houses and to abandon others, so that the work done at Farnham and Wolvesey gave the Bishops of Winchester two modern palaces and they had no need to restore that at Bishop's Waltham, which had been burnt in 1644 and gradually fell into ruin.[117]

The chronology of rebuilding of all types of property can be compared with the speed of recovery after accidental fires during the period. Most towns were restored fairly quickly, usually within ten years of a blaze. The houses were rebuilt within two or three years of the major fire at Warwick in 1694, although the new square and those parts of the church that had been gutted took ten years to complete.[118] Rebuilding was virtually completed within five-and-a-half years of the fire at Gravesend in 1727, which destroyed 105 houses, and Wareham was said to have been rebuilt 'in about two years' after the conflagration there in 1762.[119] The largest single such disaster destroyed 13,000 houses in London in September 1666. As London was the national and commercial capital, and the largest and wealthiest city in the country, the response may not have been typical. Yet, despite London's uniqueness, and the enormous scale of the losses, the chronology of reconstruction was not dissimilar from many provincial towns, with the secular buildings mostly finished by 1670 and their rebuilding completed within the next two years.[120] It was only those towns which were suffering from economic problems that were slow to recover. Roughly one-third of the houses burnt down at Buckingham in 1725 had not been replaced thirty years later, for example.[121] This pattern was reflected in the differential rate of recovery after the Civil War, with quite brisk rates of rebuilding at such places as Banbury and Denbigh, but with cities and towns like Lincoln, Gloucester, York, Scarborough and Stafford making distinctly heavy weather of recovering to their pre-war size.

The recovery of continental towns from the damage caused by wartime destruction shows some parallels with the English experience. Reconstruction of the suburbs of Rouen after the siege of 1591–2 lasted for a number of years, with no rebuilding in them before July 1593, and they had only a half of their pre-war population in 1603.[122] The reconstruction of Magdeburg – the greatest such task of the period – was accomplished within fifty years of the fire there, and Haarlem was rebuilt within a similar time following its losses of property in the siege of 1572–3 and a major blaze in 1576.[123] The speed of recovery varied from place to place, depending a great deal on the prosperity of the affected community, the length of time during which it was affected by military operations and the extent of outside aid which was received. Because of their strategic importance, the Dutch towns of Naarden and Coevorden, razed by Spanish troops in 1572 and 1592 respectively, were reconstructed as fortress towns, largely financed by the government, with Coevorden rebuilt in under ten years.[124] This points to an important difference in rebuilding between English towns and many of those on the continent, which was that continuing warfare, or the threat of it, not only inhibited restoration of suburbs, but in some cases caused a long delay before rebuilding of any kind could get under way, and produced a very slow recovery. The Moravian town of Zlín lost at least a half of its population in the course of the Thirty Years' War, and three whole streets and a subsidiary settlement had not been replaced by 1700. Similarly, almost 100 houses were destroyed when Nördlingen was bombarded in 1647 and in 1721 the town petitioned 'that the many houses which were burnt down in the bombardment have still not been rebuilt'.[125] A renewal of deliberate destruction was expensive and demoralising. That was always likely to occur at a fortified town in a strategically important region. Danzig's suburbs were destroyed in 1520 and subsequently rebuilt, only to be cleared away again in 1576.[126] It was also liable to be the fate of buildings in the countryside. Following the rigours of the wars with Spain and a period of rapid urbanisation, a 'country culture' evolved in the United Provinces from the 1620s, but this was sharply interrupted when many country houses were burnt during the French invasion in 1672.[127] This was an experience from which England and Wales were spared, apart from such rare incidents as the burning of the greater part of Teignmouth in a French raid in 1690.[128] It was accidental fires, rather than military operations, which posed a danger to those places seeking to recover from the Civil War, and in that respect Marlborough was unfortunate to suffer a devastating blaze which gutted 224 houses in 1653.[129]

The general impression of the progress of reconstruction after the Civil Wars is that there was a rather sluggish start in the 1640s, gathering pace towards the end of that decade, with the bulk of activity taking place during the 1650s and 1660s, and in some places continuing into the 1670s and even beyond. Some buildings were not replaced until later in the seventeenth century or even in the eighteenth. The rate of recovery varied from place to place, but the evidence does suggest that it was generally more prolonged than was renewal after the majority of town fires, and that it was many years before the physical evidence of wartime destruction was eradicated.

CHAPTER SIX

The Legacy

Colchester: During the Siege many of the Churches were ruined, a sad
Monument to this day of the Civil Wars. . . .

Guy Miège, The New State of England, *1701*

The memory of the destruction carried out during the Civil Wars gradually
receded with the passage of time and as the process of rebuilding covered many of
the scars. There were occasional reminders nevertheless. One of the most
dramatic of these was the fall of the steeple of St Mary's church at Scarborough
on 10 October 1659, which did extensive damage to other parts of the fabric.
Buildings do fall down from time to time; the result of inadequate foundations,
poor materials, faulty design, bad workmanship, age and neglect. Accidental
collapses are one thing, those resulting from damage deliberately inflicted by
forces from outside the community are quite another. The citizens of
Scarborough were in no doubt that it was the damage that had been done when
the steeple had been the target of artillery fire during the siege of the castle which
had caused the later collapse, and they said so.[1]

The numbers of such incidents declined, as did references to wartime
destruction, although there was a burst of petitions at the Restoration from those
who hoped that their adherence to the royalist cause would produce a
sympathetic response. Even after the early 1660s, the devastation of the war years
was still referred to by those trying to demonstrate a connection between the
physical damage to their buildings and their subsequent economic difficulties.
Such statements were made by both individuals and communities. Many were
associated with appeals for permission to raise funds for specific purposes, such
as a new church, but they were also used when the petitioners were requesting
support in dealing with other issues. Those inhabitants of St Clement's who, in
1684, were trying to defeat a move to incorporate their parish within the city of
Oxford, claimed in their petition to the king that they would then be subjected to
increased levels of local taxation and they had been 'great sufferers' in the Civil
War, 'many of their houses being demolished and their orchards and gardens
destroyed by the raising of fortifications for the service of your Majesty's royal
father of blessed memory'.[2] Such rhetoric was less appropriate after the
Revolution of 1688, and for that reason, and as the Civil Wars became more
remote, there were few appeals of that kind thereafter. It was also an ill-judged
form to adopt when addressing an appeal to a body such as the Common Council

of Gloucester. Although the previously dominant pro-parliamentarian group had been replaced at the Restoration by a leadership that was more royalist in sympathy, the city was still smarting from its losses when, in 1673, a citizen justified a request for assistance on the grounds that his house had been burnt at the time of the siege and he had 'suffered much . . . by his loyalty'. The Council felt the need to note that he had not suffered for his loyalty 'but in a common calamity' before recommending that he be given a place in an almshouse by way of compensation.[3]

Not all references to wartime destruction in the late seventeenth and early eighteenth centuries came in requests for assistance. Many were statements of fact explaining or justifying the post-war situation and the absence of buildings. One of the most poignant was made in 1677 by the schoolmaster at Bridgnorth, who explained that the school's records were 'burnt with the town' in 1646 and that the library had been lost at the same time, 'only some relics remaining'. Other towns suffered similar losses that were difficult, even impossible, to restore.[4] Damage done in another town could also have an injurious effect. The Master of Rugby school received a reduced salary for several years after the Civil War because a part of the school's endowment was a third share in Conduit Close in Holborn, which had been damaged when earthwork defences surrounding London were constructed on it. The endowment of Northwich school included buildings in Chester that were burnt down during the Civil War, and the school's library had also been destroyed.[5]

The long-term loss of such social resources as schools or almshouses, lasting well beyond the general period of recovery, was one of the detrimental effects of wartime destruction. The school building at Scarborough was destroyed during the second Civil War and for the next two centuries lessons were held in the south transept of St Mary's church.[6] Recovery could be delayed for some years if the property forming the endowment had been demolished and the rents from it lost. In 1631 the Oxford cleric Samuel Fell – who was to become Dean of Christ Church and Vice Chancellor of the university – was appointed Master of St Oswald's hospital in Worcester's northern suburb. After the Reformation the hospital had been allowed to fall into ruin and its income had been alienated, but Fell successfully recovered its property and sufficient rents for a new almshouse and chapel to be built. Their erection began in 1633 and some work was still being done to complete the buildings in 1642. Disaster struck in 1646, when the new buildings and the houses in the suburb were destroyed by the garrison. The burning of the houses which formed the recently recovered endowment of the hospital meant that its revenue was 'very much impaired' and the task of rebuilding could only begin when the suburb itself had been reconstructed and the property there was again providing St Oswald's with an adequate income. Fell's son John was appointed Master after the Restoration and by 1682 enough funds were available for the hospital to be rebuilt.[7] The legacy of the Civil War in that district was the demolition of a group of new buildings serving a social and spiritual function, which then stood in ruins for almost forty years on a prominent site alongside the main road into the city from the north. Other cities had similar problems reviving almshouses destroyed in the conflict. St John's hospital at Chester was re-established after the Civil War, with a handsome group erected in 1717, but St Giles's hospital in nearby Boughton was never rebuilt, and St Nicholas's hospital in the suburbs of York was ruined during the siege of 1644 and was not reconstructed.[8]

Difficulties restoring almshouses were encountered where the endowment was in unsympathetic hands, or it produced enough income in normal circumstances to maintain the occupants, but insufficient funds to reconstruct the buildings. Wynard's almshouses in Exeter had been founded in 1436 and the buildings were badly damaged in the Civil War. Because the tenant of the lands which formed the endowment refused to provide enough money for the repair of the almshouses – he was allegedly guilty of 'the misemployment of the lands' – there was a considerable struggle between him and the city council which dragged on in the courts for many years. Although the city obtained orders in Chancery in 1656, 1657 and 1661 that required him to restore the buildings to their pre-war condition, it was not until 1675 that they were rebuilt. Exeter corporation was particularly tenacious in that instance, and it was also instrumental in the rebuilding of the almshouses at the St Mary Magdalen hospital, further along the same street, in 1655–6.[9]

The records relating to church property also contain repeated references to the destruction carried out in the Civil War; churchwardens mentioned it in order to account for the absence of parsonages, for example. In the diocese of Worcester in 1674 there were reports of former parsonages at Madresfield, St Edmund's at Dudley, St Lawrence's at Evesham, and Middle Littleton, all of which had been destroyed in the war and not replaced. In 1714 the churchwardens at St Edmund's were still referring to the absence of a parsonage, writing that it and the church were 'buried in their ruins'.[10] The reason for the lack of a parsonage was gradually forgotten in some places, and the Civil War made only a small contribution to the problem of benefices that did not have a house for their incumbents. By 1835, 2,878 parishes were without a parsonage.[11] The house was the financial responsibility of the incumbent. In small parishes held in plurality the lack of a separate parsonage may not have been a problem, or the living may have generated such a small income that the minister could not afford to build a new one. Some were replaced only after a long delay. That at Coleorton in Leicestershire was destroyed in the Civil War, and the rectors coped without one for almost eighty years, until a new house was built in 1721.[12] Some incumbents seem to have contrived to gain from the situation. Dr Nicholas Gibbon, rector of Corfe Castle, allegedly sold the timber retrieved from the ruins of the parsonage demolished in the Civil War, but failed to build a new one. His successor was left to face that task, in 1681.[13]

More conspicuous than either almshouses or parsonages were those churches that had been destroyed or damaged and were left unrepaired for many years. They were all too obvious at towns such as Lincoln and Colchester, both of which contained several churches that had suffered in the Civil War. By 1674 St Michael's-on-the-Mount at Lincoln was 'in so ruinous a condition as to be past repair, nothing left but bare walls'. These were the kind of remains which attracted the attention of observers and reminded contemporaries of the effects of the wars. Of the churches in Lincoln ruined during the Civil War, only St Mary Magdalen was replaced in the seventeenth century, and that not until 1696. The new St Botolph's was built in 1721, St Martin's in 1739, St Michael's in 1740, St Peter's in 1781 and St Swithin's in 1801–2.[14] The damaged churches at Colchester also remained, as monuments of the siege of 1648.[15] St Mary's-at-the-Walls was rebuilt in 1713–14, while St Botolph's and the belfry of St Martin's are still in ruins. An appeal made in 1811 for a subscription to rebuild St Botolph's noted that 'a large part' of the former priory church had been battered down in 1648. That appeal was not successful, and not until 1837 was a new church built adjacent to the ruins.[16]

Small and poor urban parishes were a problem inherited from the Middle Ages, which some towns had attempted to solve in the sixteenth century, when fifteen parishes at York were dissolved and the twenty-four parishes in Lincoln were reduced to nine.[17] Nevertheless, many superfluous churches remained on the eve of the Civil War. All Saints', Wallingford, had been disused for more than fifty years before it was finally pulled down in 1643, and it has not been rebuilt.[18] The mergers of parishes effected in the 1640s and 1650s were mostly cancelled after the Restoration, although that did not necessarily lead to the rebuilding of a church which had been destroyed. In 1648 St Owen's parish in Gloucester was united with two others as part of a general reorganisation of the city's parishes. The arrangement was annulled in 1662, but the parochial duties in St Owen's continued to be carried out by the rector of St Mary de Crypt.[19] At Beverley the parish of St Nicholas was united to St Mary's after the Restoration, in 1667, although the tower of the church remained standing until 1693, when it was demolished and the materials used to repair the Minster and St Mary's. St Nicholas's church was not rebuilt until 1877.[20] Some of the other churches destroyed in the Civil War were never replaced, including St Owen's in Hereford, and St Mary Ditton, Droitwich.

Some churches were temporarily restored shortly after the war and a major rebuilding was carried out later. The nave and tower of St Thomas's, Portsmouth, were seriously damaged, but they survived until they were completely rebuilt between 1683 and 1693. Similarly, repairs carried out on the fabric of St Leonard's church in Wallingford in the late seventeenth century enabled it to be kept in use despite its wartime damage, but it was found to be in a dilapidated condition by 1700 and was rebuilt in 1704–5.[21] Such patching up of the fabric left a number of churches looking unbalanced, even mutilated. The demolition of much of the nave of Carlisle cathedral has given it a distinctly truncated and battle-scarred appearance, while the south transept of All Saints' at Faringdon was not replaced until 1853, and the church still lacks a spire.[22] Perhaps the most bizarre of the war-damaged churches is that at Dodderhill in Worcestershire, where in 1674 it was reported that 'the body of the church . . . was fired and destroyed by the soldiers in the time of the late distractions and is not rebylt yet. But the chancell and what remains is in good order'. The pre-war church had been cruciform, with a central tower, the upper parts of which were taken down after the Civil War. A massive new tower, incorporating materials from the ruined parts of the building, was built in 1708 in place of the south transept, and in the

This engraving from the 1780s shows the ruins of the nave of St Augustine's church at Dodderhill, Worcestershire, burnt during the Civil War

early nineteenth century the north transept was rebuilt and a small vestry was added on the south side of the chancel. The church therefore consists of the fourteenth-century chancel and the base of the thirteenth-century tower, which is flanked by an early eighteenth-century tower and a nineteenth-century north transept. It does not have a nave.[23]

The majority of the churches reconstructed during the decades immediately after the Civil War were built in a restrained Gothic style, so much so that Pevsner, considering Shropshire, wondered if this period should not be thought of as one of Gothic revival rather than Gothic survival.[24] Elements such as window heads could have been recovered from ruins or preserved when the undamaged parts of a church were dismantled, and re-used in the new building, but some of them were presumably copies made by the seventeenth-century masons. The churches built during the period were typically of stone, with uncomplicated and conventional plans. In many cases the opportunity to make changes was restricted by the need to use the site and foundations of the former church, and to incorporate its surviving features. That was done at Farndon in Cheshire, where the lower part of the tower was retained. Only where a completely new church was raised could a different layout be adopted, as at Taynton, where a simple hall-church with a north-south orientation was erected.[25] Most of the churches put up to replace those destroyed or damaged in the Civil War are aesthetically pleasing buildings. Indeed, St Mary's, Westport, at

Malmesbury is one of the few truly undistinguished churches of the post-war period. Ironically, this plain building, erected in the 1670s, replaced 'a prettie Church, where there were very good windows and a fair steeple . . . which much adorned the Towne of Malmesbury' before it was pulled down because of its proximity to the defences.[26]

Many of the churches constructed as replacements for wartime losses were themselves later modified or supplanted. All of those built for that reason in Lincoln were reconstructed or totally rebuilt during the second half of the nineteenth century. The simple design of St Nicholas's at Nottingham, built in 1671–82, was obscured when side aisles were added in the eighteenth century, while St Mary's-at-the-Walls in Colchester was rebuilt in 1872, except the tower, which has a medieval base surmounted by successive additions of 1729 and 1911.[27] Others were built so long after the Civil War that their Baroque and Classical styles tend to conceal their origins as the successors of churches destroyed during the conflict. Some were not erected until the nineteenth century, such as St Thomas's, Scarborough, in 1840, St Martin's, Hereford, in 1845, and St Nicholas's, Droitwich, in 1869.[28] Partly for these reasons, the legacy of the Civil War in terms of church buildings is comparatively small, and the late 1640s and the 1650s are regarded as a period when there was little or no church building, a feature which is popularly attributed to the hostility of the Commonwealth authorities. This view owes something to the success of royalist propaganda, in particular the oft-quoted inscription in Sir Robert Shirley's church of 1653 at Staunton Harold in Leicestershire, that it was built 'When all things sacred were throughout ye nation Either demollisht or profaned'.[29] It overlooks the role played by some who were active supporters of the parliamentarian cause in financing the building of churches to replace those destroyed, such as Thomas Pury the younger at Taynton. An even more apposite example is provided by Sir Robert Harley's expenditure on the new church at Brampton Bryan, for he had been chairman of the committee that had supervised the smashing of stained glass and images in London's churches and the chapels in the royal palaces around the capital during the mid-1640s.[30] The financial difficulties faced by patrons and parishioners, and demographic changes, are more likely to have caused delays in rebuilding than the hostility of the Commonwealth regime or the theological objections of the puritans, which were concerned more with the contents than the places of worship themselves. Such problems continued in some parishes into the eighteenth century. The new church of St Edmund's in Dudley was not begun until 1724 and was not ready for use before 1739. The time taken to finish the building and the fact that the elaborate design of the lower part of the tower was not extended to the remainder indicate that the parish found it difficult to provide adequate finance.[31]

A similar pattern can be detected for the country houses destroyed. Some stood ruinous for many years after the end of the Civil War, but were eventually restored, or demolished and replaced. Nevertheless, a few were completely abandoned and remained in ruins as reminders of the process which had caused a burst of destruction in the war years. This was the case with the Earl of Middlesex's house at Milcote, for example. Sir John Winter's late-sixteenth-

The remains of the west front are all that is left of the Jermyns' fortified manor house at Torksey in Lincolnshire, burnt by the royalists in 1645

century mansion known as Whitecross at Lydney in Gloucestershire was destroyed on his own instructions to prevent it from falling into parliamentarian hands, and by the early eighteenth century its remains had been 'turned into a furnace for iron'. Bagworth Park in Leicestershire was 'demolished' during the war and the ruins remained until 1769, when they were cleared and a farmhouse was built on the site.[32] Some houses had no replacements at all. The Pophams' house at Wellington in Somerset was burnt following its capture in 1645 and was not rebuilt, nor was Abbotsbury House, after the damage it sustained in the explosion and fire during the parliamentarian assault. The process of decay, the use of the remains as quarries, and the clearance of the sites for later buildings, have removed the remnants of most houses that were abandoned, although there are still substantial ruins at Basing House in Hampshire, Moreton Corbet, Shropshire, Stapleton Castle, Herefordshire, and Torksey in Lincolnshire.[33] One of the most spectacular losses, and one which attracted the especial attention of contemporaries, was the mansion built by the wealthy London mercer Sir Baptist Hickes at Chipping Campden in 1613, which was left in ruins after it was fired by the royalists in 1645. The two flanking pavilions and a small fragment of the

The medieval castle and Elizabethan house at Moreton Corbet, Shropshire, were burnt by the parliamentarians in 1645 to prevent their occupation by the royalists

house are all that is left of this fine building. The clearance of the ruins of Lathom House was even more complete, so much so that it is even uncertain where its site actually was.[34]

The impact of the destruction of housing was more apparent in the towns, where entire areas had to be rebuilt, than in the countryside. Yet in some respects the effects were not all that great, for the generally low quality of the new buildings and the lack of attempts to control reconstruction produced districts which were broadly similar in character, and probably in appearance, to those that had been destroyed. This certainly seems to have been true of the suburbs, which were the poorest and least salubrious parts of early modern towns, for many of the typical features present before the war can be recognised after rebuilding. The nature of suburban society at Exeter seems to have been unaltered, with unlicensed alehouses, drinking on the sabbath, gaming, swearing, prostitution, theft, fighting and disorderly behaviour all reported there in the 1650s.[35] The characteristic pattern of relatively prosperous inner parishes and poor ones around the urban fringe also persisted after the Civil War. This is apparent from the Hearth Tax returns for Newcastle-upon-Tyne and Exeter, both of which suffered considerable suburban destruction.[36] The St Clement's suburb of Worcester also emerged from its enforced rebuilding as one of the poorest parts of the city, with few large houses, four-fifths of its dwellings having only one or two hearths in 1678, and over a half of its householders exempted from payment of the Hearth Tax.[37] It is not unduly surprising that the post-war rebuilding produced similar societies to those that had existed before the Civil War, for it would have required large-scale changes of population, wealth, and property ownership to bring about their transformation.

Nor is it clear that wartime destruction invariably produced significant structural changes in local economies. A district containing a specialised industry was probably able to retain it in the long term despite the destruction of the buildings. Much depended upon the degree to which a substantial amount of property destruction resulted in long-distance migration, for the chief resource of an industry was the skills of the workforce. As long as the craftsmen were able to return and replace their lost equipment and tools, then the industry would probably survive. Although some of the homeless were completely displaced and became refugees seeking new homes outside the area, it seems that the majority did not travel far, perhaps no more than a few miles, and were therefore able to return once new houses were built. Given the pervasive effects of the war in many regions, prospects may have been no more attractive in other communities nearby, and so there were no great incentives to make a permanent move. On the other hand, there was always the enticing economic lure of London. In August 1646 William Adams of Peterchurch, Pembrokeshire, had been in London for over a year trying to get some compensation following the burning of his houses. Similarly, one Widow Jane, whose husband had been killed by the royalists at York, had left Birmingham when her house was burnt down by Rupert's troops, and she and her children were in lodgings in London by March 1645. They were still there in September 1646, when they were allotted new accommodation in Holborn.[38] Others may have gone to the capital originally with the intention of seeking help, but eventually settled there rather than return to a community which they knew to have been devastated.

The debate on the part the Civil War played in the decline of Chichester's needle industry has shown that the destruction of the suburbs occupied by the needle makers before 1642 did not do excessive damage to the industry, which survived well into the eighteenth century.[39] Despite the slow rate of rebuilding, enough of the workforce returned for the industry to revive. The survival of the intra-mural property may have helped to maintain continuity of personnel there, but at Banbury the wartime devastation was more general, and it coincided with a downturn in its footwear industry. From being the largest single trade amongst the citizens in the late sixteenth and early seventeenth centuries, the number of shoemakers suddenly fell in the mid-seventeenth century and thereafter they constituted a much smaller proportion of the town's tradesmen. The shoemaker described as formerly of Banbury who was recorded in Chipping Norton in 1645 may have been only one of many shoemakers who had left the town. How far the decline is attributable to the effects of the war is uncertain, although it did coincide with the rise of Northampton as a centre of the trade, boosted by orders for the parliamentarian armies and its good fortune in not being captured during the war.[40] Coventry also benefited from orders for the army for its hosiery, and it, too, was held by the parliamentarians throughout the war. In contrast, Leicester's stuttering economy received a heavy blow when the town was stormed in 1645, and it was unable to provide shoes for Cromwell's army three years later. Leicester's industries eventually recovered, but Lichfield's capping trade, which had been in decline since the late sixteenth century, was finally extinguished when Beacon Street, where most of the cappers were based, was destroyed in the Civil War.[41] The evidence suggests that property destruction was one of the deleterious effects of the war which could temporarily check the prosperity of a well-established industry, and do considerable, even fatal, harm to one which was already faltering.

The damaging effects of the Civil War in terms of economy and fabric were gradually superseded and obscured by subsequent changes. Liverpool and Bristol both prospered considerably in the eighteenth century and the building booms that accompanied their affluence covered most of the remaining evidence of the physical damage that they had sustained during the Civil War. The process was already under way at Liverpool by the end of the seventeenth century when Celia Fiennes found it 'a large fine town' with 'mostly new built houses of brick and stone after the London fashion'.[42] The 'urban renaissance' of the late seventeenth

Liverpool suffered considerable damage during the Civil War. This view of c. 1680 shows the new town hall and the prominent remains of the castle

and eighteenth centuries produced considerable changes in the townscapes of England and Wales through the gradual introduction of Classical styles in architecture, requiring the almost universal adoption of brick and tile.[43] Among the towns which had suffered damage in the Civil War that benefited from the process were Winchester, Lichfield and Ludlow, while in the eighteenth century York revived, profiting from its role as the centre of society in the north, as it had earlier done from being the focus of its administration. The patronage of the county gentry, the growth of organised leisure activities, and the development of a prosperous urban gentry brought a growing wealth to provincial towns, which percolated through their economies and was manifested in their appearance. Fashion, emulation and conspicuous consumption were all factors behind the rebuilding which took place in many towns during the period. In the social environment which resulted the poor quality timber-and-plaster buildings erected to replace wartime losses were both unfashionable and unsightly, and so were replaced, or at least were refronted. Thus, even in the central areas of towns where there had been much rebuilding after the Civil War, subsequent reconstruction and refronting disguised the fact that many of the buildings had been erected within a few years in the late 1640s and 1650s. None of the places that had to replace the wartime loss of most of their property – such as Axminster, Bridgnorth or Faringdon – has attracted the attention and admiration accorded to Warwick and Blandford Forum, where phases of more or less coherent building followed the fires in 1694 and 1731 respectively.[44]

Furthermore, the social geography of towns underwent a transformation in the eighteenth century, as the comparatively well-to-do urban dwellers moved into the suburbs, gradually changing them into socially and architecturally respectable districts. That process involved the construction of larger and better houses to replace the low-grade buildings erected after the Civil War. In some cases the seventeenth-century houses were concealed under the new fabric, rather than demolished. A Regency terrace in Magdalen Street in Exeter that was cleared away in 1977 was found to conceal the framework of a building dated 1659 that was a replacement for a house destroyed in the Civil War.[45] The effect was the same, however, with the physical evidence of the post-war rebuilding effectively removed. The increasing pace of urban expansion in the late eighteenth and nineteenth centuries and the replacement of the relatively poor post-Civil War buildings as they deteriorated left little behind from the mid-seventeenth century in many of those places where there had been extensive destruction. Only a few ruins created during the Civil War, such as those of the bishops' palaces in Lincoln and Winchester, remain in an urban context.[46]

The physical evidence of earthworks was also slowly obliterated as towns grew beyond their early modern confines and covered their immediate environs with railway yards, factories and streets of red-brick houses. Many vestiges of defences and siegeworks remained into the eighteenth century, and some of them into the nineteenth. The fort at Whitechapel was still a prominent feature until it was finally levelled in 1807, and in 1885 it was said that some earthworks at Hackney had been cleared in the recent past.[47] But there are few survivals of the many works thrown up in the 1640s. This is partly due to deliberate clearance carried

The remains of the bastioned fort known as the Queen's Sconce at Newark show the scale of such fortifications. The similar King's Sconce on the opposite side of the town was destroyed as late as c. *1887*

out during or soon after the Civil War to prevent them being refortified – which was done either by the local population, out of sheer exasperation, or by official command – and the use of their sites for other purposes. It is also because, once they were no longer maintained, the stone and wood were removed and they were gradually reduced by erosion. Their destruction has been so complete in many cases that their sites are now uncertain. Even the location of such a substantial work as the fort built by the royalists at Handbridge in Chester is now unknown.[48] Among the identifiable remains in urban areas are those at Newark, Fort Royal at Worcester, and at Brandon Hill in Bristol. In the countryside, there are some fine works at Donnington Castle, Berkshire, Horsey Hill in Huntingdonshire and elsewhere. Others are more readily visible from the air than on the ground and can hardly be regarded as prominent topographical features.[49]

Although reconstruction or clearance removed much of the physical evidence of the impact of the Civil War, some remains were left. They took their place in a landscape which already contained substantial numbers of ruined buildings. These were the products of abandonment and neglect, the visible effects of the Henrician and Edwardian dissolutions, and the vestiges of changes in taste and style, as mansions replaced castles and fortified houses as the residences of the aristocracy. The landscape of early seventeenth-century England was scattered with ruins, in both towns and the countryside, and the Civil War added to the number, speeding the decay of some structures already in decline and contributing others. As time passed, the distinction between the buildings ruined in the 1640s and the remains from earlier periods gradually became blurred.

The clear recollection of the damage done in the 1640s lasted into the early eighteenth century, until the death of those who had either witnessed the destruction caused by the war, or had been told about it at first hand. Thereafter, the prominence of the events of the Civil War naturally declined with time, and they seemed of less significance to later generations that had seen other disasters. Marlborough in 1653 and Northampton in 1675 experienced fires which caused far more damage than either town had suffered in the Civil War, and it may be that the spectacular catastrophe of the Great Fire of London in 1666 overshadowed the losses of the 1640s, both in the minds of contemporaries and of posterity.

The memory of the effects of the 1640s eventually faded to such an extent that the possibility that a building could have been destroyed in the Civil War was not even considered, even where documentary evidence was available. A return made from St Helen's, Abingdon, in 1666 explained that the vicarage had been demolished in the war and not replaced, but by 1783 the circumstances of the loss had been forgotten and the rather bemused vicar noted that 'there neither is, nor can I discover the most distant traces that there ever has been a house' for the minister.[50] Not surprisingly, there was also a tendency for confusion to creep in, with some remains not perceived as being the result of military action during the Civil War, but others, perhaps less understandably, wrongfully attributed to it. No later than 1736 Francis Drake, the reputable local historian of York, was reluctant to accept that the large fort outside Micklegate was in fact a fortification constructed during the Civil War, preferring to regard it as of Roman origin. Drake's aberration is all the more surprising because Defoe, writing in the previous decade, had had no doubt that 'the old additional Works' had been 'cast up in the late Rebellion'.[51] Another error perpetrated in the eighteenth century was that the desertion of Sezincote in Gloucestershire followed the wartime destruction of the village. Samuel Rudder, whose history of the county was published in 1779, wrote that the parish 'was totally depopulated . . . and the church demolished' during the Civil War, but it is clear that the depopulation was due to a change in agricultural practices, that it was already complete by the early seventeenth century, and that the church was probably demolished around 1700.[52] In other cases the memory of the local impact of the war was not entirely lost, although it may have been somewhat distorted. In 1934 the traveller and journalist Wilfrid Byford-Jones visited High Ercall in Shropshire and asked an elderly villager if there was anything of interest to be seen there, only to be told: 'Nothing's happened 'ere not since that varmint Cromwell tried to blow up the hall and the church.'[53] Apart from the common misattribution of responsibility to Cromwell – the royalists' excesses have generally been blamed on Prince Rupert – this remark was a reasonable summary of events almost three hundred years earlier.

With the modification or replacement of many of the buildings erected in the aftermath of the Civil War, the structures that became associated with wartime damage and destruction were ruined castles. Many of these are prominent features in the landscape, standing on such spectacular sites as those at Corfe and Bridgnorth, but the association is rather misleading, for many of the slightings and demolitions of the 1640s were carried out during the periods of peace. Some castles were damaged during the conflict, with sections of curtain walls brought down by artillery fire or undermining, and the timber buildings burnt, leaving parts of the structure in disrepair. Few decisions to demolish castles were made during the first Civil War, however, and it was not until the early months of 1647 that the parliamentary authorities gave full consideration to the problems presented by the costs of garrisons and the risks of defensible castles being captured by hostile forces during an uprising. Even then, there were differences of opinion between the two Houses of Parliament regarding the castles to be slighted. The second Civil War perfectly illustrated the consequences of leaving castles that were still largely intact either empty or in the hands of small garrisons, and there was a further burst of orders for slighting or destruction in 1648 and the subsequent years. The distinction between slighting and demolition was an important one. Some castles, such as Pontefract and Banbury, were totally demolished, but the costs were high, and slighting, which involved the wrecking of the outer walls, while leaving many of the other buildings intact, was preferred in many cases. It was ordered that Kenilworth Castle should be slighted so as to be untenable as a fortification, but with the house left undamaged. Because of the reluctance of the local committees to carry out the work of demolition or slighting that was ordered – perhaps because of the expense, or the considerable practical difficulties – a number of directives were issued before some castles were dealt with. The order of July 1646 to slight the defences at Sudeley Castle was not fully effected before September 1649, for example. The work of destroying parts of Montgomery Castle was also delayed until 1649, but when it was carried out it was not only the fabric of the medieval building that was demolished but also the mansion built within the outer bailey by Lord Herbert in the early 1620s.[54] The surviving ruins of many castles are in fact the results of neglect and abandonment, the removal of stone for other buildings, and such accidents as the fire which burnt for several days in 1750 in the former residential ranges of Dudley Castle.[55]

The parliamentarians' iconoclasm has also been perceived as an important destructive effect of the Civil Wars. Among the handsome structures that were destroyed were Cheapside Cross in London, pulled down in 1643, and the cross in the market-place at Abingdon, which the parliamentarians demolished when they captured the town in 1644.[56] Much of the damage was inflicted upon the interiors of churches, with many defaced by the smashing of stained glass, the disfigurement or destruction of statues, and the removal and burning of woodwork. When Richard Symonds visited St Peter's church in Buckingham he

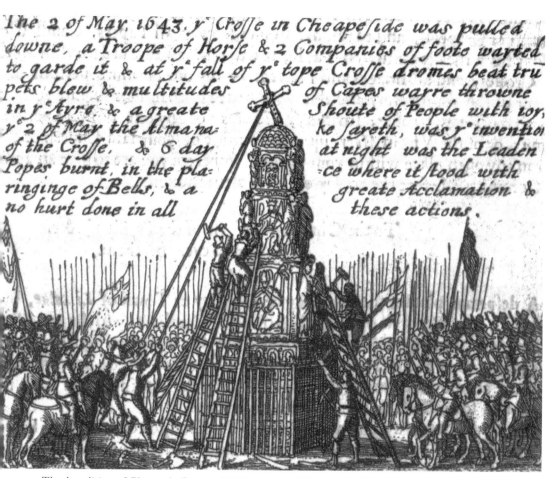

The 2 of May. 1643. y^e Crosse in Cheapeside was pulled downe, a Troope of Horse & 2 Companies of foote wayted to garde it & at y^e fall of y^e tope Crosse dromes beat trū pets blew & multitudes of Capes warre throwne in ye Ayre & a greate Shoute of People with ioy, ye 2 of May the Almana ke sayeth, was ye invention of the Crosse. & 6 day at night was the Leaden Popes burnt, in the pla- ce where it stood with ringinge of Bells, & a greate Acclamation & no hurt done in all these actions.

The demolition of Cheapside Cross in 1643 was part of the process of the destruction of idolatrous images. It was watched by an enthusiastic crowd, according to this parliamentarian account

found that the destruction of the stained glass had been very thorough: 'Never were any windows more broken, in May, 1644, by the rebels of Northampton.'[57] Yet the extent of the damage to church interiors deliberately executed by the troops was limited; most was carried out under the direction of local civilian officials, such as William Dowsing, whose activities in East Anglia, as recorded in his journal, indicate the scale of the damage done to the interiors of many parish churches. It has been estimated that no more than a few dozen churches suffered from deliberately inconoclastic actions by parliamentarian soldiers.[58] The effects of the troops of both sides using church buildings for fortified strongpoints, prisons, barracks, stables and storehouses were no less damaging than the attempts to 'cleanse' them of the idolatorous images associated with popery. The results of neglect during a period of disruption which saw many parishes lose their incumbents because they had been expelled, or had found it prudent to

Iconoclasm was a feature of the years of the Civil Wars, with the destruction and removal of the more theologically contentious church fittings and decorations. The process is neatly captured in this woodcut

withdraw, were also deleterious. Iconoclasm, misuse and negligence left many churches in a sorry state. But in many cases it is difficult to determine whether the damage occurred in the 1640s, or during the burst of iconoclastic fury a century earlier, or indeed at the hands of the earnest nineteenth-century reformers.[59] In many cases there is no contemporary evidence for damage said to have been caused during the Civil Wars and the attribution is based upon a later tradition.

The association of the destructive impact of the Civil Wars primarily with castles and churches is understandable, for they are the largest and most prominent of the buildings that were defaced to have survived. Yet the damage which they sustained was uncharacteristic – the destruction of houses was far more widespread and caused much greater disruption and distress, but produced less spectacular and relatively short-lived results.

Even when the physical remains of the majority of the buildings destroyed had been replaced or become less conspicuous, the archival evidence remained. Much of it was made accessible through the accounts of the Civil War published by antiquarians in county and civic histories, and, from the mid-nineteenth century, in the volumes of the growing number of record societies. Many local historians gave some attention to the destructive effects of the war, but the evidence which they presented was not translated into an overall view of the extent of destruction. Rather, historians summarising the impact of the Civil War were at pains to stress that it was relatively insignificant compared with the destruction carried out during the Thirty Years' War. Indeed, their awareness of the scale of the devastation in Germany may have caused them to understate the damage carried out in the British Isles. Defoe was an early exponent of the view that the full horrors of the German wars had not been repeated in Britain, with his fictional narrator of *Memoirs of a Cavalier: Or a Military Journal of the Wars in Germany, and the Wars in England; From the Year 1632, to the Year 1648*, published in 1720, concluding that even in the areas that were most fought over during the Civil War 'there never was seen that Ruin and Depopulation' which he had witnessed in Germany.[60] Historians tended to reach similar conclusions, G.M. Trevelyan writing that 'no part of England was burnt to a desert, like all Germany of that day'.[61] The reassessment of the effects of the wars in Germany has replaced the earlier view of almost universal desolation with an awareness of the variety in the extent of the damage from region to region, the differing lengths of time to which areas were subjected to military operations, and differing speeds with which communities recovered.[62] The perspective of historians of the Civil War has also changed, producing a more detailed and critical evaluation of the impact of the conflict.[63]

A contemporary observer from the continental wars would have found the methods of warfare and their consequences entirely familiar, but the fears of those who in 1642 had anticipated a replication of the worst destructive effects of the German wars were not fully realised. The destruction during the years of civil war did not prove to be an absolute and irrevocable disaster for communities in England and Wales, although some suffered badly enough. The difference was one of scale rather than of kind. This was largely because of the length of the first Civil War, the failure of the royalists to recover to any degree after 1646, and the relatively short duration of the campaigns in 1648 and 1651. The shortness of the conflict limited the physical damage and restricted the impact of its other deleterious effects, allowing an economic recovery that came quickly enough to permit most places to recover and rebuild within a generation. Even so, the scale of the destruction, concentrated within a few years, was undoubtedly one of the harmful consequences of the war. It affected not only those who are well represented in the documentary record as participants or prominent members of the community – the gentry, clergy, and civic élite – but also the common people who were caught up in the conflict simply because of the location of their houses, and found themselves homeless and without a large part of their possessions as a result. The relatively little surviving physical evidence from the period of rebuilding should not be allowed to obscure the scale of the losses produced by military action during the Civil Wars, and the human distress that was caused by 'that fearfull fruit of wasting wars'.[64]

Gazetteer

This gazetteer includes some of the ruins resulting from destruction during the Civil War and buildings erected to replace those destroyed. Most of the sites are accessible or can be seen from a public road or footpath. It is not a list of those places affected by destruction, for in many cases the evidence has been obliterated, either by the process of destruction itself, or by development and rebuilding since the seventeenth century.

Ashby de la Zouch, Leicestershire. The Royalist garrison of the castle surrendered in February 1646, but the buildings were not slighted until 1649. The most imposing part of the ruins is the Hastings Tower, erected by William, Lord Hastings, in 1474–83.

Basing House, Hampshire. Little remains of the Marquis of Winchester's mansion house, destroyed by fire when the New Model Army captured it in October 1645, but the Civil War earthworks are still impressive and include three angled bastions. Much of the nearby village was also destroyed.

Berwick-upon-Tweed, Northumberland. The town played little part in the Civil War, but its sixteenth-century defences are among the most important surviving bastioned fortifications in Europe.

Bishop's Waltham, Hampshire. This was one of the palaces of the bishops of Winchester. It was garrisoned by the royalists and burnt down when it was captured by the parliamentarians in 1644, although considerable sections of ruins still survive.

Boarstall, Buckinghamshire. The village and church were destroyed by the royalist garrison of the house. The village has not been rebuilt – its site can be identified in the fields to the south of the moated site – but a new church was erected in 1663. The house itself was later demolished, but its fine fourteenth-century gatehouse has survived.

Brampton Bryan, Hereford and Worcester. The remains of the castle that was twice besieged during the Civil War stand in the grounds of the eighteenth-century house. The village and church of St Barnabas were destroyed. The church was rebuilt in 1656, evidently using materials from the castle.

Bridgnorth, Shropshire. Most of the High Town was destroyed in 1646 when the royalist garrison withdrew into the castle and the parliamentarians occupied the town. St Leonard's church blew up when the magazine stored in it was detonated. It was rebuilt after the Restoration, but the present structure dates largely from the 1860s, although incorporating parts of the roof from the seventeenth-century building. The castle was slighted after the war and its ruins occupy a spectacular site above the River Severn. Castle Street is largely eighteenth century.

Bristol. Key to much of the West Country, Bristol's defence required extensive fortifications, parts of which survive, although much eroded, at Brandon Hill, to the west of the city centre. The castle was totally demolished in 1656, but a part of the site has been uncovered by recent excavations.

Castle Bolton, Wensleydale, North Yorkshire. The castle was a royalist garrison until it surrendered in November 1645. Much of the fourteenth-century keep is still standing, although in ruins. The village was burnt down by the garrison in March 1645.

Castlemorton, Hereford and Worcester. This village was the scene of a clash between Sir Jacob Astley's forces and the inhabitants in 1646. The villagers retreated to the church, which the royalists then set on fire, together with some of the houses. St Gregory's church was repaired c.1647 with part of the proceeds from the sale of the materials of a bell tower close to Worcester Cathedral, and at least a part of the nave was rebuilt at that time.

Chester. A major royalist base for much of the war, Chester eventually surrendered in February 1646, after the destruction of many of its buildings. Most of the physical evidence of the siege has been obliterated, although a section of the city walls rebuilt after being breached by the parliamentarian artillery can be seen close to St John's church. King Charles's Tower on the city walls has a museum devoted to the Civil War.

Chipping Campden, Gloucestershire. The fine Jacobean mansion built by the wealthy London mercer Sir Baptist Hickes was burnt by the royalists in 1645, and all that remains is a section of wall and the two flanking pavilions on a terrace.

Colchester, Essex. This town was the scene of a particularly vicious siege in 1648, when many buildings were destroyed. The churches damaged were later rebuilt, although St Botolph's priory is still in ruins. The so-called Siege House in East Street is pock-marked with bullet holes. The castle keep contains a museum.

Corfe Castle, Dorset. A royalist garrison for most of the Civil War, it was surrendered in February 1646 and almost immediately slighted, creating some of the most dramatic ruins to have survived from the period. The village also suffered considerable damage during the war.

Denbigh, Clwyd. The castle was held by the royalists until October 1646, but the garrison had burnt much of the town in the previous autumn. The castle was later slighted, but extensive ruins remain.

Dodderhill, Hereford and Worcester. This village lies to the north of Droitwich. Parts of St Augustine's church were destroyed in the Civil War and the building is now a curious mixture of medieval and post-seventeenth-century elements, including a substantial tower of 1708.

Donnington, Berkshire. Only the late-fourteenth-century gatehouse survives of the castle defended by the royalists in 1645–6; the remainder was demolished by the besiegers' artillery. Most of the earthwork defences added around the castle during the Civil War are still visible. The nearby village was destroyed in 1645 on the orders of Sir John Boys, the governor of the castle.

Dudley, West Midlands. The medieval market town was dominated by its castle, which now forms part of Dudley Zoo. The castle was a royalist fortress for much of the Civil War and was later slighted; further damage was caused by a fire in 1750. St Edmund's church, close to the castle, was pulled down in the Civil War and rebuilt in 1724–39.

Exeter, Devon. Fortified by the parliamentarians and captured by the royalists in September 1643, Exeter finally surrendered to the New Model in April 1646. Most of the extra-mural buildings were destroyed; St Thomas's church in West Exe and Wynard's almshouses in Magdalen Street are among those that were subsequently rebuilt. Stretches of the city walls survive in the vicinity of Southernhay and Northernhay.

Faringdon, Oxfordshire. The village was burned down by the garrison of Faringdon House in 1646. All Saints' church was damaged during the siege of the house in that year and not all of the elements that were destroyed have been replaced.

Farndon, Cheshire. The village was partly destroyed in clashes between parliamentarian forces and the royalist garrison of Holt Castle on the opposite bank of the River Dee. St Chad's church, except the tower, had to be rebuilt after the Civil War. A unique stained-glass window in the Barnston chapel depicts members of Sir Francis Gamull's regiment and arms and armour of the period. There are some ruins of Holt Castle, and the north door of St Mary's church close by still has loopholes for muskets.

Farnham, Surrey. The castle, a palace of the bishops of Winchester, was a parliamentarian garrison for most of the Civil War and was restored after the Restoration, although the keep is in ruins. Part of the town was burnt down during the war.

Gloucester. Most important parliamentarian garrison in the Severn valley throughout the first Civil War, Gloucester sustained a major siege in the summer of 1643. Virtually all of its suburbs were destroyed. A part of the early sixteenth-century friary church of the Greyfriars, ruined by artillery fire during the siege, stands close to Southgate Street. The folk museum in Westgate Street has displays of Civil War material.

Great Torrington, Devon. The royalists' powder magazine in St Michael's church blew up during the New Model Army's attack on the town in February 1646. Much of the building was rebuilt during the Interregnum.

Hereford. Held by both sides at various times, Hereford resisted a major siege by the parliamentarians in the summer of 1645. Most of the suburbs were destroyed, including St Owen's church outside St Owen's Gate and St Martin's church on the south side of Wye Bridge. St Martin's was rebuilt in 1845 on another site. Stretches of the city walls have survived and the castle bailey is preserved as Castle Green. Hereford Museum has the mortar Roaring Meg, cast for the parliamentarians and used in a number of operations in the region.

Hillesden, Buckinghamshire. The medieval mansion was burnt after being captured by parliamentarians in March 1644. Slight remains of the Civil War earthworks can be traced, and All Saints' church, a royalist outpost, bears the marks of the skirmish during which its garrison was expelled.

Lichfield, Staffordshire. The cathedral close was enclosed by a wall with two gates and was a garrison during the Civil War. It was besieged on three occasions. The cathedral itself was badly damaged and was restored in the 1660s, when the central spire was replaced. There was also considerable destruction elsewhere in the city, especially in Beacon Street.

Lilleshall, Shropshire. The house created within the abbey buildings following the Dissolution was used by the royalists as a garrison, which only surrendered after a destructive bombardment followed by an assault in 1645. The imposing ruins include the splendid west doorway of the former abbey church.

Lincoln. The city suffered considerably during the Civil War and several of its churches were damaged. Most of them were rebuilt in the eighteenth century and again in the nineteenth, but parts of the medieval building of St Benedict's have survived, although the nave and north aisle were demolished after the Civil War. There are extensive remains of the castle. The bishop's palace, close to the cathedral, fell into ruin after the Civil War, but part of it was rebuilt in 1838.

Lostwithiel, Cornwall. The Earl of Essex's army arrived here in August 1644 and used the church as a prison. When some of the prisoners got into the tower their gaolers exploded a gunpowder charge in an attempt to force them down and the explosion 'blew off the slates' from the roof, which was later replaced. The line of the earlier roof can be seen on the tower.

Montgomery, Powys. Despite its strong hilltop position, in September 1644 the castle was surrendered to the parliamentarians without a siege. A decision to preserve the castle was later reversed, and in 1649 both it and the house built within it in the 1620s were demolished. There are still extensive ruins of the castle, and stretches of the bank and ditch of the thirteenth-century town walls also survive.

Moreton Corbet, Shropshire. The medieval keep and Elizabethan domestic buildings formed a perfect site for a garrison. Held by both sides at various times, the buildings were burnt by the parliamentarians from Shrewsbury in March 1645, although extensive ruins remain.

Newark-upon-Trent, Nottinghamshire. The town was defended by its royalist garrison in three sieges, and sustained considerable damage. The ruins of the castle show marks of the parliamentarian bombardment. Several earthwork defences from the Civil War have survived in the vicinity of the town, most notably the Queen's Sconce to the south of the town centre.

Nottingham. This town was held for parliament from late 1642. The castle was rebuilt after the Restoration and again in the nineteenth century. St Nicholas's church, demolished by the garrison, was rebuilt in 1671–82, with side aisles added in the eighteenth century.

Oswestry, Shropshire. The town and castle were garrisoned by the royalists, but captured by the parliamentarians in 1644. The suburbs and the church, which stood outside the walls, were destroyed. St Oswald's was rebuilt in 1675, with the tower added in 1692, but the only remains of the castle are some ruins in the public park on the site of the motte.

Oxford. This was the royalists' headquarters throughout the first Civil War. Only fragments now remain of the city's elaborate earthwork defences, but the castle motte still stands to a considerable height. The city museum has displays on the Civil War. There are ruins of Godstow House near Wolvercote, to the north of the city, where a royalist garrison was placed until May 1645, when it was withdrawn and the buildings were burnt.

Pembroke, Dyfed. The sieges in both Civil Wars caused considerable destruction. There are substantial remains of the castle, and stretches of the town wall have also survived.

Pontefract, West Yorkshire. Although badly damaged during the three prolonged sieges of the castle, some of the castle fabric has survived. The nave of All Saints' church still stands in ruins.

Raglan, Gwent. The Marquis of Worcester garrisoned his castle here for the king, and it did not surrender until August 1646, after a long siege. The fabric was badly damaged by artillery fire during the siege and deliberate destruction after the surrender, but the remaining ruins are still impressive. Some of the Civil War earthworks can be seen close to the castle. The nearby village was destroyed by the garrison in May 1646.

Rockingham, Northamptonshire. The castle was garrisoned during the Civil War and was badly damaged, although parts of it were subsequently rebuilt and have remained in occupation. The church and part of the village were also destroyed. The present church, below the castle, is largely nineteenth-century. The village now stands further away from the castle than did its predecessor.

Rushall, West Midlands. This is now in the north-east suburbs of Walsall. In May 1644 the Earl of Denbigh's parliamentarian troops bombarded the hall and church and did considerable damage, setting the church alight. The present church is Victorian, but there are remains of the hall, including the ruins of the fifteenth-century gatehouse.

Scarborough, North Yorkshire. Prolonged sieges of the castle in both Civil Wars led to considerable destruction within the town. The castle ruins stand on a cliff top above the town and are still impressive. St Mary's church close to the castle was badly damaged and only a fragment of the original building is still standing.

Shrawardine, Shropshire. The village stands on the banks of the River Severn, six miles west of Shrewsbury. There are only slight remains of the medieval castle which the royalists occupied in 1644 and was burnt following their surrender at the end of June 1645. The garrison pulled down the church in two stages in February and June 1645, and destroyed the village in June that year. The nave was rebuilt in 1649 and the chancel in 1722.

Stapleton Castle, Hereford and Worcester. The house was a royalist garrison until it was abandoned and burnt in the summer of 1645. The ruins stand on a hill overlooking the Lugg valley to the north of Presteigne.

Stokesay Castle, Shropshire. The castle survived the Civil War and is a fine example of a late-thirteenth-century fortified manor house. The church of St John the Baptist stood too close to the castle for the garrison's comfort, however, and much of it was destroyed. It was rebuilt in 1654, with the tower added in 1664, and has retained many of its mid-seventeenth-century fittings.

Sudeley Castle, Gloucestershire. The castle was twice captured by parliamentarian forces and sustained considerable damage then and during the slighting ordered in 1649. Although the house was later rebuilt, the ruins of the fifteenth-century banqueting hall remain.

Taynton, Gloucestershire. This is three miles south of Newent. The garrison of the manor house here destroyed the church and the present simple aisleless building was erected on a new site in or soon after 1648. The chancel was added in 1894.

Torksey Castle, Lincolnshire. The Elizabethan manor house here, close to the River Trent south of Gainsborough, was destroyed by the royalists in 1645. The ruined remains of the west front are all that has survived.

Wallingford, Oxfordshire. The town was one of the ring of royalist garrisons around Oxford, with the castle serving as a citadel. The castle was not slighted until 1652; its site has now been laid out as gardens. Three churches were destroyed. The site of All Saints' lies between the castle and Castle Street, St Leonard's was rebuilt in 1704–5 and St Peter's in the 1760s, with its distinctive spire added in 1777.

Wardour Castle, Wiltshire. This was damaged in two sieges during the Civil War and there was no attempt to restore the buildings. Wardour House was built outside the bailey in the 1680s.

Woolsthorpe, Lincolnshire. There are some remains of the church, which was held as an outpost by the garrison of nearby Belvoir Castle and was ruined during an attack by parliamentary forces.

Worcester. One of the royalists' most important fortresses, Worcester sustained damage in both the first Civil War and the Scottish invasion in 1651 that culminated in the battle here. Stretches of the medieval city wall have survived, but little now remains of the Civil War fortification of Fort Royal on the south side of the city centre. The commandery buildings in Sidbury are now a museum devoted to the Civil War.

Wormleighton, Warwickshire. This house stands in an isolated spot, eight miles north of Banbury. The village was depopulated following enclosure in the late fifteenth century and the manor was bought by the Spencer family in 1506. Their manor house was badly damaged during the Civil War and the surviving parts were later converted into a farmhouse. One range of the house and the fine gatehouse survive.

Yate, Avon. The moated medieval manor house was garrisoned by both sides and it was reduced to ruins by the end of the Civil War. It was not rebuilt, but some of the remains were incorporated into a later farmhouse.

York. The city sustained major damage in the Civil War, when most of its suburbs were destroyed. St Mary's Tower in Bootham was partially ruined when a mine was exploded beneath it during the siege of 1644, and the ruined section was later rebuilt with thinner walls, giving the building a distinctly patched appearance. Long stretches of the city wall have survived. Walmgate Bar, in the south-east, was badly damaged by the parliamentarian batteries and was reconstructed in 1648. The tower of St Lawrence's church outside Walmgate Bar is all that remains of the pre-Civil War building; the remainder of the present fabric was erected in 1881.

Notes

ABBREVIATIONS

B.L.	British Library
C.J.	Journals of the House of Commons
Cal. State Papers Dom.	Calendar of State Papers, Domestic
ECA	Exeter City Archives
H.M.C.	Historical Manuscripts Commission
L.J.	Journals of the House of Lords
N.L.W.	National Library of Wales
P.R.O.	Public Record Office
R.C.H.M.	Royal Commission on the Historical Monuments of England
Thomason	Thomason Tracts in the British Library
V.C.H.	Victoria County History

CHAPTER ONE

1. *C.J.*, *VII, 1651–9*, p. 306.
2. P.R.O., SP 28/35, f. 732.
3. Johan Goudsblom, *Fire and Civilization*, 1992, pp. 64, 74, 88–91, 99–100, 105–9.
4. J.R. Hale, 'Armies, navies and the art of war', in *The New Cambridge Modern History*, II, ed. G.R. Elton, 2nd edn, Cambridge, 1990, pp. 550–3; 'Armies, navies and the art of war', in *The New Cambridge Modern History*, III, ed. R.B. Wernham, Cambridge, 1968, pp. 195–201. Geoffrey Parker, *The Military Revolution*, Cambridge, 1988, pp. 6–16.
5. Geoffrey Parker, *The Dutch Revolt*, 1977, pp. 157–8.
6. Geoffrey Parker, *The Army of Flanders and the Spanish Road 1567–1659*, Cambridge, 1972, p. 11.
7. Michael Roberts, *The Military Revolution, 1560–1660*, Belfast, 1956. Geoffrey Parker, 'The "Military Revolution 1560–1660" – a Myth?', in *Spain and the Netherlands*, 1979, pp. 86–103; *Military Revolution*, pp. 6–44.
8. Christopher Duffy, *Siege Warfare. The Fortress in the Early Modern World 1494–1660*, 1979, p. 145.
9. Iain MacIvor, 'The Elizabethan Fortifications of Berwick-upon-Tweed', *The Antiquaries Journal*, XLV, 1965, pp. 64–96.
10. Ian Roy, 'England turned Germany? The Aftermath of the Civil War in its European Context', *Trans. Royal Historical Soc.*, fifth series, 28, 1978, p. 130. Parker, *Army of Flanders*, p. 52. J.P. Kenyon, *The Civil Wars of England*, 1988, pp. 44, 46.
11. J.W. Stoye, *English Travellers Abroad 1604–1667*, 1952, pp. 29–30, 239–67.
12. Edward, Earl of Clarendon, *The History of the Rebellion and Civil Wars in England*, ed. W.D. Macray, 6 vols, Oxford, 1888, I, pp. 78, 509.
13. *D.N.B.* Ian Roy, 'The Profession of Arms', in *The Professions in Early Modern England*, ed. Wilfrid Prest, 1987, pp. 191–3. *Alter Britanniae Heros: Or the life of the most Honourable Knight Sir Henry Gage*, 1645, p. 8.
14. Parker, *Military Revolution*, pp. 51–3, 175–6.

15. P.R. Newman, 'The Royalist Officer Corps 1642–1660: Army Command as a reflection of the social structure', *The Historical Journal*, 26, 1983, p. 953.
16. *Diary of Henry Townshend of Elmley Lovett, 1640–1663*, ed. J.W. Willis Bund, Worcestershire Historical Soc., 1915–20, I, p. 149.
17. Richard Gough, *The History of Myddle*, ed. David Hey, 1981, pp. 133–4.
18. *Cal. State Papers Dom.*, *1644–5*, pp. 516–17.
19. Joshua Sprigge, *Anglia Rediviva*, 1647, p. 60. *Cal. State Papers Dom.*, *1644*, p. 97. Thomason, E 531(16) *A Perfect Diurnall*, 2–9 July 1649, p. 2,636. *C.J.*, VI, 1648–51, p. 253. *Mercurius Aulicus*, 8 June 1644, p. 1,007.
20. P.R.O., SP 28/36, ff. 596–8.
21. Duffy, *Siege Warfare*, pp. 146–7.
22. Shakespeare Birthplace Trust R.O., DR 98/1704, 25 Nov. 1642.
23. *Cal. State Papers Dom.*, *1644–5*, pp. 248–9.
24. *Cal. State Papers Dom.*, *1644–5*, p. 516. C.H. Firth, *Cromwell's Army*, 3rd edn, 1921, p. 177.
25. P.R.O., SP 28/251, unfol.
26. Kenyon, *Civil Wars of England*, p. 42.
27. Ernest Broxap, *The Great Civil War in Lancashire (1642–1651)*, 2nd edn, Manchester, 1973, pp. 40–1.
28. Keith Roberts, 'Lessons in revolution: the impact of the London Military Companies' *Cromwelliana*, 1992, pp. 36–9.
29. Herman Hugo, *The Siege of Breda Written In Latin. . . . Translated into English By C.H.G.*, 1627; *The Seige of Breda By The Armes of Phillip The Fovrt Vnder the Gouernment Of Isabella Atchived By The Conduct Of Amr. Spinola*, 1627.
30. Roger Williams, *The Actions of the Lowe Countries*, 1618. *The Commentaries Of Sir Francis Vere*, 1657.
31. Robert Monro, *Monro His Expedition with the Worthy Scots Regiment called Mac-Keyes Regiment*, 1637, pt II, pp. 9–11, 31–8, 138, 213.
32. H.S. Bennett, *English Books and Readers, 1603–1640*, Cambridge, 1970, pp. 186–9. Joseph Frank, *The Beginnings of the English Newspaper 1620–1660*, Cambridge, Mass., 1961, pp. 3–18.
33. Maurice J.D. Cockle, *A Bibliography of British Military Books up to 1641*, 1957, pp. 58–126.
34. David Papillon, *A Practicall Abstract of the Arts, of Fortification and Assailing*, 1645, pp. 9–10, 14. Nathaniel Nye, *The Art of Gunnery*, 1647, pp. 50–3.
35. J.R. Hale, *War and Society in Renaissance Europe 1450–1620*, 1985, p. 56.
36. Peter Clark, 'The Ownership of Books in England, 1560–1640: The Example of Some Kentish Townsfolk', in *Schooling and Society: Studies in the History of Education*, ed. Lawrence Stone, 1976, pp. 97, 101.
37. F.J. Varley, *Cambridge during the Civil War 1642–1646*, Cambridge, 1935, pp. 125–6.
38. *Diary of the Marches of the Royal Army during the Great Civil War: kept by Richard Symonds*, ed. C.E. Long, Camden Soc., LXXIV, 1859, p. 278.
39. Geoffrey Parker, *The Thirty Years' War*, 2nd edn, 1987, p. 125.
40. *The Letter Books 1644–45 of Sir Samuel Luke*, ed. H.G. Tibbutt, Historical Manuscripts Commission, JP4, 1963, p. 555.
41. Barbara Donagan, 'Codes and Conduct in the English Civil War', *Past and Present*, 118, 1988, pp. 67–70.
42. Paul S. Seaver, *Wallington's World. A Puritan Artisan in Seventeenth-Century London*, 1985, pp. 156, 160–1.
43. A.H. Johnson, *The History of the Worshipful Company of the Drapers of London, III, 1603–1920*, Oxford, 1922, p. 180.
44. Julian Cornwall, *The Revolt of the Peasantry 1549*, 1977, pp. 106, 173, 217–18. Francis Blomefield, *An Essay Towards A Topographical History of . . . Norfolk*, III, 1806, pp. 244, 250.
45. *Cal. State Papers Dom.*, *1595–7*, pp. 77, 79. Richard Carew, *The Survey of Cornwall*, 1749, pp. 156–7.
46. *History of Newcastle and Gateshead, vol. III Sixteenth and Seventeenth Centuries*, ed. Richard Welford, 1887, p. 396.
47 E.L. Jones, S. Porter and M. Turner, *A Gazetteer of English Urban Fire Disasters, 1500–1900*, Historical Geography Research Series, 13, Norwich, 1984, p. 16.
48. Seaver, *Wallington's World*, pp. 49, 54.

49. G.V. Blackstone, *A History of the British Fire Service*, 1957, pp. 21–6. Stephen Porter, 'Fire Precautions in Early-Modern Abingdon', *Berkshire Archaeological Journal*, 71, 1981–2, pp. 71–7; 'Fire Precautions in 17th Century Bath', *Notes & Queries for Somerset and Dorset*, XXXI, 1981, pp. 109–12. J.B.P. Karslake, 'Early London Fire-Appliances', *The Antiquaries Journal*, IX, 1929, pp. 229–38. Worcester R.O., Worcester Corporation Records, Audit of Annual Accounts, 3, 1640–9, *sub* 1641. Norfolk and Norwich R.O., Norwich City Records, case 18a, Chamberlains' Accounts, 1626–48, f. 367. B. Howard Cunnington, *Some Annals of the Borough of Devizes 1555–1791*, Devizes, 1925, p. 98.

50. *Acts of the Privy Council, 1615–16*, p. 420; *1618–19*, pp. 401, 462–3; *1619–21*, p. 74. *Privy Council Registers*, III, 1967, p. 19.

51. W.M. Barnes, 'The Diary of William Whiteway, of Dorchester, from November, 1618, to March, 1634', *Proceedings of the Dorset Natural History and Antiquarian Field Club*, XIII, 1891, p. 75. Essex R.O., T/R 5/1/4, Chelmsford St Mary's, Briefs 1615–1733, unfol. E.H. Bates, 'Great Fire at Yeovil, in 1640', *Notes and Queries for Somerset and Dorset*, I, 1890, pp. 69–73.

52. Stephen Porter, 'Fires in Stratford-upon-Avon in the Sixteenth and Seventeenth Centuries', *Warwickshire History*, III, 1976, pp. 97–8.

53. Peter Wenham, *The Great and Close Siege of York, 1644*, Kineton, 1970, p. xi. R.C.H.M, *Newark on Trent, the Civil War Siegeworks*, 1964, pp. 22–4.

54. *Reactions to the English Civil War 1642–1649*, ed. John Morrill, 1982, p. 17. Charles Carlton, *Going to the Wars: The Experience of the British Civil Wars 1638–1651*, 1992, pp. 204–11.

CHAPTER TWO

1. Anthony Fletcher, *The Outbreak of the English Civil War*, 1981, pp. 397–8.

2. Great Yarmouth Town Hall, Great Yarmouth Assembly Book C 19/6, f. 513. I owe this reference to the kindness of Professor Anthony Fletcher.

3. Ernest Broxap, 'The Sieges of Hull during the Great Civil War', *English Historical Review*, XX, 1905, pp. 457–83. John Webb, *The Siege of Portsmouth in the Civil War*, The Portsmouth Papers, 7, 1969, pp. 15–21.

4. Anthony Fletcher, 'The Coming of War', in *Reactions to the English Civil War 1642–1649*, ed. John Morrill, 1982, pp. 30–8.

5. C.V. Wedgwood, 'The Chief Passages in Middlesex', *Middlesex Local History Bulletin*, 14, 1962, pp. 1–7; *The King's War 1641–1647*, 1958, p. 142.

6. *Cal. Committee for the Advance of Money*, p. 155.

7. Thomason, E 245(8) *Marlborowe's Miseries, or, England turned Ireland. Cal. State Papers, Venetian, 1642–3*, p. 219.

8. Sir Henry Ellis, 'Letters from a Subaltern Officer of the Earl of Essex's Army . . .', *Archaeologia*, XXXV, 1864, p. 319.

9. Duffy, *Siege Warfare*, p. 157. Peter Harrington, 'English Civil War fortifications', *Fort*, 15, 1987, pp. 39–60.

10. Wenham, *York*, pp. 4–5. Ellis, 'Letters from a Subaltern Officer . . .', p. 332.

11. Philip Styles, 'The city of Worcester during the Civil Wars, 1640–1660', in *Studies in Seventeenth Century West Midlands History*, Kineton, 1978, pp. 227, 299. Wenham, *York*, pp. 143–52, 200–11.

12. *L.J., V, 1642–3*, p. 447. Corporation of London R.O., Common Council Journal, 40, 1640–9, f. 52v. Devon R.O., ECA, B 1/8 Act Book 1634–47, f. 143.

13. Mark Stoyle, *The Civil War Defences of Exeter and the Great Parliamentary Siege of 1645–46*, Exeter, 1990, p. 14. Malcolm Atkin and A.P. Garrod, 'Archaeology in Gloucester 1989', *Trans. of the Bristol and Gloucestershire Archaeological Soc.*, 108, 1990, p. 185. Sprigge, *Anglia Rediviva*, p. 67. Peter Harrington, *Archaeology of the English Civil War*, Princes Risborough, 1992, pp. 27–36.

14. Stephen Porter, 'Property Destruction in Civil-War London', *Trans. London & Middlesex Archaeological Soc.*, 35, 1984, p. 60. Bodleian, MS Add. D 114, ff. 7–8, 12.

15. P.R.O., SP23/184, pp. 65, 409; /185, p. 173; E 317 Carmarthenshire 2, f. 1. John Latimer, *The Annals of Bristol in the Seventeenth Century*, Bristol, 1900, p. 264. *Records of the Borough of*

Leicester . . ., 1603–1688, ed. Helen Stocks, Cambridge, 1923, p. 430. John Besley Gribble, *Memorials of Barnstaple*, Barnstaple, 1830, p. 460. Robert Gibbs, *A History of Aylesbury*, Aylesbury, 1885, p. 172. Luke, *Letter Book*, p. 519.

16. *Bibliotheca Gloucestrensis*, ed. John Washbourn, Gloucester, 1825, p. 99.
17. Sprigge, *Anglia Rediviva*, p. 67.
18. Clarendon, *History*, III, pp. 109, 113, 134.
19. Thomason, E 292(31) *A True Experimental and Exact Relation upon That famous and renowned Siege of Newcastle*, 1645, p. 11.
20. P. Warwick, *Memoires of the Reigne of King Charles I*, 1701, p. 264. *The Diary of Sir Henry Slingsby, of Scriven, Bart.*, ed. Daniel Parsons, 1836, p. 100.
21. Thomason, E 29(7) *Occurrences of Certain Special and Remarkable Passages in Parliament*, 12–19 January 1645, unpag.
22. Townshend, *Diary*, I, p. 115.
23. James Dallaway, *The Parochial History of the Rape of Arundel, in the Western Division of the County of Sussex*, ed. Edmund Cartwright, 1832, p. 106. 'John Byron's Account of the Siege of Chester 1645–1646', *The Cheshire Sheaf*, fourth series, 1971, pp. 7, 9, 13. B.L., Harleian 2155, f. 113v. Hutchinson, pp. 95–6.
24. Townshend, *Diary*, I, p. 102.
25. Thomason, E 572(5) *The First Publique Lecture, Read at Sir Balthazar Gerbier His Accademy, Concerning Military Architecture, or Fortifications*, 1649, p. 2.
26. David Sturdy, 'The Civil War Defences of London', *The London Archaeologist*, 2, 1975, pp. 334–8. Brett-James estimated the defences to be eighteen miles in length: N.G. Brett-James, *The Growth of Stuart London*, 1935, pp. 274–9.
27. Merton College, Oxford, MS 115.
28. Brett-James, *Stuart London*, p. 274.
29. Brett-James, *Stuart London*, pp. 268–95. Sturdy, 'Civil War defences of London', pp. 334–7. A. Kemp, 'The Fortification of Oxford during the Civil War', *Oxoniensia*, 42, 1977, pp. 237–46. R.H. Morris, *The Siege of Chester 1643–1646*, Chester, 1924, pp. 59, 221.
30. S. Ward, *Excavations at Chester: The Civil War Siegeworks 1642–6*, Chester, 1987, pp. 6–12. R.H. Morris, *The Siege of Chester 1643–1646*, Chester, 1924, pp. 59, 221.
31. T.B. Howell, *A Complete Collection of State Trials . . .*, IV, 1816, p. 255.
32. Based upon information in Townshend, *Diary*, I, p. 102, and Thomason, E266(10) *Perfect Occurrences of Parliament*, 24–31 October 1645, unpag.
33. For example in Robert Norton, *The Gunner*, 1628, p. 113.
34. A.R. Bayley, *The Great Civil War in Dorset 1642–1660*, Taunton, 1910, p. 142. *Journal of Sir Samuel Luke*, ed. I.G. Philip, Oxfordshire Record Soc., 3 vols, 1947–53, II, p. 88. *Cal. State Papers Dom., 1645–7*, p. 128.
35. Bulstrode Whitelocke, *Memorials of the English Affairs*, 1732, p. 167. J.R. Bramble, 'Ancient Bristol Documents VIII: Three Civil War Retournes', *Proceedings of the Clifton Antiquarian Club*, II, 1888–93, pp. 155–6. *Quarter Sessions Records for the County of Somerset, III Commonwealth 1646–60*, ed. E.H.B. Harbin, Somerset Record Soc., 28, 1912, p. 202. Sprigge, *Anglia Rediviva*, pp. 89, 113. *Cal. State Papers Dom., 1654*, p. 268, *1661–2*, p. 393. Samuel Seyer, *Memoirs of Bristol*, II, Bristol, 1823, p. 432. Thomason, E 299(8) *The Moderate Intelligencer*, 28 Aug.–4 Sept. 1645, p. 211; E 301(2) *A True Relation of the Storming of Bristol*, p. 16.
36. B.L., Harleian 2125, ff. 66v, 135, 148; 2155, f. 112v; 7568, f. 169. Chester City R.O., A/F/26/5, A Particular of the losses . . . at Spittle Boughton. Cheshire R.O., DCC/26, An Account of the Siege of Chester . . ., pp. 2, 10, 37. *Cal. State Papers Dom., 1655*, pp. 136, 206, 211, 217.
37. R.W. Ketton-Cremer, *Norfolk in the Civil War*, 1969, p. 211. Thomason, E 67(3) *Certaine Informations*, 4–11 Sept. 1643, p. 264.
38. Whitelocke, *Memorials*, pp. 75–6. Luke, *Journal*, I, pp. 43–4; II, pp. 173–4, 176, 178.
39. R.C.H.M., *Newark on Trent*, pp. 35–6, 67. Philip Morant, *The History and Antiquities of the County of Essex*, I, 1748, p. 63.
40. P.R.O., SP 28/144/9/2. Devon R.O., DD 62701, Captain Nicholas Roop's account.
41. Duffy, *Siege Warfare*, p. 157.
42. Sprigge, *Anglia Rediviva*, p. 55. Lucy Hutchinson, *Memoirs of the Life of Colonel Hutchinson*, ed. James Sutherland, 1973, p. 162.

43. *The Diary of Bulstrode Whitelocke 1605–1675*, ed. Ruth Spalding, Oxford, 1990, p. 166.

44. Bristol Archive Office, Common Council Minute Book, 1627–42, f. 127v.

45. Thomason, E 313(2) *The Weekly Account*, 10–17 Dec. 1645, unpag. Luke, *Letter Book*, pp. 690, 693.

46. Bodleian, MS Clarendon 26, f. 114. B.L., Add. MS 27,402, ff. 95v–6. Adrienne Rosen, 'Winchester in transition, 1580–1700', in *Country towns in pre-industrial England*, ed. Peter Clark, Leicester, 1981, pp. 165, 169–70.

47. Howell, *State Trials*, IV, pp. 243, 246. *The Writings and Speeches of Oliver Cromwell, I, 1599–1649*, ed. Wilbur Cortez Abbott, Cambridge, Mass., 1937, pp. 376–8. Sprigge, *Anglia Rediviva*, p. 108.

48. Thomason, E 21(21) *The true Informer*, 7–14 Dec. 1644, p. 432.

49. *They Saw It Happen: Contemporary Accounts of the Siege of Basing House*, ed. John Adair, Winchester, 1981, p. 39.

50. Thomason, E 333(9) *A Letter . . . Concerning the Surrender of Ruthin Castle*, 1646, p. 4. N.L.W., Wynnstay MS 113, 'An account of the rebellion . . .', p. 8. Bodleian, MS Tanner 59, f. 28. *Reliquiae Baxterianae: Or Mr Richard Baxter's Narrative of . . . his Life and Times*, ed. Matthew Sylvester, 1696, p. 21. H.M.C., *Tenth Report, Appendix IV, Corporation of Bridgnorth MSS*, p. 428.

51. V.C.H., *Oxfordshire*, X, 1972, pp. 9–10, 24–5. Alfred Beesley, *History of Banbury*, 1854, pp. 331–421.

52. Hutchinson, p. 176.

53. David Underdown, *Somerset in the Civil War and Interregnum*, Newton Abbot, 1973, p. 104. John Vicars, *The Burning-Bush not Consumed, or The Fourth and last Part of the Parliamentarie Chronicle*, 1646, p. 192. Abbott, *Cromwell*, p. 366.

54. G.N. Godwin, *The Civil War in Hampshire (1642–1645)*, 1904, p. 184. H.M.C. *Fourteenth Report, Appendix II, Portland II*, p. 109. Thomason, E 40(1) *A Fuller Relation of the Great Victory obtained at Alsford . . .*, 1644, p. 7.

55. Malcolm Falkus and John Gillingham, *Historical Atlas of Britain*, 2nd edn, 1987, pp. 94–5. Donald Pennington, 'The War and the People', in *Reactions*, ed. Morrill, p. 124.

56. Bodleian, MS Tanner 59, f. 97. William Phillips, 'The Ottley Papers relating to the Civil War', *Trans. Shropshire Archaeological Soc.*, 2nd series, VIII, 1896, p. 230.

57. Luke, *Letter Book*, pp. 458–9.

58. Bodleian, MS North adds c.11, f. 5. P.R.O., SP 28/42, f. 287v. *Diary of Bulstrode Whitelocke*, p. 154.

59. Clarendon, *History*, IV, p. 37.

60. Ian Roy, 'The English Civil War and English Society', in *War and Society, A Yearbook of Military History, I*, eds Brian Bond and Ian Roy, 1975, p. 40.

61. Thomason, E254(3) *A Diary, or an Exact Journall*, 11–19 July 1644, p. 60.

62. Thomason, E 293(4) *The Weekly Account*, 9–16 June 1645, unpag. R.C.H.M., *Herefordshire, II North-West*, 1934, p. 182.

63. *Mercurius Aulicus*, p. 1610. *The Life and Times of Anthony Wood, antiquary, of Oxford, 1632–1695, described by Himself*, ed. Andrew Clark, Oxford Historical Soc., 4 vols, 1891–5, I, p. 271; II, p. 449. *The Life, Diary, and Correspondence of Sir William Dugdale*, ed. William Hamper, 1827, p. 79.

64. Eliot Warburton, *Memoirs of Prince Rupert and the Cavaliers*, 3 vols, 1849, II, p. 91. Bayley, *Dorset*, p. 233.

65. Fritz Redlich, *De Praeda Militari. Looting and Booty 1500–1815*, Wiesbaden, 1956, pp. 44–8; 'Contributions in the Thirty Years War', *Economic History Review*, 2nd series, 12, 1959–60, pp. 247–54.

66. Worcester R.O., Droitwich Borough Records, BA 1006/33/638, f. 16.

67. Stephen Porter, 'The Fire-raid in the English Civil War', *War and Society*, 2, 1984, pp. 27–40.

68. Warburton, *Prince Rupert*, III, p. 69.

69. Porter, 'Fire-raid', pp. 34–5.

70. Luke, *Letter Book*, p. 675.

71. Henry Symonds, 'A By-Path of the Civil War', *Somerset Archaeological & Natural History Soc. Proceedings*, LXV, 1919, pp. 54, 58–61.

72. Warburton, *Prince Rupert*, II, p. 193.

73. N.L.W., Gwysaney MS 32A.

74. Thomason, E 310(19) *The Kingdomes Weekly Intelligencer*, 25 Nov.–3 Dec. 1645, pp. 1026–7; E 315(7) *Special and Remarkable Passages*, 2–9 Jan. 1646, p. 7.

75. Clarendon, *History*, III, p. 105.

76. John Vicars, *God on the Mount, or A Continuation of England's Parliamentary Chronicle*, 1646, p. 304.

77. A.C. Wood, *Nottinghamshire in the Civil War*, 1937, p. 51. Thomason, E21(13) *Perfect Passages of Each Dayes Proceedings in Parliament*, 4–11 Dec. 1644; E21(21) *The true Informer*, 7–14 Dec. 1644, p. 429.

78. Broxap, *Lancashire*, pp. 121–4, 127–8.

79. Styles, *Worcester*, p. 250.

80. Margaret Toynbee and Peter Young, *Strangers in Oxford. A Side Light on the First Civil War, 1642–1646*, 1973, pp. 10, 12.

81. *Bibliotheca Gloucestrensis*, Washbourn, p. 184. C.S. Terry, 'The Siege of Newcastle-upon-Tyne by the Scots in 1644', *Archaeologia Aeliana*, 2nd series, XXI, 1899, pp. 226, 245–6.

82. Brian Manning, *The English People and the English Revolution 1640–1649*, 1976, pp. 202–5.

83. Wedgwood, *King's War*, pp. 321–2. David Underdown, *Fire from Heaven: The Life of an English Town in the Seventeenth Century*, 1992.

84. Underdown, *Fire from Heaven*, p. 204. Bayley, *Dorset*, pp. 194, 204. Luke, *Journal*, I, p. 83. *Cal. State Papers Dom., 1655–6*, p. 334. Thomason, E 262(21) *A Perfect Diurnall of Some Passages in Parliament*, 7–14 July 1645, p. 810.

85. *Tracts relating to Military Proceedings in Lancashire during the Great Civil War*, ed. George Ormerod, Chetham Soc., II, 1844, pp. 46, 53, 78, 82–3, 116, 129. Vicars, *God on the Mount*, p. 175. *Bibliotheca Gloucestrensis*, ed. Washbourn, pp. 167, 171.

86. *The Pythouse Papers*, ed. William Ansell Day, 1879, pp. 45–6. Thomason, E 245(8) *Marlborowe's Miseries, or, England turned Ireland*, 1643, p. 3; E 96(22) *A Letter Written from Walshall . . .*, 1643, p. 4; E 78(22) *A Narration of the great Victory . . . at Alton*, 1643.

87. *A Letter: Being A full Relation of the Siege of Banbury Castle . . .*, 1644, p. 5. Thomason, E 10(29) *The Countrey Foot-Post*, 2 Oct. 1644, p. 7; E 254(26)(29) *A Perfect Diurnall . . .*, 26 Aug.–2 Sept. 1644, p. 456, 2–9 Sept. 1644, p. 461; E 327(2) *The Moderate Intelligencer*, 26 Feb.–5 March 1646, p. 316. *A Journal of the first and second sieges of Pontefract Castle, 1644–1645, by Nathan Drake*, Surtees Soc., 37, 1860, pp. 12–13, 20, 27, 31–2, 34–6, 40, 44–5, 48.

88. Underdown, *Somerset*, pp. 94–5. Wedgwood, *King's War*, p. 444. Thomason, E 285(7) *The Moderate Intelligencer*, 15–22 May 1645, p. 94; E 260(40) *Perfect Occurrences of Parliament*, 16–23 May 1645, unpag.

89. *Bibliotheca Gloucestrensis*, ed. Washbourn, p. 48.

90. Underdown, *Somerset*, pp. 108–10. Sprigge, *Anglia Rediviva*, pp. 80–2. H.G. Tibbutt, *The Life and Letters of Sir Lewis Dyve 1599–1669*, Bedfordshire Historical Record Soc., XXVII, 1948, p. 67.

91. Thomason, E 330(1) *The Three Kingdomes Case*, 1645, preface, unpag; E 42(13) *A True Relation of the Routing of His Majesties Forces in the County of Pembroke*, 1644, pp. 6, 13. Bodleian, MS Tanner 62, pt I, f. 208.

92. Thomason, E 53(11) *The Weekly Account*, 26 June–3 July 1644, unpag. Ian Roy and Stephen Porter, 'The Population of Worcester in 1646', *Local Population Studies*, 28, 1982, pp. 32–8.

93. B.L., Add MS 11,364, f. 18; Harleian 2135, ff. 112–34v. V.C.H., *Warwickshire*, VIII, 1969, p. 5. Toynbee and Young, *Strangers in Oxford*, pp. 10, 12.

94. *Diary of Bulstrode Whitelocke*, p. 150.

95. Gloucestershire R.O., GBR, F4/5 Chamberlains' Accounts 1635–53, ff. 144–6, 299. Oxford City Archives, P.5.2 Audit Book 1592–1682, ff. 257, 259, 262v, 263v.

96. *Bibliotheca Gloucestrensis*, ed. Washbourn, p. 212. Worcester Cathedral Library, A 28 Treasurers' Accounts, 1643.

97. B.L., Harleian 2155, f. 119v. P.R.O., SP 23/191, p. 375.

98. John Wroughton, *The Civil War in Bath and North Somerset*, Bath, 1973, p. 103.

99. Devon R.O., ECA, B 1/8 Act Book, 1634–47, f. 149v; B 1/10 Act Book, 1652–63, f. 74.

100. At Oxford, Leighton Buzzard, Diss, Lowestoft and Wrexham: Jones et al., *Gazetteer*, p. 17. H.M.C., *Seventh Report, House of Lords MSS*, p. 19. *C.J.*, V, *1646–8*, p. 603.
101. Luke, *Journal*, I, pp. 20–1. Edmund Venables, 'A List and Brief Description of the Churches of Lincoln previous to the period of the Reformation'. *Reports and Papers of the Associated Architectural Societies*, 19, 1888, p. 340. P.R.O., SP 28/332, f. 502. Ketton-Cremer, *Norfolk*, pp. 335–47.

CHAPTER THREE

1 H.J. Dyos, *Victorian Suburb, A Study of the Growth of Camberwell*, Leicester, 1961, pp. 34–5. Fernand Braudel, *The Structures of Everyday Life*, 1981, pp. 503–4.
2. Stocks, *Leicester*, pp. 334–5. Cornelius Brown, *A History of Newark-on-Trent*, II, Newark, 1907, p. 84.
3. D.H. Pennington and I.A. Roots, *The Committee at Stafford 1643–1645*, Manchester, 1957, pp. 67, 72–3.
4. Coventry City R.O., A 10, ff. 70v, 73.
5. B.L., Egerton 3054, Diary of Joyce Jefferies, f. 18. I owe this reference to the kindness of Dr Joan Thirsk.
6. Welford, *History of Newcastle and Gateshead*, III, p. 396. *Yorkshire Royalist Composition Papers*, ed. J.W. Clay, Yorkshire Archaeological Soc., Record Series, XV, 1893, p. 29; XVIII, 1895, p. 5.
7. Gloucestershire R.O., GBR B3/2 Corporation Minute Book, 1632–56, pp. 294, 314, 459; F4/5 Chamberlains' Accounts, 1635–53, ff. 242, 282.
8. At Bridgnorth, Bristol and Chester, for example: H.M.C., *Tenth Report, Appendix IV, Corporation of Bridgnorth MSS*, p. 436. *The Royalist Ordnance Papers, 1642–1646*, ed. Ian Roy, Oxfordshire Record Soc., XLII, XLIX, 1964, 1975, pp. 371, 508. B.L., Harleian 2158, f. 338v.
9. B.L., Harleian 1994, f. 52; 2158, f. 338v. R.C.H.M., *The City of York*, V, 1981, p. 23. V.C.H., *The City of York*, 1961, p. 397.
10. H.M.C., *Bridgnorth*, p. 436.
11. Alfred Kingston, *East Anglia and the Great Civil War*, 1897, p. 295. B.L., Egerton 3054, f. 58v.
12. Cumbria R.O., TL 1036, An Historical Record of the City of Carlisle . . ., f. 59; TL 1037, Register of the Dean and Chapter, 1660–68, p. 475.
13. Thomason, E 313(2) *The Weekly Account*, 10–17 Dec. 1645, unpag.
14. Townshend, *Diary*, p. 128. Thomason, E 313(31) *The Weekly Account*, 16–30 Dec. 1645, unpag.
15. Thomason, E 13(18) *The London Post*, 23 Oct. 1644, p. 4; E 244(26) *England's Memorable Accidents*, 19–25 Dec. 1642, p. 127. H.M.C., *Eleventh Report, appendix 7, Reading Corporation Records*, p. 217. Isaac Tullie, *A Narrative of the Siege of Carlisle, in 1644 and 1645*, ed. Samuel Jefferson, Carlisle, 1988 edn, pp. 15–16, 19.
16. Tullie, *Carlisle*, p. 25. Underdown, *Somerset*, p. 95. Matthew Carter, *A True Relation of that Honorable, though unfortunate Expedition of Kent, Essex, and Colchester*, 1789 edn, p. 146.
17. Tullie, *Carlisle*, p. 12.
18. H.M.C., *Thirteenth Report, Portland Manuscripts*, I, p. 483; *Fourteenth Report, appendix 9, Round Manuscripts*, pp. 283–90. Whitelock, *Memorials*, p. 321. 'A Diary of the Siege of Colchester' in W.G. Ross, 'Military Engineering During the Great Civil War, 1642–9', *Professional Papers of the Corps of Royal Engineers*, Royal Engineers Institute Occasional Papers, XIII, Chatham, 1887, pp. 196–200.
19. Francis Drake, *Eboracum: or the History and Antiquities of the City of York*, 1736, pp. 163–4. Thomason, E 50(30) *An Exact Relation of the Siege before Yorke*, 1644, p. 3.
20. Thomason, E 287(6) *A More Exact Relation of the Siege Laid to the Town of Leicester*, 1645, p. 5; E 261(3) *An Examination of a Printed Pamphlet Entitled 'A Narration of the Siege of the Town of Leicester . . .'*, 1645, p. 2.
21. Thomason, E 51(9) *A Continuance of True Intelligence From . . . the North . . .*, 1644, unpag. B.L., Harleian 2155, f. 114. Byron, *Siege of Chester*, p. 8. Chester City R.O., MF/71/177, Portmote court papers, 27 Aug. 1650. Devon R.O., ECA, Bk 60F, L391, f. 41.
22. Underdown, *Somerset*, p. 95.
23. B.L., Add MS 18,982, Prince Rupert's letter book, f. 25. East Sussex R.O., Danny MSS, 46 47. *Cal. State Papers Dom., 1644–5*, p. 205.

24. *Diary of . . . Richard Symonds*, pp. 166–7. *Diary of Sir Henry Slingsby*, pp. 143–5.
25. Menna Prestwich, *Cranfield: Politics and Profits under the early Stuarts*, Oxford, 1966, pp. 582–3. P.R.O., SP 28/246, unfol.
26. *Memoirs, Letters, and Speeches of Anthony Ashley Cooper, First Earl of Shaftesbury*, ed. W.D. Christie, 1859, pp. 98–9.
27. *The Life of Adam Martindale, Written by Himself*, ed. R. Parkinson, Chetham Soc., IV, 1845, p. 39. Thomason, E 315(7) *Special and Remarkable Passages*, 2–9 Jan. 1646, p. 7.
28. *The Compleat Gunner, in Three Parts*, 1672, 3rd part, p. 12. Thomas Smith, *The Art of Gunnery*, 1643 edn, pp. 89–94. Robert Ward, *Animadversions of Warre*, 1639, pp. 389–90.
29. *Bibliotheca Gloucestrensis*, ed. Washbourn, p. 167. Warburton, *Prince Rupert*, II, pp. 250–2.
30. Hutchinson, pp. 113–14. John Vicars, *God's Arke Overtopping the Worlds Waves, or The Third Part of the Parliamentary Chronicle*, 1646, p. 135.
31. Bayley, *Dorset*, pp. 135–6. Richard Hine, *The History of Beaminster*, Taunton, 1914, pp. 118–19.
32. Vicars, *God on the Mount*, p. 160. Webb, *Portsmouth*, p. 18. Thomas Hinderwell, *The History and Antiquities of Scarborough*, 2nd edn, York, 1811, pp. 76, 84, 102, 104. D.A. Johnson and D.G. Vaisey, *Staffordshire and the Great Rebellion*, Stafford, 1964, p. 35. Birmingham Reference Library, MS 595,611, Sir William Brereton's letter book, 1646, pp. 250, 263–4. Thomas Harwood, *The History and Antiquities of the Church and City of Lichfield*, 1806, p. 57.
33. Clarendon, *History*, III, p. 411.
34. Ormerod, *Lancashire*, p. 55.
35. Thomason, E 99(3) *Continuation of Certain Special and Remarkable Passages*, 13–20 April 1643, unpag; E 99(15) *Certain Informations . . .*, 17–24 April 1643, p. 106; E 42(13) *A True Relation of the Routing of His Majesties Forces in the County of Pembrokeshire*, 1644, pp. 6, 13.
36. Townshend, *Diary*, I, pp. 125–8.
37. *The Compleat Gunner*, third part, p. 11. Casimir Simienowicz, *The Great Art of Artillery*, 1729, pp. 303–5.
38. *Bibliotheca Gloucestrensis*, ed. Washbourn, pp. 51, 220. Luke, *Journal*, p. 146.
39. Thomason, E 70(4) *The true Informer*, 30 Sept.–7 Oct. 1643, p. 18; E 51(11) *Hull's Managing of the Kingdoms Cause*, 1644, p. 16; E 330(1) *The three Kingdomes Case*, 1645, preface, unpag. *Stuart Tracts 1603–1693*, ed. C.H. Firth, Westminster, 1903, p. 388. *Diary of Sir Henry Slingsby*, p. 100.
40. Vicars, *God's Arke . . .*, p. 253. *Documents Relating to the Civil War 1642–1648*, edd. J.R. Powell and E.K. Timings, Navy Records Soc., CV, 1963, p. 151. Sprigge, *Anglia Rediviva*, p. 72.
41. *Military Memoir of Colonel John Birch*, eds J. and T.W. Webb, Camden Soc., second series, VII, 1873, p. 21.
42. Thomason, E 274(7) *A Brief Relation of the Surprise of the Forts of Weymouth . . .*, 1645, pp. 4–5; E 332(3) *The Moderate Intelligencer*, 2–9 April 1646, p. 377.
43. *Bibliotheca Gloucestrensis*, ed. Washbourn, pp. 47, 216.
44. *Royalist Ordnance Papers*, ed. Roy, pp. 32–3.
45. Norton, *The Gunner*, pp. 59–61. Thomas Malthus, *A Treatise of Artificial Fire-workes*, 1629, pp. 3–15. Robert Ward, *Animadversions of Warre*, 1639, pp. 363–5. Smith, *Art of Gunnery*, p. 104. Henry Hexham, *The Third Part of the Principles of the Art Military practised in the Warres of the United Provinces*, Rotterdam, 1643, pp. 28, 31. Nye, *Art of Gunnery*, pp. 59–64.
46. *Royalist Ordnance Papers*, ed. Roy, p. 226. Shakespeare Birthplace Trust R.O., DR 98/1704, unfol. Firth, *Cromwell's Army*, p. 158.
47. Byron, *Siege of Chester*, pp. 18–19. *The Letter Books of Sir William Brereton*, Vol. 2, ed. R.N. Dore, Record Soc. of Lancashire and Cheshire, CXXVIII, 1991, pp. 335, 350, 522. B.L., Harleian 2155, ff. 121, 124v–6.
48. Nottinghamshire R.O., PRNW, will of Thomas Waite, 1645. Brown, *Newark-on-Trent*, II, pp. 73, 227.
49. Thomason, E 330(1) *The three Kingdomes case . . .*, preface, unpag; E 333(4) *The Kingdomes Weekly Intelligencer*, 7–13 April 1646, p. 74; E 333(11) *The Weekly Account*, 8–15 April 1646, unpag; E 10(5)(23) *The London Post*, 24 Sept. 1644, p. 2; 1 Oct. 1644, p. 4. *Mercurius Aulicus*, 8 Sept. 1643, p. 496. John Rushworth, *Historical Collections*, V, 1721, p. 280. Sprigge, *Anglia Rediviva*, p. 72. Whitelock, *Memorials*, pp. 163, 200. Bodleian, MS Tanner 62, f. 208. John Davies, *The Civill Warres of Great Britain and Ireland*, 1661, p. 160.

50. Sprigge, *Anglia Rediviva*, pp. 123, 130. Ormerod, *Lancashire*, p. 177.

51. Byron, *Siege of Chester*, p. 21.

52. Norton, *The Gunner*, p. 157. Nye, *Art of Gunnery*, pp. 65–6. Smith, *Gunnery*, pp. 95, 108–9. *The Compleat Gunner*, third part, p. 12. Simienowicz, *Great Art of Artillery*, pp. 223–32, 238–45.

53. B.L., Harleian 2155, f. 120. *Letter Books of Sir William Brereton*, Vol. 2, p. 179. Byron, *Siege of Chester*, p. 8. Bodleian, MS Clarendon 26, f. 33v. Chester City R.O., CR 63/2/691/16, letter of Sir William Brereton, 30 Oct. 1645.

54. Bayley, *Dorset*, pp. 149, 171. Thomason, E 50(25) *A true and perfect Diurnall of all Passages since Colonell Weres comming to the Towne of Lyme Regis*, 1644, p. 7.

55. *Cal. State Papers Dom., 1591–1594*, pp. 203, 421.

56. J.R. Partington, *A History of Greek Fire and Gunpowder*, Cambridge, 1960, pp. 28–32. Du Praissac, *The Art of Warre, or Militarie discourses*, Cambridge, 1639, pp. 152–3. Ward, *Animadversions of Warre*, pp. 363–4. Malthus, *Treatise of Artificial Fire-Works*, pp. 16–19.

57. Thomason, E 91(5) *Speciall Passages . . .*, 21–28 Feb. 1643, p. 241.

58. Luke, *Journal*, pp. 43, 135. Vicars, *God on the Mount*, p. 236. Godwin, *Civil War in Hampshire*, p. 57.

59. At Nantwich and Plymouth, for example: Thomason, E 252(19) *A Perfect Diurnall . . .*, 29 Jan.–5 Feb. 1644, p. 222; E 19(9) *The true Informer*, 23–30 Nov. 1644, pp. 421–2.

60. *The Harleian Miscellany*, VI, 1810, p. 401.

61. Thomason, E 454(3) *The Perfect Weekly Account*, 19–25 July 1648, unpag.

62. *Royalist Ordnance Papers*, ed. Roy, p. 227.

63. *The Compleat Gunner*, third part, pp. 7–9.

64. Stephen Porter, 'Fireships in the English Civil War', *The Mariner's Mirror*, 70, 1984, pp. 85–6.

65. Thomason, E 330(1) *The three Kingdomes Case . . .*, preface, unpag. Rushworth, *Historical Collections*, V, pp. 279–80.

66. *Bibliotheca Gloucestrensis*, ed. Washbourn, p. 220.

67. V.C.H., *Worcestershire*, IV, 1924, p. 387. William H. Turner, *Selections from the Records of the City of Oxford, 1509–1583*, Oxford, 1880, p. 424. *Reading Charters, Acts and Orders. 1253–1911*, ed. C. Fleetwood Pritchard, Reading, 1913, pp. 68–70.

68. Derek Portman, *Exeter Houses 1400–1700*, Exeter, 1966, p. 54.

69. John C. Tingey, *Records of the City of Norwich*, II, 1910, pp. 139–40.

70. H.M.C., *Various Collections, IV, Corporation of Aldeburgh MSS*, 1910, p. 286. Chester City R.O., MF/67/143, Portmote court papers, 13 July 1644.

71. *Stuarts Tracts*, ed. Firth, p. 388. B.L., Lansdowne 890, The History . . . of Kingston upon Hull . . ., f. 127. John Tickell, *History of the Town and County of Kinston upon Hull*, 1798, p. 482. Alec Clifton-Taylor, *The Pattern of English Building*, 1972, pp. 212–13.

72. B.L., Harleian 2135, f. 40. Byron, *Siege of Chester*, p. 19.

73. Bayley, *Dorset*, pp. 171, 177.

74. For the range of the various sizes of guns during the period see: A.R. Hall, *Ballistics in the Seventeenth Century*, Cambridge, 1952, pp. 166–70.

75. Thomason, E 452(41) *Joyfull Newes from Colchester*, 1648, pp. 2–3; E 453(29) *The Moderate Intelligencer*, 13–20 July 1648, unpag.

76. *Bibliotheca Gloucestrensis*, ed. Washbourn, p. 162. Ormerod, *Lancashire*, p. 172.

77. Thomason, E 51(11) *Hull's Managing . . .*, p. 16.

78. *Bibliotheca Gloucestrensis*, ed. Washbourn, pp. 48, 217. Sprigge, *Anglia Rediviva*, pp. 82–5.

79. Sprigge, *Anglia Rediviva*, p. 297.

80. Thomason, E 316(5) *Relation of the fight at Bovey Tracy*, 1646.

81. *Journal of Nathan Drake*, pp. 6–81.

82. *Royalist Ordnance Papers*, ed. Roy, p. 490. *Bibliotheca Gloucestrensis*, ed. Washbourn, pp. 51, 220, 279.

83. *Royalist Ordnance Papers*, ed. Roy, pp. 111, 264, 269–70, 485. Luke, *Journal*, p. 135.

84. B.L., Harleian 2155, ff. 125r–v. *Letter Books of Sir William Brereton*, Vol. 2, p. 522.

85. Ormerod, *Lancashire*, pp. 172–86.

86. Thomason, E 252(19) *A Perfect Diurnall . . .*, 29 Jan.–5 Feb. 1644, p. 222.

87. Wenham, *York*, p. 109.

88. Townshend, *Diary*, I, pp. 124–59.

89. Luke, *Letter Books*, p. 453.
90. B.L., Harleian 2043, f. 30.
91. Thomason, E 322(9) *The Citties Weekly Post*, 3–10 Feb. 1646, pp. 2–3; E 506(31) *Perfect Occurrences of Both Houses of Parliament*, 17 April 1646, unpag.
92. P.R.O., SP28/31, f. 442; SP28/37, f. 382; SP28/60, f. 146.
93. *Memorials of the Civil War in Cheshire*, ed. John Hall, Lancashire and Cheshire Record Soc., 19, 1889, p. 101. Thomason, E 274(7) *A Brief Relation of the Surprise of the Forts of Weymouth . . .*, 1645, p. 4. Bodleian, MS Tanner 59, f. 28.
94. Malthus, *Treatise of Artificial Fire-workes*, p. 33.
95. *Records of the County of Wilts, being extracts from the Quarter Sessions Great Rolls of the Seventeenth Century*, ed. B. Howard Cunnington, Devizes, 1932, p. 200.
96. Chester City R.O., M/L/2 Great Letter Book 1599–1650, p. 293.
97. *Cal. State Papers Dom., 1644–5*, pp. 503, 508.
98. Byron, *Siege of Chester*, pp. 11, 19, 21.
99. *The Commentaries of Blaise de Monluc*, ed. Ian Roy, 1971, p. 155.
100. Hutchinson, p. 163. Prestwich, *Cranfield*, p. 582.
101. B.L., Add MS 18,982, f. 7.
102. Thomason, E293(27) *Sir Thomas Fairfaxes Entring Bridgewater*, 1645, pp. 2–3, 5. John Collinson, *The History and Antiquities of the County of Somerset*, Vol. III, Bath, 1791, p. 76.
103. Mark Stoyle, *Exeter City Defences Project: Documentary Evidence for the Civil War Defences of Exeter, 1642–3*, Exeter, 1988, p. xxiv; *Civil War Defences of Exeter and the Great Parliamentary Siege*, fig. 2. I am very grateful to Mr Stoyle for drawing my attention to this example.
104. *Letter Books of Sir William Brereton*, Vol. 2, p. 335.
105. Walter Raleigh, *The History of the World*, 1687 edn, p. 319.
106. Thomason, E 127(3) *Orders and Institutions of War . . .*, 1642, p. 6; E 127(31) *Lawes and Ordinances of Warre . . .*, 1642, p. 20.
107. Hutchinson, pp. 200–1. William Sanderson, *A Compleat History of the Life and Raigne of King Charles*, 1658, p. 888.
108. *Cal. State Papers Dom., 1645–7*, p. 409.
109. Ian Gentles, *The New Model Army in England, Ireland and Scotland, 1645–1653*, Oxford, 1992, pp. 421–2.
110. *Cal. State Papers Dom., 1644–5*, pp. 85, 100–1, 275.
111. H.M.C., *Seventh Report, House of Lords MSS*, p. 77. *L.J.*, VIII, 1645–6, p. 591. *Cal. State Papers Dom., 1645–7*, pp. 154, 236.
112. *Cal. State Papers Dom., 1645–7*, pp. 402–3.

CHAPTER FOUR

1. John Taylor, *Wanderings to see the Wonders of the West*, 1649, p. 5; *A Short Relation of a Long Journey*, 1652, p. 15. Thomason, E 344(6) George Newton, *Mans Wrath and Gods Praise*, 1646, p. 14. Sprigge, *Anglia Rediviva*, p. 251.
2. *C.J.*, V, 1646–8, pp. 424–5.
3. H.L.R.O. (House of Lords Record Office), Main Papers, 10 July–2 Aug. 1645, f. 113; 23 Aug.–2 Sept. 1648, f. 182. P.R.O., SP 18/69/21, II.
4. Gwent R.O., D/PA/86.1.
5. *Cal. State Papers Dom., 1645–7*, p. 160.
6. *The Agrarian History of England and Wales*, V, part II, ed. Joan Thirsk, Cambridge, 1985, p. 134.
7. Based upon a population for England and Wales of 5.25 million, of which London's share of 400,000 was equal to that of the provincial urban population. Jonathan Barry, *The Tudor and Stuart Town*, 1990, pp. 2–3, 39–41.
8. *Cal. State Papers Dom., 1655*, pp. 136, 211, 217. Seyer, *Bristol*, p. 432.
9. Whitelock, *Memorials*, p. 207. John and T.W. Webb, *Memorials of the Civil War between King Charles I and the Parliament of England as it affected Herefordshire and the adjacent counties*, I, 1879, p. 319.

10. Arthur Clark, *Raglan Castle and the Civil War in Monmouthshire*, Chepstow, 1953, pp. 33–4, 36–9. *Bibliotheca Gloucestrensis*, ed. Washbourn, p. 124. *Cal. State Papers Dom., 1644–5*, p. 43.

11. H.M.C., *Eleventh Report, part 3, Corporation of King's Lynn MSS*, pp. 181–2; *part 7, Hamon Le Strange MSS*, p. 102. Kingston, *East Anglia*, pp. 295–6.

12. *C.J.*, *VI, 1648–51*, p. 271.

13. Porter, 'Property Destruction in Civil-War London', pp. 59–62. M.A. Tierney, *The History and Antiquities of the Castle and Town of Arundel*, II, 1834, pp. 713–14.

14. Great Yarmouth Town Hall, Great Yarmouth Assembly Book, C 19/6, f. 513. R.K.G. Temple, 'Discovery of a manuscript eye-witness account of the battle of Maidstone', *Archaeologia Cantiana*, XCVII, 1981, pp. 209–20. Morant, *Essex*, I, p. 72.

15. Bayley, *Dorset*, pp. 135–6. John Hutchins, *The History of Dorset*, II, 3rd edn, 1863, p. 119. Hine, *Beaminster*, pp. 118–19.

16. Bayley, *Dorset*, pp. 136–91. Vicars, *God's Arke*, pp. 246, 254. Bodleian, MS Clarendon 23, f. 86. Thomason, E 50(25) *A true and perfect Diurnall of all Passages since Colonell Weres comming to the Towne of Lyme Regis*, 1644, pp. 7–8. *Cal. State Papers Dom., 1644*, pp. 205, 207, 239–40.

17. *Cal. State Papers Dom., 1644–5*, p. 231. Bayley, *Dorset*, p. 275.

18. *Memoirs . . . of Anthony Ashley Cooper*, ed. Christie, pp. 97–9.

19. Stephen Porter, 'The Destruction of Axminster in 1644', *Devon & Cornwall Notes & Queries*, XXXV, 1985, pp. 243–6.

20. Thomason, E 333(4) *The Kingdomes Weekly Intelligencer*, 7–13 April 1646, p. 76; E 506(29) *A Perfect Diurnall . . .*, 6–13 April 1646, p. 1,133.

21. H.F. Killick, 'Memoirs of Sir Marmaduke Rawden, Kt. 1582–1646', *Yorkshire Archaeological Journal*, 25, 1920, pp. 326, 330. G.W.B. Huntingford, 'Church Building and Restoration in North Berkshire in the Seventeenth, Eighteenth and Nineteenth Centuries', *Berkshire Archaeological Journal*, 40, 1936, p. 94.

22. H.L.R.O., Main Papers 23 Aug.–2 Sept. 1648, ff. 177–85.

23. Berkshire R.O., Archdeaconry Papers c.100, f. 8; c.139, ff. 7, 10–20; A/FAc3, 1643–4. Christ's Hospital, Abingdon, Minute Book 1577–1694, ff. 146, 171. Thomason, E 15(1) *Mercurius Civicus*, 24–31 Oct. 1644, p. 698; E 52(3) *The Scotish Dove*, 14–21 June 1644, p. 258; E 252(47) *A Perfect Diurnall of some Passages in Parliament*, 17–24 June 1644, p. 373. John Kirby Hedges, *The History of Wallingford*, II, 1881, pp. 171, 334, 339, 392, 400. Luke, *Journal*, I, p. 75; II, p. 88; *Letter Books*, pp. 690, 693.

24. For Godstow House and the Bishop's Palace at Cuddesdon: Wood, *Life and Times*, I, p. 271; II, p. 449. Whitelock, *Memorials*, pp. 147, 163. Thomason, E 294(8) *The Weekly Account*, 29 July 1645, unpag. E 285(17) *A Copy of A Letter from An Eminent Commander in Sir Thomas Fairfax Army . . .*, 1645, p. 2.

25. Warburton, *Prince Rupert*, II, p. 193. *L.J.*, VI, *1643–4*, p. 52. Luke, *Journal*, pp. 99–100.

26. Stephen Porter, 'The Civil War Destruction of Boarstall', *Records of Bucks*, 26, 1984, pp. 86–91.

27. Bodleian, MS Clarendon 26, f. 112. *C.J.*, *IV, 1644–6*, p. 503.

28. Stephen Porter, 'The Oxford Fire of 1644', *Oxoniensia*, XLIX, 1984, pp. 289–300

29. Wood, *Life and Times*, I, pp. 99–100. Bodleian, MS Add. D 114, ff. 7, 8, 12. P.R.O., SP29/436/79.

30. *Oxford Council Acts 1626–1665*, eds M.G. Hobson and H.E. Salter, Oxford Historical Soc., 1933, pp. 125–6.

31. Whitelock, *Memorials*, pp. 147, 163. Thomason, E 278(14) *The Moderate Intelligencer*, 10–17 April 1645, p. 55; E 286(2) *Perfect Passages of Each Dayes Proceedings in Parliament*, 21–27 May 1645, p. 248; E 294(8)(10) *The Weekly Account*, 23–29 July, 20–26 Aug. 1645, unpag.

32. Southampton Civic R.O., SC 4/2/376.

33. Bodleian, MS Clarendon 26, ff. 114–15. Rosen, 'Winchester', pp. 165, 169–70. Webb, *Portsmouth*, pp. 18–21.

34. Thomason, E 258(14) *Perfect Occurrences of Parliament*, 10–17 Jan. 1645, unpag. Nehemiah Wallington, *Historical Notices*, ed. R. Webb, II, 1869, pp. 247–8. Vicars, *God's Arke*, p. 97. Thomason, E 78(22) *A Narration of the great Victory . . . at Alton*, 1643; E 40(1) *A Fuller Relation of the Victory obtained at Alsford . . .*, 1644. H.M.C., *Fourteenth Report, Appendix II, Portland MSS III*, p. 109.

35. Adair, *Basing*. Abbott, *Cromwell*, I, p. 386.

36. Thomason, E26(13) *Mercurius Civicus*, 23–30 Jan. 1645, p. 806. *The Diary of John Evelyn*, ed. E.S. de Beer, Oxford, 1955, III, p. 111.

37. Berkshire R.O., Reading Corporation archives LI, no. 44. Bodleian, MS Tanner, f. 76v. Thomason, E99(2) *Good and true Newes from Redding*, 1643, pp. 3–4; E99(3) *Continuation of special and remarkable Passages*, 13–20 April 1643, unpag; E99(15) *Certain Informations from several parts of the Kingdom*, 17–24 April 1643, p. 106. Vicars, *God on the Mount*, pp. 306–7.

38. Tierney, *Arundel*, II, pp. 714–15.

39. John Adair, *Roundhead General*, 1969, p. 52. H.M.C., *Seventh Report, House of Lords MSS*, p. 2. Vicars, *God on the Mount*, pp. 236–7. W.D. Peckham, 'The Parishes of the City of Chichester', *Sussex Archaeological Collections*, 74, 1933, pp. 86–7. John Ogilby, *Britannia*, 1675, p. 8.

40. Ann Hughes, 'Coventry and the English Revolution', in *Town and Countryside in the English Revolution*, ed. R.C. Richardson, Manchester, 1992, pp. 77–81.

41. Coventry City R.O., A 14(B) Council Book 2, 1640–96, ff. 35v–6.

42. P.R.O., SP 18/69/21.

43. *Bibliotheca Gloucestrensis*, ed. Washbourn, pp. 22–30, 40–1, 211. Gloucestershire R.O., GBR B 3/2, p. 266.

44. Clarendon, *History*, III, pp. 133–4. *Bibliotheca Gloucestrensis*, ed. Washbourn, p. 45.

45. *Bibliotheca Gloucestrensis*, ed. Washbourn, pp. 379–87.

46. Stoyle, *Civil War Defences of Exeter, 1642–3*, pp. x, xiii–xvii, xxiv, 40, 42–3, 50; *Civil War Defences of Exeter and the Great Parliamentary Siege*, pp. 9, 12, 16, 27. Sprigge, *Anglia Rediviva*, p. 150. Devon R.O., Exeter St Petrock PW4, Churchwardens' Accounts 1615–69, account for 1643–4. Thomason, E 296(1) *The Weekly Account*, 6–13 Aug. 1645, unpag; E 296(33) *Mercurius Civicus*, 7–14 Aug. 1645, unpag; E 262(44) *Perfect Occurrences of Parliament*, 8–18 Aug. 1645, unpag; E 300(20) *The Moderate Intelligencer*, 4–11 Sept. 1645, p. 224; E 266(10) *Perfect Occurrences of Parliament*, 24–31 Oct. 1645, unpag; E 308(25) *The true Informer*, 1–8 Nov. 1645, p. 226; E 309(8) *The City Scout*, 4–11 Nov. 1645, p. 4; E 322(7) *The Moderate Messenger*, 3–10 Feb. 1646, p. 16; E 222(12) *The Scotish Dove*, 4–11 Feb. 1646, p. 962; E 333(23) *Sir Thomas Fairfax's Further Proceedings in the West*, 1646, p. 1.

47. Wallace T. MacCaffrey, *Exeter, 1540–1640. The Growth of an English County Town*, 3rd edn, Cambridge, Mass., 1975, p. 105.

48. *Diary of Sir Henry Slingsby*, p. 163. John Duncumb, *Collections towards the History and Antiquities of the County of Hereford*, I, Hereford, 1804, pp. 250, 275, 371, 373, 426, 603.

49. John Nash, *Collections for the History of Worcestershire*, II, 1782, app. p. cvi.

50. Abbott, *Cromwell*, pp. 376–7. *C.J., IV, 1644–6*, p. 371. Warburton, *Prince Rupert*, II, p. 241. Bristol Archive Office, Common Council Minute Book 1627–42, f. 127.

51. Thomason, E 246(13) *A Perfect Diurnall of the Passages in Parliament*, 6–13 Feb. 1643, unpag; E 378(8) *Perfect Occurrences of Every Daie Journall in Parliament*, 19–26 Feb. 1647, p. 63; E 378(17) *The Moderate Intelligencer*, 25 Feb.–2 March 1647, pp. 937–8. Latimer, *Annals of Bristol*, p. 216.

52. *Quarter Sessions Records for . . . Somerset, Volume III . . .*, ed. Harbin, p. 202. Sprigge, *Anglia Rediviva*, pp. 89, 113. Thomason, E 513(13) *Perfect Occurrences of Both Houses of Parliament*, 2 Oct. 1646, unpag.

53. H. Owen and J.B. Blakeway, *A History of Shrewsbury*, I, 1825, pp. 435–6. Gough, *Myddle*, p. 1.

54. P.R.O., SP 18/155/100. Gough, *Myddle*, p. 4. F.S. Acton, *The Garrisons of Shropshire during the Civil War, 1642–48*, Shrewsbury, 1867, pp. 80–1. W.J. Farrow, *The Great Civil War in Shropshire (1642–49)*, Shrewsbury, 1926, p. 52.

55. Acton, *Garrisons of Shropshire*, p. 61. Hall, *Cheshire*, p. 206. P.R.O., SP 23/180, pp. 54, 60.

56. Emanuel Green, *The Siege of Bridgwater, July 1645*, Bath, 1905. Sprigge, *Anglia Rediviva*, pp. 71–4. Tibbutt, *Sir Lewis Dyve*, p. 67. Whitelock, *Memorials*, pp. 162–3. Bell, *Fairfax*, I, p. 240.

57. H.M.C., *Third Report, Corporation of Bridgwater MSS*, p. 319. *Cal. State Papers Dom., 1656–7*, p. 207. Thomason, E 261(7) *Mr Peters Report from the Army to the Parliament*, 1645, p. 3. There were 642 names in the Protestation Returns; *The Somerset Protestation Returns and Lay Subsidy Rolls 1641/2*, edd. A.J. Howard and T.L. Stoate, Almondsbury, Bristol, 1975, pp. 84–7.

58. Thomason, E 262(27) *Perfect Passages of Each Dayes Proceedings in Parliament*, 16–23 July 1645, p. 311; E 293(23) *The Moderate Intelligencer*, 17–24 July 1645, p. 166.

59. Sprigge, *Anglia Rediviva*, p. 196. Thomason, E 324(17) *The Citties Weekly Post*, 17–24 Feb. 1646, p. 7.

60. N.L.W., Wynnstay MS 113, 'An account of the rebellion . . .'. *Letter Books of Sir William Brereton*, Vol. 2, p. 192. B.L., Harleian 7568, f. 423. Bodleian, MS Clarendon 26, f. 33v. *Cal. State Papers Dom., 1644–5*, p. 182. Thomason, E 21(13) *Perfect Passages of Each Dayes Proceedings in Parliament*, 4–11 Dec. 1644, p. 64. Taylor, *Short Relation*, p. 16.

61. *C.J., V, 1646–8*, p. 603. H.M.C., *Seventh Report, House of Lords MSS*, p. 19.

62. *L.J., VIII, 1645–6*, p. 23. Bodleian, MS Tanner 59, f. 337. Rushworth, *Historical Collections*, VII, p. 1159. Thomason, E 262(3) *Perfect Occurrences of Parliament*, 30 May–6 June 1645, unpag; E 288(3) *The Exchange Intelligencer*, 4–11 June 1645, p. 26.

63. Thomason, E 313(2) *The Weekly Account*, 10–17 Dec. 1645, unpag. G. Bellett, *The Antiquities of Bridgnorth*, 1856, pp. 144–7.

64. Bodleian, MS Tanner 59, f. 28. Thomason, E 333(4) *The Kingdomes Weekly Intelligencer*, 7–13 April 1646, p. 74. *Reliquiae Baxterianae*, p. 21.

65. *L.J., IX, 1646–7*, p. 657. Bodleian, MS Tanner 59, f. 787. *Orders of the Shropshire Quarter Sessions, I, 1638–1708*, ed. R.L. Kenyon, Shropshire County Records, 14, undated, p. 71.

66. E. Rowley-Morris, 'Royalist Composition Papers', *Montgomeryshire Collections*, 18, 1885, pp. 270–2. W.G.D. Fletcher, 'The Sequestration Papers of Sir Thomas Whitmore, Knight and Baronet, of Apley', *Trans. Shropshire Archaeological Soc.*, 4th series, IV, 1914, pp. 287, 294.

67. N.L.W. Wynnstay MS 113, 'An account of the rebellion . . .', p. 8; Chirk Castle MSS, Denbighshire Quarter Sessions Records, B 20/d/4, cited in J. Gwynn Williams, 'The Castles of Wales during the Civil War, 1642–1647', *Archaeologia Cambrensis*, CXXXVII, 1988, p. 14. Vicars, *Burning Bush*, p. 409.

68. Hall, *Cheshire*, pp. 162–3. *The Siege of Chester: Nathaniel Lancaster's Narrative*, ed. John Lewis, Leeds, 1987, pp. 11, 14.

69. Bodleian, MS Top. Northants c.9, Memorandums of . . . Northampton . . . Collected by Henry Lee, p. 99. Papillon, *Fortification and Assailing*, p. 10.

70. P.R.O., SP 28/184, returns for Market Place, High Pavement and Saltisford wards, unfol.

71. *Cal. State Papers Dom., 1644–5*, p. 434. Walker, *Historical Discourses*, p. 128. *Diary . . . of Richard Symonds*, p. 180. Thomason, E 287(6), *A More Exact Relation of the Siege laid to the Town of Leicester*, 1645, p. 5; E 261(3) *An Examination of a Printed Pamphlet Entitled 'A Narration of the Siege of the Town of Leicester . . .'*, 1645, p. 2; E 303(14) *An Examination Examined: Being a full and moderate Answer to Maior Innes Relation concerning the Siege and taking of the Town of Leicester*, 1645, p. 3.

72. Alan Everitt, *Change in the Provinces: the Seventeenth Century*, University of Leicester, Department of Local History, Occasional Papers, 2nd series, 1, 1969, p. 6.

73. Rushworth, *Historical Collections*, VI, pp. 50–1.

74. Stocks, *Leicester*, p. 349.

75. Birmingham Reference Library, MS 595,611, Sir William Brereton's Letter Book, pp. 116, 137, 140, 172. Charles Twamley, *History of Dudley Castle and Priory*, 1867, pp. 74–5. J.W. Willis Bund, *The Civil War in Worcestershire*, 1905, pp. 180–1.

76. Ogilby, *Britannia*, p. 44. Johnson and Vaisey, *Staffordshire*, p. 35. Stebbing Shaw, *History and Antiquities of Staffordshire*, I, 1798, p. 240. Birmingham Reference Library, MS 595,611, pp. 234, 250, 263–4. P.R.O., SP 24/6, f. 65v; SP 24/74, Saxon v. Biddulph. V.C.H., *Staffordshire*, XIV, 1990, p. 18.

77. Willis-Bund, *Worcestershire*, pp. 84–9. V.C.H., *Warwickshire*, VII, 1964, p. 271. *Four Tracts relative to the Battle of Birmingham Anno Domini 1643*, ed. L. Jaye, Birmingham, 1931.

78. *Cal. State Papers Dom., 1658–9*, pp. 1–2. Philip B. Chatwin, 'Edgbaston', *Trans. Birmingham Archaeological Soc.*, XXXIX, 1913, pp. 20–1.

79. *Diary of Sir Henry Slingsby*, pp. 144–5. *Diary . . . of Richard Symonds*, pp. 167, 277. V.C.H., *Worcestershire*, IV, p. 13. Thomason, E 269(21) *The true Informer*, 8–15 Feb. 1645, pp. 499–500.

80. P.R.O., SP 16/501, f. 222v. *Cal. State Papers Dom., 1644*, p. 178. *Diary . . . of Richard Symonds*, p. 279.

81. Thomason, E 252(36) *Perfect Occurrences of Parliament*, 24–31 May 1644, unpag. P.R.O., SP 28/226, unfol, petition of Thomas Street.

82. Hutchinson, p. 100. *Cal. State Papers Dom., 1644–5*, p. 508.

83. Pennington and Roots, *Committee at Stafford*, pp. 6, 35, 64, 67, 72–3, 82, 98, 105–6, 119, 173,

195, 220, 224–5, 228, 297, 302–3. *Cal. State Papers Dom., 1653–4*, p. 407. P.R.O., SP 24/3, ff. 7v, 51v, 100.

84. William Phillips, 'The Ottley Papers Relating to the Civil War, Part II', *Trans. Shropshire Archaeological Soc.*, 2nd series, VII, 1895, pp. 345–6. Shaw, *Staffordshire*, I, pp. 9, 18.

85. R.C.H.M., *Newark on Trent. Cal. State Papers Dom., 1661–2*, p. 45. B.L., Add. MS 18,981, f. 65. Thomason, E 506(35) *A Perfect Diurnall of Some Passages in Parliament*, 20–27 April 1646, p. 1144; E 509(1) *A Perfect Diurnall . . .*, 27 April–4 May 1646, p. 1158.

86. J.W.F. Hill, *Tudor and Stuart Lincoln*, Cambridge, 1956, pp. 162–3, 199–200. William Dugdale, *A Short View of the Late Troubles in England*, Oxford, 1681, p. 560. Lincolnshire Archives Office, CC 27/2, pp. 6, 9–11, 16–18, 20, 24; CC 27/3, pp. 8, 11; CC27/7, pp. 15, 21, 23, 27–8; Dean and Chapter of Lincoln MSS, ciii/29/2/1, pp. 2–3, 7–8; ciii/48/1/1, p. 23; ciii/48/1/3, pp. 15, 61, 67–8. Venables, 'A List and Brief Description of the Churches of Lincoln . . .', pp. 330, 334, 338–44. P.R.O., SP 28/35, f. 63; SP 23/183, p. 566; SP 23/332, f. 502.

87. Edward Peacock, 'Gainsburgh during the Great Civil War, A.D. 1642–1660', *Reports and Papers of the Associated Architectural Societies*, 8, 1866, p. 265. Bodleian, MS Tanner 62, pt I, f. 208. Hutchinson, pp. 163–4. Whitelock, *Memorials* p. 159.

88. Whitelock, *Memorials*, p. 106. *Cal. State Papers Dom., 1652–3*, p. 214. P.R.O., SP 28/171, unfol, A particular of Lord Rockingham's account.

89. 'Chorographia: Or, a Survey of Newcastle upon Tine, 1649', *Harleian Miscellany*, III, 1809, p. 281. Bodleian, MS Tanner, 62, pt II, f. 575. *Records of the Committees for Compounding . . . in Durham and Northumberland . . . 1643–1660*, Surtees Soc., CXI, 1905, p. 168. Thomason, E 33(33) *A Continuation of Certaine Speciall and Remarkable passages informed to the Parliament*, 15–22 Feb. 1644, p. 4.

90. H.M.C., *Hastings Manuscripts, Volume II*, 1930, p. 119.

91. Tullie, *Carlisle*, p. 12. Bodleian, MS Tanner 59, f. 716. Cumbria R.O., TL 1036, ff. 48–60; TL 1040, pp. 4–10.

92. Thomason, E4(6) *A Continuation of true Intelligence . . .*, 10–27 July 1644, p. 9. Sir Thomas Widdrington, *Analecta Eboracensia: Or, some remaynes of the ancient City of York*, ed. Caesar Caine, 1897, pp. 120, 128. Wenham, *York*, pp. 41, 98.

93. B.L., Harleian 2135, f. 40. Cheshire R.O., DCC/26, p. 38. Chester City R.O., A/F/26/5. *An Account of the Siege of Chester during the Civil Wars between King Charles I and his Parliament*, Chester, 1790, pp. 70–2.

94. *C.J., IV, 1644–6*, p. 277. George Chandler and E.K. Wilson, *Liverpool under Charles I*, Liverpool, 1965, pp. 422–3.

95. *L.J., V, 1642–3*, p. 495. *Cal. State Papers Dom., 1656–7*, p. 175. George Poulson, *Beverlac; or, The Antiquities and History of the town of Beverley*, 1829, Vol. II, p. 723. Keith Miller, John Robinson, Barbara English and Ivan Hall, *Beverley. An archaeological and architectural study*, R.C.H.M.E., Supplementary series, 4, 1982, pp. 42–3, 48. Wedgwood, *King's War*, p. 177.

96. H.P. Kendall, 'The Civil War as affecting Halifax and the surrounding towns', *Halifax Antiquarian Soc.*, 1910, pp. 37–40.

97. Ormerod, *Lancashire*, pp. 131–2. *A Discourse of the Warr in Lancashire*, ed. William Beamont, Chetham Soc., LXII, 1864, pp. 28–9. Warburton, *Prince Rupert*, II, p. 143.

98. Hinderwell, *Scarborough*, pp. 76, 80–4, 104, 126. J. Binns, 'Scarborough and the Civil Wars 1642–1651', *Northern History*, XXII, 1986, pp. 117–19.

99. *Journal of the . . . Sieges of Pontefract Castle, 1644–1645, by Nathan Drake*, pp. 12–13, 20, 27, 31–2, 34–6, 40, 44–5, 48. Thomason, E 24(9) *The London Post*, 14 Jan. 1645, p. 6; E 274(11) *A Diary, or an Exact Journall*, 13–20 March 1645, unpag. *The Booke of Entries of the Pontefract Corporation 1653–1726*, ed. Richard Holmes, Pontefract, 1882, pp. 14, 27–8. H.M.C., *Eighth Report: Corporation of Pontefract MSS*, pp. 274–5.

100. *Diary of Sir Henry Slingsby*, p. 126. Geoffrey Ridsdill Smith, *Without Touch of Dishonour. The Life and Death of Sir Henry Slingsby 1602–1658*, Kineton, 1968, pp. 81–3.

101. Wroughton, *Bath*. Bath City R.O., corporation leases. Thomason, E 262(38) *Perfect Passages of Each Dayes Proceedings in Parliament*, 30 July–6 Aug. 1645, p. 325.

102. D.J. Schove, 'Fire and Drought', *Weather*, XXI, 1966, pp. 311–14.

CHAPTER FIVE

1. Stoyle, *Civil War Defences of Exeter . . . 1645–6*, p. 11.
2. Styles, *Worcester*, pp. 231–2. *Cal. State Papers Dom., 1643–7*, p. 63. Roy, 'England turned Germany?', p. 140.
3. P.R. Mounfield, 'The Footwear Industry of the East Midlands: II Northamptonshire', *The East Midlands Geographer*, 3, 1964–5, pp. 396, 406–9.
4. W.A. Bewes, *Church Briefs*, 1896, p. 19. *C.J., IV, 1644–6*, p. 154; *V, 1646–8*, pp. 695–6. *L.J., VII, 1644–5*, p. 393; *VIII, 1645–6*, pp. 69–70, 78.
5. *C.J., V, 1646–8*, pp. 603, 629. *L.J., X, 1647–8*, p. 318.
6. *The Register of Baptisms, Marriages & Burials of the Parish of Ottery St. Mary, Devon, 1610–1837*, ed. H. Tapley-Soper, Devon and Cornwall Record Soc., 1908–29, p. 828. Essex R.O., T/R 5/1/4 Chelmsford St Mary Briefs, 1615–1753, unfol.
7. *L.J., IX, 1646–7*, p. 657. Gloucestershire R.O., P86 VE 2/1, f. 28v, W.D. Macray, *A Register of . . . St Mary Magdalen College, Oxford*, III, 1901, p. 19.
8. Bewes, *Church Briefs*, pp. 20, 172–4. Bodleian, MS Tanner 59, f. 787. *L.J., IX, 1646–7*, p. 657. N.L.W., Aston Hall MS 2400. J.E. Thorold Rogers, *A History of Agriculture and Prices in England*, 1866–1900, VI, p. 668.
9. *C.J., V, 1646–8*, pp. 424–5; *VII, 1651–9*, p. 306.
10. C.H. Firth and R.S. Rait, *Acts and Ordinances of the Interregnum*, 1911, II, pp. 737–8. *Cal. State Papers Dom., 1656–7*, p. 194. Gloucestershire R.O., GBR B3/2 Corporation Minute Book, 1632–56, p. 658. *C.J., VII, 1651–9*, pp. 322–3.
11. Gloucestershire R.O., GBR B3/3 Corporation Minute Book, 1656–86, pp. 19, 32–3, 37, 68, 75, 178–9; 1421/1541 Letter Book, 1640–60, pp. 211–16, 221. J.A. Picton, *City of Liverpool: Selections from the Municipal Archives and Records, from the 13th to the 17th century*, Liverpool, 1883, pp. 148–51.
12. *C.J., III, 1642–4*, pp. 108, 123, 331; *IV, 1644–6*, p. 168; *V, 1646–8*, p. 399; *VI, 1648–51*, p. 584. *L.J., VI, 1643–4*, p. 102.
13. *C.J., IV, 1644–6*, p. 277; *VI, 1648–51*, p. 203. Chandler and Wilson, *Liverpool under Charles I*, pp. 363–4, 423.
14. *L.J., VIII, 1645–6*, p. 434. *C.J., V, 1646–8*, pp. 367, 663. *Original Papers illustrative of the Life and Writings of John Milton*, ed. W.D. Hamilton, Camden Soc., 1859, p. 111. H.M.C., *Seventh Report, House of Lords MSS*, p. 43. Rushworth, *Historical Collections*, V, p. 682.
15. House of Lords R.O., Main Papers 23 Aug.–2 Sept. 1648, f. 179. H.M.C., *Eleventh Report, Appendix 7: Le Strange MSS*, p. 102.
16. *C.J., V, 1646–8*, p. 29. Bayley, *Dorset*, p. 136. Hutchins, *Dorset*, II, p. 119.
17. *C.J., V, 1646–8*, p. 592; *VI, 1648–51*, p. 291. *Cal. State Papers Dom., 1657–8*, pp. 91–2, 199.
18. P.R.O., SP 18/69/21.
19. *Cal. State Papers Dom., 1653–4*, p. 281.
20. Robert Tittler, *Architecture and Power. The Town Hall and the English Urban Community c.1500–1640*, Oxford, 1991, pp. 51–66.
21. Trevor Rowley, *The Shropshire Landscape*, 1972, p. 191. V.C.H., *Oxfordshire*, X, p. 82.
22. *Records of the County of Wilts*, ed. Cunnington, p. 207.
23. P.R.O., SP 28/246, f. 176.
24. D.H. Allen, *Essex Quarter Sessions Order Book 1652–1661*, Chelmsford, 1974, p. 139.
25. H.M.C., *Sixth Report, House of Lords MSS*, p. 188. *C.J., V, 1646–8*, p. 249.
26. *Cal. State Papers Dom., 1654*, p. 352.
27. Gloucestershire R.O., GBR 1421/1451, pp. 67–80, 108–13.
28. P.R.O., E 317 Denbighshire 3, f. 9. James Millerd, An Exactt Delineation of the Famous City of Bristol and Suburbs thereof . . ., 1673.
29. P.R.O., SP 24/84, White versus Powell.
30. *C.J., V, 1646–8*, pp. 574, 598–9. F.C. Morgan, 'Local Government in Hereford', *Trans. of the Woolhope Naturalists' Field Club*, XXXI, 1942, p. 41. *Cal. State Papers Dom., 1656–7*, p. 207.
31. H.M.C., *Eighth Report, Corporation of Pontefract Records*, pp. 274–5. *Booke of Entries of the Pontefract Corporation*, ed. Holmes, pp. 27–30. *Cal. State Papers Dom., 1654*, pp. 344–5; *1657–8*, p. 350. *C.J., VI, 1648–51*, p. 174. *Herbert Correspondence*, ed. W.J. Smith, Cardiff, 1963, p. 135.

32. *Quarter Sessions Order Book, 1642–1649*, ed. B.C. Redwood, Sussex Record Soc., 54, 1954, pp. 171–2, 196.

33. Styles, *Worcester*, p. 243. *C.J., V, 1646–8*, pp. 466–7. *L.J., X, 1647–8*, p. 64. Worcester R.O., Worcester Corporation Records, Charities: Inglethorpe's Charity, 1632–1717, unfol; D 247, Accounts approved at Quarter Sessions, 1652.

34. R. Machin, 'The Mechanism of the Pre-industrial Building Cycle', *Vernacular Architecture*, 8, 1977, pp. 816–17. Lawrence Stone and Jeanne C. Fawtier Stone, *An Open Elite? England 1540–1880*, Oxford, 1984, pp. 354–5. Malcolm Airs, *The Making of the English Country House 1500–1640*, 1975, pp. 82–90.

35. Airs, *Country House*, pp. 82, 88, 90.

36. P.R.O., SP 23/179, pp. 610, 613, 618, 620–1. Maurice Barley, *Houses and History*, 1986, p. 223.

37. *Cal. State Papers Dom., 1645–7*, p. 454. Devon R.O., ECA, B 1/9, Act Book, 1647–52, f. 96v.

38. John Aleyn, *Select Cases*, 1688, pp. 26–8. I owe this reference to the kindness of Ian Edge.

39. P.R.O., SP 24/11, f. 118; SP 24/36 Brand versus Reynolds.

40. West Sussex R.O., Cap. I/30/I Survey of the Lands of the Dean and Chapter of Chichester, f. 108.

41. H.M.C., *Bridgnorth*, p. 428.

42. Lincolnshire Archive Office, Dean and Chapter MSS, Bii/4/1 Lease register, 1664–7, ff. 7v–9, 17v–19, 22–23v, 48v–49v.

43. Coventry City R.O., A14(B), ff. 52, 85v, 106, 128. Gloucestershire R.O., GDR D936 E12/4, Lease book of the Dean and Chapter of Gloucester, 1667–77, pp. 9–10, 77–9, 83–5, 311–14.

44. Devon R.O., ECA B 1/9–11, Act Books, 1647–52, 1652–63, 1663–84, passim.

45. Worcester R.O., BA 7811/11, 13, 14, 22, 22(i).

46. Devon R.O., ECA B 1/8, Act Book, 1634–47, f. 209v.

47. Worcester R.O., BA 2636/161.

48. E.M. Platt, 'Liverpool during the Civil War', *Trans. of the Historical Soc. of Lancashire and Cheshire*, 61, 1909, pp. 196–7.

49. Colchester Castle Muniment Room, Assembly Book 4, 1646–66, f. 24v.

50. R, Machin, 'The Great Rebuilding: A Reassessment', *Past and Present*, 77, 1977, pp. 36–42.

51. P.R.O., C3/453/33. J.T. Cliffe, *Puritans in Conflict: the Puritan Gentry during and after the Civil Wars*, 1988, pp. 90–1.

52. House of Lords R.O., Main Papers 23 Aug.–2 Sept. 1648, f. 180. Gloucestershire R.O., GBR 1454/1543 Town Clerk's Notebook, f. 35. Wenham, *York*, p. 171.

53. Exeter Cathedral Library, MS 1098, ff. 6, 11. J.F. Chanter, *The Bishop's Palace Exeter*, 1932, pp. 83–93. W.J. Harte, 'Ecclesiastical and Religious Affairs in Exeter 1640–1662', *Trans. of the Devonshire Association*, LXIX, 1937, p. 51.

54. West Sussex R.O., Cap. I/30/2 Survey of the Lands of the Dean and Chapter of Chichester, ff. 49–50. Gloucestershire R.O., GDR, G 3/19 Survey of the Estates of the Bishop of Gloucester, pp. 48–9.

55. *Quarter Sessions Records for . . . Somerset, III*, ed. Harbin, pp. 15, 52–3, 85, 126, 135.

56. B.L., Harleian 2125, f. 149; 7568, f. 161. Chester City R.O., A/F/29/17.

57. Gloucestershire R.O., GBR, B 3/2, pp. 277, 280–1, 297, 342–3. John Dorney, *Certain Speeches made upon the day of the Yearly Election of Officers in the City of Gloucester*, 1653, p. 21.

58. Colchester Castle Muniment Room, Examinations and Recognisances, 1646–1687, unfol.

59. V.C.H., *Staffordshire*, VI, 1979, p. 191.

60. 'Henry Townshend's "Notes of the Office of a Justice of the Peace", 1661–1663', ed. R.D. Hunt, *Miscellany II*, Worcestershire Historical Soc., new series, 5, 1967, pp. 92–3. P.R.O., ASSI 2/1, Crown Book, Assizes, Oxford Circuit, 1656–78, f. 10. *Diary of Francis Evans, Secretary to Bishop Lloyd, 1699–1706*, ed. David Robertson, Worcestershire Historical Soc., 1903, pp. 38–40.

61. Machin, 'Great Rebuilding', pp. 42, 46.

62. Taylor, *Wanderings to see the Wonders of the West*, p. 5. H.M.C., *Thirteenth Report, Appendix 2, Portland II*, p. 297.

63. H.M.C., *Seventh Report, House of Lords MSS*, p. 19.

64. Taylor, *Short Relation*, pp. 10, 13, 15–16, 19.

65. *Diary of John Evelyn*, III, p. 176.

66. Lincolnshire Archive Office, CC 27/5; C iii/29/2/1.

67. P.R.O., E 317 Cheshire 6A, ff. 3, 5–6; Cheshire 13A, ff. 1–9. *Lancashire and Cheshire Church Surveys, 1649–1655*, ed. Henry Fishwick, Lancashire and Cheshire Record Soc., I, 1879, pp. 232–3. West Sussex R.O., Cap. 1/30/I, ff. 52–5, 72–4, 93–5, 103–8, 144–5, 163–5. *The Parliamentary Survey of the Lands and Possessions of the Dean and Chapter of Worcester*, edd. Thomas Cave and Rowland A. Wilson, Worcestershire Historical Soc., 1924, pp. 169–217.

68. P.R.O., E 317 Denbighshire 3, f. 9; Oxon. 8, ff. 1–8. V.C.H., *Oxfordshire*, X, 1972, pp. 25, 29–30; *Staffordshire*, XIV, 1990, p. 18.

69. Chester City R.O., A/B/2, ff. 107v, 109v, 129v; A/F/34/29, 30, 34, 38–40; A/F/35/24; A/F/36/18, 20; QSF/78/1.

70. B.L., Harleian 7568, f. 137v.

71. Chester City R.O., C/Ch/2A/4; A/F/34/34, 38–40; A/F/37a/12; QSF/78/1.

72. Chester City R.O., A/B/2, f. 109. Cheshire R.O., P 51/12/1 St John's, Chester, churchwardens' accounts 1634–85, unfol. A.M. Johnson, Some Aspects of the Political, Constitutional, Social, and Economic History of the City of Chester, 1550–1662, unpublished D.Phil. thesis, University of Oxford, 1971, pp. 197, 202, 211–13.

73. Harte, 'Ecclesiastical and Religious Affairs in Exeter', p. 55. Bridget Cherry and Nikolaus Pevsner, *The Buildings of England: Devon*, 1989, p. 396.

74. Portman, *Exeter Houses*, p. 59. Devon R.O., ECA, B 1/9–11; Bk 190, Survey and rental of the City's property, 1671; Bk 69, Sessions of the Peace, depositions 1642–60, ff. 177, 251, 255, 266, 292v, 342v, 345v, 349v, 372, 378v, 380v, 392v, 406, 423, 434; Bk 11, Act Book 1663–84, ff. 170, 236. W.B. Stephens, *Seventeenth-century Exeter*, Exeter, 1958, pp. 64, 72.

75. Porter, 'Oxford Fire of 1644', pp. 298–9.

76. House of Lords R.O., Main Papers 1641–2, Protestation Returns. Roy and Porter, 'Population of Worcester', pp. 32–43. P.R.O., E179/260/8, 11–13; E179/355. Worcester R.O., BA3790/1(i) St Nicholas, Worcester, parish register, 1563–1694.

77. Worcester R.O., B.A. 7811/14(i).

78. *C.J.*, VII, 1651–9, p. 103.

79. Binns, 'Scarborough and the Civil Wars', pp. 118–19.

80. K.R. Adey, 'Seventeenth-century Stafford: A County Town in Decline', *Midland History*, II, 1974, pp. 154–7.

81. D.M. Palliser, 'York under the Tudors: the trading life of the northern capital', in *Perspectives in English Urban History*, ed. Alan Everitt, 1973, pp. 56–9. Kevin Sharpe, *The Personal Rule of Charles I*, New Haven and London, 1992, pp. 448–50.

82. Gloucestershire R.O., GBR 1421/1541, pp. 262–3. Peter Clark, '"The Ramoth-Gilead of the Good": Urban change and political radicalism at Gloucester 1540–1640', in *The English Commonwealth 1547–1640*, eds Peter Clark, Alan G.R. Smith and Nicholas Tyacke, Leicester, 1979, pp. 167–87.

83. Wenham, *York*, p. 173.

84. Widdrington, *Analecta Eboracensia*, p. 128.

85. Wenham, *York*, p. 108. R.C.H.M., *The City of York: IV Outside the City Walls East of the Ouse*, 1975, pp. xxxviii–ix, xlix, 87.

86. Francis Drake, *Eboracum: or the History and Antiquities of the City of York*, 1736, p. 245. Penelope Corfield, 'Urban Development in England and Wales in the Sixteenth and Seventeenth Centuries', in *Trade, Government and Economy in Pre-Industrial England*, edd. D.C. Coleman and A.H. John, 1976, pp. 228–9, 239.

87. Dorney, *Certain Speeches*, p. 20. Ogilby, *Britannia*, p. 30.

88. Gloucestershire R.O., GBR B3/2 Corporation minute book, 1632–56, pp. 461–2; GBR 1407/1521B, 1408/1522 Lease books of corporation property, 1646–64, 1664–84; GDR D936 E12/2, 4, 5, Lease books of the Dean and Chapter of Gloucester, 1660–7, 1667–77, 1677–87.

89. Clark, '"The Ramoth Gilead of the Good" . . .', p. 168. V.C.H. *Gloucestershire*, IV, 1988, p. 102.

90. York Corporation Archives, B.36 House Book, 1637–50, f. 122v.

91. Devon R.O., ECA Bk 64, Sessions of the Peace minute book, 1642–60, ff. 255v–6. Guildhall Library, MSS 11,936/26, 33, Sun Fire Office policy registers, 1728, 1730–1, passim.

92. 'The Travels of Cosmo III, Grand Duke of Tuscany, Through England, By Count L. Magalotti', in *Early Tours in Devon and Cornwall*, ed. A. Gibson, Newton Abbot, 1967, p. 111.

93. Alan Dyer, 'Urban housing: a documentary study of four Midland towns 1530–1700', *Post-*

Medieval Archaeology, 15, 1981, pp. 209, 212, 217. Kenneth H. Docton, 'Lancaster, 1684', *Trans. of the Historical Soc. of Lancashire and Cheshire*, 109, 1957, pp. 127, 129.

94. *L.J., VI, 1643–4*, pp. 88, 102. *C.J., III, 1643–4*, p. 108; *VII, 1651–9*, p. 36. *Cal. State Papers Dom., 1655*, p. 211. Hutchins, *Dorset*, I, p. 99.

95. *C.J., V, 1646–8*, p. 679. *Letters of the Lady Brilliana Harley*, ed. Thomas Taylor Lewis, Camden Soc., 58, 1853, pp. xi–xii, 230. R.C.H.M., *Herefordshire, III North-West*, 1934, p. 19. Webb, *Herefordshire*, II, p. 15.

96. J.E. Auden, 'Ecclesiastical History of Shropshire during the Civil War, Commonwealth and Restoration', *Trans. of the Shropshire Archaeological Soc.*, 3rd series, VII, 1907, pp. 273–6. Nikolaus Pevsner, *The Buildings of England: Shropshire*, 1958, pp. 247, 296.

97. William Dugdale, *The Antiquities of Warwickshire*, II, 2nd edn, 1730, p. 897. *Cal. State Papers Dom., 1658–9*, pp. 1–2. Chatwin, 'Edgbaston', pp. 20–1.

98. Nikolaus Pevsner and Edward Hubbard, *The Buildings of England: Cheshire*, 1971, p. 218. V.C.H., *Warwickshire*, V, 1949, p. 66. *Inspections of Churches and Parsonage Houses in the Diocese of Worcester in 1674, 1676, 1684 and 1687*, ed. Paul Morgan, Worcestershire Historical Soc., new series, 12, 1986, pp. 57, 96.

99. *L.J., IX, 1647–8*, p. 665. Samuel Rudder, *A New History of Gloucestershire*, Cirencester, 1779, p. 726. John Nichols, *The History of Antiquities of the County of Leicester*, II, 1795, p. 84. John Marius Wilson, *The Imperial Gazetteer of England and Wales*, 1866–9, II, p. 1116.

100. Pevsner, *Shropshire*, p. 72. Paul Benthall, *Benthall Hall, Shropshire*, 1976, pp. 16–17, 24.

101. Porter, 'Civil War Destruction of Boarstall', pp. 86–91.

102. Nichols, *Leicestershire*, II, p. 81.

103. Nicholas Kingsley, *The Country Houses of Gloucestershire*, Cheltenham, 1989, p. 6. Geoffrey Tyack, *Warwickshire Country Houses in the Age of Classicism 1650–1800*, Warwickshire Local History Soc., Occasional Paper No. 3, 1980, pp. 4, 65. R.C.H.M.E., *The Country Houses of Northamptonshire*, 1996, p. 33.

104. *Country Houses of Northamptonshire*, p. 72.

105. *Diary of John Evelyn*, III, p. 111. V.C.H., *Wiltshire*, VII, 1953, p. 179. C.H. Talbot, 'Notes on Spye Park and Bromham', *Wiltshire Archaeological Magazine*, XV, 1975, pp. 320–8.

106. Kingsley, *Country Houses of Gloucestershire*, pp. 106–7.

107. John Bold, *Wilton House and English Palladianism*, 1988, p. 9. Tyack, *Warwickshire Country Houses*, pp. 33–4.

108. R.C.H.M., *Dorset: V East Dorset*, 1975, p. 46.

109. A.J. Taylor, *Raglan Castle*, 1975, pp. 22–3. T.L. Jones, *Ashby de la Zouch Castle*, 1972, p. 13.

110. R.B. Pugh and A.D. Saunders, *Old Wardour Castle*, 1968, pp. 9–13, 17–20. Mark Girouard, 'Wardour Old Castle', *Country Life*, 14 Feb. 1991, pp. 44–9, 21 Feb. 1991, pp. 76–9.

111. H. Thorpe, 'The Lord and the Landscape', *Transactions and Proceedings of the Birmingham Archaeological Soc.*, 80, 1962, p. 71. *Country Houses of Northamptonshire*, p. 52.

112. Mark Girouard, 'Wootton Lodge, Staffordshire', *Country Life*, 125, 1959, pp. 522–5, 596–9. Rudder, *Gloucestershire*, p. 717. David Verey, *The Buildings of England: Gloucestershire, 1. The Cotswolds*, 1970, pp. 438–40.

113. *Documents Relating to the History of the Cathedral Church of Winchester in the Seventeenth Century*, edd. W.R.W. Stephens and F.T. Madge, 1897, pp. 83, 159. Bodleian, MS Tanner 140, ff. 123–4. *Cal. State Papers Dom., 1660–1*, pp. 340–1.

114. *Cal. State Papers Dom., 1663–4*, pp. 277, 362, 386. *Documents Relating to . . . Winchester*, pp. 104–5, 114, 137, 142–3, 161.

115. Lincolnshire Archive Office, Bii/1/10. D.S. Bailey, *The Canonical Houses of Wells*, Gloucester, 1982, pp. 142–3, 145.

116. Phyllis Hembry, 'Episcopal Palaces, 1535 to 1660', in *Wealth and Power in Tudor England*, eds E.W. Ives, R.J. Knecht and J.J. Scarisbrick, 1979, pp. 164–5. I.J. Gentles and W.J. Sheils, *Confiscation and Restoration: The Archbishopric Estates and the Civil War*, Borthwick Papers No. 59, York, 1981, p. 13.

117. Nikolaus Pevsner, *The Buildings of England: Worcestershire*, 1968, pp. 28, 190. V.C.H. *Staffordshire*, XIV, 1990, pp. 18, 57, 61–3. *Agrarian History of England and Wales*, V pt II, p. 601. M.W. Thompson, *Farnham Castle Keep*, 1978, p. 14.

118. V.C.H., *Warwickshire*, VIII, 1969, p. 430, and information kindly supplied by Dr Peter Borsay.

119. Thomas Harris, *The Duty of Gratitude*, 1733, p. 8. Hutchins, *Dorset*, I, p. 81.
120. T.F. Reddaway, *The Rebuilding of London after the Great Fire*, 1940, pp. 24–83.
121. Browne Willis, *The History and Antiquities of the Town, Hundred, and Deanery of Buckingham*, 1755, p. 29.
122. Philip Benedict, *Rouen during the Wars of Religion*, Cambridge, 1981, p. 218.
123. S.H. Steinberg, *The 'Thirty Years War'*, 1966, p. 103. G.L. Burke, *The Making of Dutch Towns*, 1956, pp. 82, 84, 122–3, 133–6.
124. Parker, *Dutch Revolt*, p. 142. Burke, *Dutch Towns*, pp. 121–3.
125. J.V. Polisensky, *The Thirty Years War*, 1974, pp. 247–52. C.R. Friedrichs, *Urban Society in an Age of War: Nördlingen, 1580–1720*, Princeton, 1979, pp. 31, 168.
126. John Childs, *Armies and Warfare in Europe 1648–1789*, New York, 1982, p. 147.
127. *The Anglo-Dutch Garden in the Age of William and Mary*, eds John Dixon Hunt and Erik de Jong, 1988, p. 129.
128. *Cal. State Papers Dom., 1690–91*, pp. 81, 83.
129. Thomason, 669.f.17(5) *A Briefe representation of the sad and lamentable condition of that once flourishing Town of Marleborough . . .*, 1653.

CHAPTER SIX

1. Hinderwell, *Scarborough*, p. 104.
2. *Seventeenth-Century Economic Documents*, eds Joan Thirsk and J.P. Cooper, Oxford, 1972, p. 414.
3. Gloucestershire R.O., GBR B 3/4, Common Council Minute Book, 1673–87, ff. 14v–15.
4. Corpus Christi College, MS C.C.C. Oxon. 390/2, f. 133.
5. V.C.H., *Warwickshire*, II, 1908, pp. 361–2. Corpus Christi College, MS C.C.C. Oxon. 390/1, f. 67.
6. John Lawson, *The Endowed Grammar Schools of East Yorkshire*, East Yorkshire Local History Series, 14, 1962, p. 14.
7. Ian Roy and Stephen Porter, 'The Social and Economic Structure of an Early-Modern Suburb: the Tything at Worcester', *Bulletin of the Institute of Historical Research*, LII, 1980, pp. 205–6, 215–16. Worcester R.O., BA 7811/7.
8. V.C.H., *Cheshire*, III, 1980, pp. 179, 182. Wenham, *York*, pp. 109–10.
9. Richard Izacke, *Remarkable Antiquities of the City of Exeter*, 1681, pp. 162, 168. Alexander Jenkins, *The History and Description of the City of Exeter*, Exeter, 1806, pp. 381–2. Devon R.O., ECA, B 1/10, Act Book, 1652–63, f. 16; B 1/11, Act Book, 1663–83, ff. 10v, 13, 29v; ED/WA/13–15.
10. *Inspections . . . in the Diocese of Worcester*, ed. Morgan, pp. 23, 33, 39–40. Twamley, *Dudley Castle and Priory*, p. 75.
11. Alan Savidge, *The Parsonage in England*, cited in J.S. Leatherbarrow, *Churchwardens Presentments in the Diocese of Worcester c1660–1760*, Worcestershire Historical Soc., Occasional Publications, 1, 1977, p. 12.
12. *Diary of Richard Symonds*, p. 279. John H. Pruett, *The Parish Clergy under the Later Stuarts. The Leicestershire Experience*, Urbana, Ill., 1978, p. 137.
13. Bodleian, MS Tanner 129, f. 73v.
14. Venables, 'A List and Brief Description of the Churches of Lincoln . . .', pp. 330–44.
15. Guy Miège, *The New State of England*, 1701, p. 42.
16. Morant, *Essex*, I, p. 108. Essex R.O., D/Y 2/2. Nikolaus Pevsner, *The Buildings of England: Essex*, 2nd edn, 1965, p. 134.
17. D.M. Palliser, 'The Unions of Parishes in York, 1547–86', *Yorkshire Archaeological Journal*, XLVI, 1974, pp. 87–102. Hill, *Tudor and Stuart Lincoln*, pp. 56–8.
18. Daniel Lysons, *Magna Britannia*, I, 1806, p. 402.
19. *Bibliotheca Gloucestrensis*, ed. Washbourn, pp. 356–66. *L.J.*, X, *1647–8*, pp. 173–5. Rudder, *Gloucestershire*, p. 203.
20. George Oliver, *The History and Antiquities of the Town and Minster of Beverley*, Beverley, 1829, p. 230. Harris et al., *Beverley*, p. 48.
21. V.C.H., *Hampshire*, III, 1908, p. 197. Hedges, *History of Wallingford*, II, p. 392. Berkshire R.O., D/P 137/1/1, unfol.; Archdeaconry Papers c.139, ff. 7–23.

22. Huntingford, 'Church Building and Restoration in North Berkshire', p. 94.
23. *Inspections . . . in the Diocese of Worcester*, ed. Morgan, p. 36. V.C.H., *Worcestershire*, III, 1913, pp. 65–6.
24. Pevsner, *Shropshire*, p. 31.
25. Pevsner and Hubbard, *Cheshire*, p. 218. David Verey, *The Buildings of England: Gloucestershire, 2, The Vale and the Forest of Dean*, 1970, p. 355.
26. *Wiltshire. The Topographical Collections of John Aubrey, F.R.S.*, ed. John Edward Jackson, Devizes, 1862, p. 263.
27. J.H. Walker, 'St Nicholas' Church Nottingham', *Trans. of the Thoroton Soc.*, XLIV, 1940, pp. 56–7. Nikolaus Pevsner, *The Buildings of England: Nottinghamshire*, 2nd edn, 1979, p. 224; *Essex*, p. 134; *Lincolnshire*, pp. 495–500.
28. Nikolaus Pevsner, *The Buildings of England: Herefordshire*, 1963, pp. 174, 176; *Worcestershire*, p. 135.
29. Marcus Whiffen, *Stuart and Georgian Churches*, 1947–8, p. 13.
30. Jacqueline Eales, *Puritans and Roundheads: The Harleys of Brampton Bryan and the outbreak of the English Civil War*, Cambridge, 1990, pp. 182–4.
31. John S. Roper, *Dudley: The town in the eighteenth century*, Dudley, 1968, p. 9.
32. Robert Atkyns, *The Ancient and Present State of Glostershire*, 1712, p. 282. Nichols, *Leicestershire*, Vol. IV, pt II, p. 990.
33. *Diary of Richard Symonds*, p. 21. P.R.O., SP 28/42, ff. 253–4. Thomason, E 273(3) *The London Post*, 11 March 1645, p. 8. Whitelock, *Memorials*, p. 159. R.C.H.M., *Herefordshire: III North-West*, p. 182.
34. Clarendon, *History*, IV, pp. 37–8. *Diary . . . of Richard Symonds*, p. 166. *Diary of Sir Henry Slingsby*, p. 144. Walker, *Historical Discourses*, p. 126. Broxap, *Lancashire*, pp. xiv–xv, 110–13.
35. Devon R.O., ECA, Bk 69, Sessions of the Peace Minute Book, 1642–60, ff. 177, 255, 266, 292v, 342v, 345v, 349v, 372, 378v, 423.
36. John Langton, 'Residential patterns in pre-industrial cities: some case studies from seventeenth-century Britain', *Trans. of the Institute of British Geographers*, 65, 1975, pp. 7–11.
37. *The Hearth Tax Collectors' Book for Worcester 1678–1680*, edd. C.A.F. Meekings, S. Porter and I. Roy, Worcestershire Historical Soc., new series, 11, 1983, pp. 26–31, 112–15.
38. H.M.C., *Sixth Report, House of Lords Manuscripts*, p. 131. *Cal. Committee for the Advance of Money*, p. 519.
39. E.W. Hulme, 'History of the Chicester Needles', *Sussex Notes and Queries*, XII, 1948–9, pp. 124–8. F.W. Steer, *The Chichester Needle Industry*, The Chichester Papers, 31, 1963, pp. 2–3.
40. V.C.H., *Oxfordshire*, X, 1972, p. 64.
41. Jack Simmons, *Leicester: The Ancient Borough to 1860*, Gloucester, 1983, pp. 91–2. Harry Thorpe, 'Lichfield: A Study of its Growth and Function', *Collections for a History of Staffordshire*, 1950–1, pp. 176–7, 182.
42. *The Journeys of Celia Fiennes*, ed. Christopher Morris, 1947, pp. 183–4.
43. Peter Borsay, *The English Urban Renaissance: Culture and Society in the Provincial Town, 1660–1779*, Oxford, 1989, pp. 41–79.
44. Borsay, *Urban Renaissance*, pp. vii, 90–5, 319–20. Michael Turner, 'New Towns for old? Reconstruction after fires in the South West: the case of Blandford Forum, Dorset, 1731', in *Landscape and Townscape in the South West*, ed. Robert Heigham, Exeter, 1989, pp. 78–84.
45. Peter Thomas and Jacqueline Warren, *Aspects of Exeter*, Plymouth, 1980, p. 120.
46. Nikolaus Pevsner and John Harris, *The Buildings of England: Lincolnshire*, ed. Nicholas Antram, 1989, pp. 443, 485.
47. Daniel Lysons, *The Environs of London*, III, 1795, pp. 447, 474–5. Brett-James, *Stuart London*, p. 291.
48. Ward, *Excavations at Chester*, p. 11.
49. Harrington, 'Civil War fortifications', pp. 51–60.
50. Berkshire R.O., Archdeaconry Papers c.100, f. 8. James Townsend, *A History of Abingdon*, 1910, p. 78.
51. Wenham, *York*, p. 209. Defoe, *Tour*, p. 639.
52. Rudder, *Gloucestershire*, pp. 645–6. John S. Moore, 'The Gloucestershire section of Domesday Book: geographical problems of the text, part 4', *Trans. of the Bristol and Gloucestershire Archaeological Soc.*, 108, 1990, p. 114.

53. W. Byford-Jones, *Midland Leaves: A Travel Notebook*, Wolverhampton, 1934, p. 71.
54. M.W. Thompson, *The Decline of the Castle*, Cambridge, 1987, pp. 138–57, 179–85. J.D.K. Lloyd, 'The New Building at Montgomery Castle', *Archaeologia Cambrensis*, CXIV, 1965, pp. 60–4.
55. Twamley, *Dudley Castle and Priory*, pp. 96–8.
56. Thomason E 100(21) *The Downe-fall of Dagon, or the taking downe of Cheape-side Crosse*, 1643. M.J.H. Liversidge, 'Abingdon's 'Right Goodly Crosse of Stone'', *The Antiquaries Journal*, LXIII, 1983, pp. 315–16.
57. *Diary . . . of Richard Symonds*, p. 20.
58. Gentles, *The New Model Army*, pp. 109–10.
59. Nigel Llewellyn, *The Art of Death*, 1991, p. 121.
60. Daniel Defoe, *Memoirs of a Cavalier*, ed. James T. Boulton, Oxford, 1991, p. 168.
61. G.M. Trevelyan, *England under the Stuarts*, 1965 edn, p. 219; this work was first published in 1904.
62. Roy, 'England turned Germany?', p. 129. H. Kamen, 'The Economic and Social Consequences of the Thirty Years' War', *Past and Present*, 39, 1968, pp. 44–61. J.V. Polisensky, *War and Society in Europe 1618–1648*, 1978. Friedrichs, *Urban Society*. Parker, *Thirty Years' War*. M.S. Anderson, *War and Society in Europe of the Old Regime 1618–1789*, 1988, pp. 63–76.
63. Roy, 'England turned Germany?', pp. 127–44. *Reactions to the English Civil War*, pp. 115–35. Carlton, *Going to the Wars*.
64. Wenham, *York*, p. 40.

Bibliography

MANUSCRIPT SOURCES

Abingdon Borough Records
  Council Minute Book, 1556–1686
  Christ's Hospital Minutes, 1577–1694, transcript

Balliol College, Oxford
  Lease Log Book, 1588–1850
  Leases, 1588–1665

Bath City Record Office
  Chamberlains' accounts, 1635–65
  Corporation leases, 1642–65

Berkshire Record Office
  Archdeaconry papers, Churchwardens' presentments
  Abingdon, Chamberlains' accounts, 1633–85
  —— Bailiffs' accounts, 1642–4
  Hungerford, Hock-tide Court book, 1582–1777
  Newbury, Churchwardens' accounts, 1602–1726
  Reading, Corporation Diaries, 1655–65
  —— Petitions to the Corporation
  —— Parish records of St Giles, Reading
  Wallingford, Corporation Minute Book, 1507–1684
  —— Statute Book, 1648–1766
  —— Parish records of St Leonard and St Mary, Wallingford
  Wokingham, Common Council Book, 1630–1748
  —— By-laws of 1625

Birmingham Reference Library
  Sir William Brereton's Letter Book, 1646

Bodleian Library
  MS Add. D114, Papers relating to the siege of Oxford
  MSS Clarendon 21–28, Letters and papers of Edward, Earl of Clarendon, 1642–6
  MS Oxf. dioc. papers b.126, Accounts of Hugh Boham, parson of St Ebb's and Fellow of All
    Souls
  MS Rawlinson B.210, Byron's account of the defence of Chester
  MS Rawlinson C.125, Civil War letters
  MS Rawlinson D.687, Account Book of Smith's Hospital, Lincoln, 1612–53
  MSS Tanner 59–64, Lenthall Papers, 1642–6
  MS Tanner 140, Accounts of the Dean and Chapter of Winchester, 1660–7

MS Top. Berks d.24, Calendar of the documents at St Helen's Church, Abingdon
MS Top. Bucks b.6, Plan of the fortifications of Newport Pagnell, 1644
MS Top. Northants c.9, Henry Lee's 'Memorandums of the Antiquities of the town of
    Northampton'

Bristol Archive Office
    Common Council Minutes, 1627–75
    Great Audit Books, 1645–57
    Ordinances of the Common Council to 1674
    Sessions Order Book, 1653–71
    Dean and Chapter of Bristol, book of leases, 1660–75
    Parish records of St Jacob, St James, St John the Baptist, St Phillip, St Thomas, and St
        Werburgh, Bristol

British Library
    Add. MS 5027, Civil War town plans
    Add. MSS 11,332–3, Sir William Brereton's letter books, 1645–6
    Add. MS 11,364, Annals of Coventry
    Add. MS 18,980–2, Prince Rupert's papers
    Add. MS 27,402, 'A true Relation of my Lord Ogle's Engagements'
    Add. MS 35,297, The Journal of John Syms
    Egerton MS 3054, Diary of Joyce Jefferies of Hereford
    Harleian MSS, Randle Holme Papers
    Lansdowne MS 890, 'The History . . . of Kingston upon Hull . . . by A. de la P[ryme]'
    Stowe MS 833, Assessments of Colchester, 1643–65
    Stowe MS 842, Committee of Colchester Minute Book, 1644–56; Morant's papers concerning
        the siege of Colchester

Cheshire Record Office
    Lease Book of the Dean and Chapter of Chester, 1602–68
    Letter book of Sir William Brereton, 1645
    Chester, St John's, parish records
    Cowper MSS, 'An Account of the Siege of Chester . . .'

Chester City Record Office
    Assembly Book, 1625–84
    Assembly Files, 1642–80
    Company of Painters, Glaziers, Embroiderers and Stationers, Minute Book, 1624–51
    Copies of grants and leases, 1574–1705
    Corporation rental, 1858
    Great Letter Book, 1599–1650
    Mayors' Files: Portmote Court papers, 1642–55
    Quarter Sessions Files, 1656–8

Christ Church, Oxford
    Estates Ledger, 1659–75
    MSS Estates, vols 100, 103

Colchester Castle Muniment Room
    Corporation Assembly Book, 1646–66
    Assessments, 1649
    Examinations and Recognisances, 1646–87

Corpus Christi College, Oxford
    Wase Collection

Coventry City Record Office
    Chamberlains' accounts, 1636–1708
    Council Book, 1640–96
    Leet Book, 1588–1834

Cumbria Record Office
    Carlisle Corporation, Audit Book, 1597–1684
    —— Chamberlains' Accounts, 1649–94
    —— Court Leet papers, 1625–65
    —— Petitions to the Corporation
    —— Account book for the repair of the mills, 1653
    Dean and Chapter of Carlisle, Register, 1680–8
    —— 'An Historical Record of the City of Carlisle . . .' by Hugh Todd

Devon Record Office
    Dean and Chapter Act Books, 1642–77
    —— Sealing Books, 1640–89
    Dartmouth Borough Records, Accounts of expenditure and losses, 1642–4
    Exeter Corporation, Act Books, 1634–84
    —— General Sessions Book, 1660–72
    —— Letters, 1640–1700
    —— Petitions to the Chamber
    —— Sessions of the Peace, presentments, 1620–57
    —— Sessions rolls, 1654–6
    —— Surveys and rentals of the city property, 1640–71
    —— St Mary Magdalen Hospital leases, 1656–76
    —— Wynard's Almshouses, papers, 1657
    Parish records of Holy Trinity, St David, St Kerrian, St Mary Major, St Petrock, and St Sidwell,
        Exeter
    Parliamentary Survey, rental and lease of the Bishop's Palace, Exeter, 1646

Dorset Record Office
    Lyme Regis, Mayors' Accounts, 1549–1665
    Articles between George Penny and the Burgesses of Beaminster, 1648

East Suffolk Record Office
    Ipswich Corporation Assemblies Book, 1644–80

Essex Record Office
    Chelmsford, St Mary, Book of Briefs, 1615–1753
    —— Churchwardens' accounts, 1636–78
    Parish records of St Mary at Walls, Colchester
    Petre MSS, Civil War losses, c.1660
    Philip Morant's notebook

Gloucestershire Record Office
    Cirencester Vestry Book, 1586–1886
    Gloucester Corporation Minutes, 1632–86
    —— Chamberlains' accounts, 1635–86
    —— Charity Trustees' accounts, 1625–1742
    —— Debts owing to the City, 1645–1719
    —— Leases, 1629–84
    —— Letters, 1619–60
    —— Quarter Sessions Order Books, 1639–54
    —— Town Clerk's notebook, 1635–70
    Parish records of St John the Baptist, St Mary Crypt, and St Nicholas, Gloucester

Dean and Chapter of Gloucester, Act Book, 1617–87
—— Lease books, 1617–87
—— Parliamentary Surveys
—— Treasurers accounts, 1634–64
Parliamentary Surveys of the lands of the Bishop of Gloucester

Hampshire Record Office
Quarter Sessions Order Book, 1628–49
Winchester Corporation Ledger Books, 1625–91

Hereford Record Office
Hereford City documents, typescripts

House of Lords Record Office
Main Papers, 1641–9

Lincolnshire Archive Office
Lincoln Corporation Council Books, 1655–1710
—— 'The White Book', 1421–1729
Dean and Chapter of Lincoln, lease registers, 1660–74
—— Accounts of the rebuilding of the vicars' houses, 1664–5
—— Parliamentary Surveys
Holywell Collection, indentures of property in Birmingham, 1647–56
St Mark's, Lincoln, deeds
Sympson's survey of Lincoln parishes

London, Corporation of London Record Office
Common Council Journal, 1640–9
—— Guildhall Library
Sun Fire Office policy registers

Magdalen College, Oxford
Ledger, 1641–7

Merton College, Oxford
Register, 1567–1731
Letter of Charles I, 1643

National Library of Wales
Aston Hall MS 2400, Appointment of collectors for rebuilding Oswestry church, 1676
'Crosse of Shaw Hill MS 1115, Certificate of Prince Rupert concerning Ruthin, 1644
Wynnstay MS 113, 'An account of the rebellion in North and South Wales . . .'

New College, Oxford
Long Book, 1643–5

Norfolk and Norwich Record Office
Norwich City Records, Chamberlains' accounts, 1626–63

Northamptonshire Record Office
Northampton Borough Assembly Book, 1629–1744

Nottinghamshire Record Office
Nottingham probate records, wills, 1645

Oxford Central Library
    City Audit, 1592–1682
    Mayors' Council, Minutes, 1630–80
    Keykeepers' accounts, 1644–85
    Ledger of leases, 1636–75
    Sessions Rolls, 1657–78
    Enrolments of deeds, 1588–1689

Oxford University Archives
    Views of Frankpledge of the Chancellor's Court, 1635–65
    Court Leet presentments, 1635–65

Public Record Office
    ASSI 2/1, Crown Book, Oxford Circuit Assizes, 1656–78
    E179, Subsidy rolls
    E317, Parliamentary Surveys of crown land in Banbury, Carlisle, Carmarthen, Chester,
        Colchester, Denbigh, Lincoln, Newark, Pontefract and Reading
    SP16, 18, 21, State Papers, domestic series, 1635–60
    SP23, Papers of the Committee for Compounding
    SP24, Minute books and papers of the Committee of Indemnity
    SP28 Commonwealth Exchequer Papers

Shakespeare Birthplace Trust Record Office
    Stratford-upon-Avon Corporation, Chamberlains' accounts, 1641–2
    —— By-laws, 1665
    —— Misc. documents, i, iii, vii
    Willoughby de Broke Collection, Sir Edward Peyto's account book, 1642–3

Shropshire Record Office
    Shrewsbury Borough Records, petitions
    Shrewsbury Drapers' Company, Account Book, 1579–1745

Somerset Record Office
    Sheppard Collection, brief of 1689
    Somerset Archaeological Society Records, consent to build in Taunton St James, 1646

Wiltshire Record Office
    Marlborough General Account Book, 1572–1771

Worcester Cathedral Library
    Account of damage to the cathedral, 1661
    Account of lead taken by Parliament, 1647
    Administrators' accounts, 1655–60
    Chapter Orders, 1605–1702
    Dean and Chapter's Lease Registers, 1660–4
    Treasurers' accounts, 1639–61

Worcester Record Office
    Worcester Corporation, Chamber Order Books, 1650–1721
    —— Audit of accounts, 1623–69
    —— City deeds, 1635–65
    —— Liber Recorda, 1635–65
    —— Sessions Books, 1632–78
    Papers of Inglethorpe's Charity, 1632–1717
    Manor of Whitstones and Claines, Parliamentary Survey, 1647

Parish records of All Saints, St Andrew, St Clement, St Martin, St Michael, St Nicholas, and St
 Swithin, Worcester
St Oswald's Hospital, accounts, 1631–42
—— Deeds and leases
Worcester Royal Grammar School, Six Masters MSS

York City Library
 York Corporation Archives, House Book, 1637–50

PRINTED SOURCES

PRIMARY SOURCES

Aleyn, John, *Select Cases*, 1686
Anon., *The Compleat Gunner, in Three Parts*, 1672
Babington, John, *Pyrotechnia*, 1635
Baxter: *Reliquiae Baxterianae: Or Mr Richard Baxter's Narrative of . . . his Life and Times*, ed.
 Matthew Sylvester, 1696
Birch: *Military Memoir of Colonel John Birch*, edd. J. and T.W. Webb, Camden Soc., second series,
 VII, 1873
Birmingham: *Four Tracts relative to the Battle of Birmingham Anno Domini 1643*, ed. L. Jaye,
 Birmingham, 1931
Bourne, William, *The Arte Of Shooting In Great Ordnance*, 1643 edn
Brereton: *The Letter Books of Sir William Brereton*, ed. R.N. Dore, Record Soc. of Lancashire and
 Cheshire, CXXIII, CXXVIII, 1984, 1991
Byron: 'John Byron's Account of the Siege of Chester 1645–1646', *The Cheshire Sheaf*, fourth series,
 1971
Calendar of the Proceedings of the Committee for Advance of Money, ed. M.A.E. Green, 3 vols, 1888
Calendar of the Proceedings of the Committee for Compounding with Delinquents, ed. M.A.E. Green, 5
 vols, 1889–92
Calendar of State Papers, Domestic
Calendar of State Papers, Venetian
Carter, Matthew, *A True Relation of that Honorable, though unfortunate Expedition of Kent, Essex, and
 Colchester*, 1789 edn
Cheshire: *Memorials of the Civil War in Cheshire*, ed. John Hall, Lancashire and Cheshire Record
 Soc., 19, 1889
Chester: *The Siege of Chester: Nathaniel Lancaster's Narrative*, ed. John Lewis, Leeds, 1987
—— *An Account of the Siege of Chester during the Civil Wars betweeen King Charles I and his
 Parliament*, Chester, 1790
Clarendon, Edward, Earl of, *The History of the Rebellion and Civil Wars in England*, ed. W.D.
 Macray, 6 vols, Oxford 1888
Cooper: *Memoirs, Letters, and Speeches of Anthony Ashley Cooper, First Earl of Shaftesbury*, ed. W.D.
 Christie, 1859
Cosmo III: 'The Travels of Cosmo III, Grand Duke of Tuscany, Through England, By Count L.
 Magalotti' in *Early Tours in Devon and Cornwall*, ed. A Gibson, Newton Abbot, 1967
Cromwell: *The Writings and Speeches of Oliver Cromwell, I, 1599–1649*, ed. Wilbur Cortez Abbott,
 Cambridge, Mass., 4 vols, 1937–47
Cruso, John, *Castramentation, Or The Measuring Out Of The Quarters For The Encamping of an
 Army*, 1642
Davies, John, *The Civill Warres of Great Britain and Ireland*, 1661
Dorney, John, *Certain Speeches made upon the day of the Yearly Election of Officers in the City of
 Gloucester*, 1653
Drake, Francis, *Eboracum: or the History and Antiquities of the City of York*, 1736
Du Praissac, *The Art of Warre, or Militarie discourses*, Cambridge, 1639
Dugdale, William, *The Antiquities of Warwickshire*, II, 2nd edn, 1730

—— *A Short View of the Late Troubles in England*, Oxford, 1681

—— *The Life, Diary, and Correspondence of Sir William Dugdale*, ed. William Hamper, 1827

Durham and Northumberland: *Records of the Committees for Compounding . . . in Durham and Northumberland . . . 1643–1660*, Surtees Soc., CXI, 1905

Essex: D.H. Allen, *Essex Quarter Sessions Order Book 1652–1661*, Chelmsford, 1974

Evelyn: *The Diary of John Evelyn*, ed. E.S. de Beer, 6 vols, Oxford, 1955

Fiennes: *The Journeys of Celia Fiennes*, ed. Christopher Morris, 1947

Firth, C.H., ed., *Stuart Tracts 1603–1693*, Westminster, 1903

—— and Rait, R.S., *Acts and Ordinances of the Interregnum*, 3 vols, 1911

Gloucestershire: *Bibliotheca Gloucestrensis*, ed. John Washbourn, Gloucester, 1825

Gough, Richard, *The History of Myddle*, ed. David Hey, 1981

H.M.C., *Third Report, Corporation of Bridgwater MSS*, 1872

—— *Sixth Report, House of Lords MSS*, 1877

—— *Seventh Report, House of Lords MSS*, 1879

—— *Eighth Report, Corporation of Pontefract MSS*, 1881

—— *Tenth Report, appendix 4, Corporation of Bridgnorth MSS*, 1885

—— *Eleventh Report, appendix 3, Corporation of King's Lynn MSS*, 1887

—— *Eleventh Report, appendix 7, Corporation of Reading MSS*, 1888

—— *Eleventh Report, appendix 7: Le Strange MSS*, 1888

—— *Thirteenth Report, Portland MSS I and II*, 1891, 1893

—— *Fourteenth Report, appendix 2, Portland MSS III*, 1894

—— *Fourteenth Report, appendix 9, Round MSS*, 1895

—— *Various Collections, IV, Corporation of Aldeburgh MSS*, 1910

—— *Hastings MSS II*, 1930

Harleian: *The Harleian Miscellany*, VI, 1810

Harley: *Letters of the Lady Brilliana Harley*, ed. Thomas Taylor Lewis, Camden Soc., 58, 1853

Harris, Thomas, *The Duty of Gratitude*, 1733

Herbert Correspondence, ed. W.J. Smith, Cardiff, 1963

Hexham, Henry, *The Principles of the Art Militarie Practised in the Warres of the United Netherlands*, 1637; *An Appendix of the Quarter for the ransoming of Officers of all Qualities, and Souldiers, concluded betweene the King of Spayne his side, and the side of the States General of the United Netherlands*, 1637

—— *The Third Part of the Principles of the Art Military practised in the Warres of the United Provinces*, Rotterdam, 1643

Howell, T.B., *A Complete Collection of State Trials . . .*, IV, 1816

Hugo, Herman, *The Siege of Breda Written In Latin . . . Translated into English By C.H.G.*, 1627; *The Seige of Breda By The Armes Of Phillip The Fovrt Vnder the Gouernment Of Isabella Atchived By The Conduct Of Amr. Spinola*, 1627

Hutchinson, Lucy, *Memoirs of the Life of Colonel Hutchinson*, ed. James Sutherland, 1973

Journals of the House of Commons

Journals of the House of Lords

Lancashire: *Tracts relating to Military Proceedings in Lancashire during the Great Civil War*, ed. George Ormerod, Chetham Soc., II, 1844

—— *A Discourse of the Warr in Lancashire*, ed. William Beamont, Chetham Soc., LXII, 1864

—— *Lancashire and Cheshire Church Surveys, 1649–1655*, ed. Henry Fishwick, Lancashire and Cheshire Record Soc., I, 1879

Leicester: *Records of the Borough of Leicester . . ., 1603–1688*, ed. Helen Stocks, Cambridge, 1923

Luke: *The Letter Books 1644–45 of Sir Samuel Luke*, ed. H.G. Tibbutt, Historical Manuscripts Commission, JP4, 1963

—— *Journal of Sir Samuel Luke*, ed. I.G. Philip, Oxfordshire Record Soc., 3 vols, 1947–53

Malthus, Thomas, *A Treatise of Artificial Fire-works*, 1629

Martindale: *The Life of Adam Martindale, Written by Himself*, ed. R. Parkinson, Chetham Soc., IV, 1845

Miège, Guy, *The New State of England*, 1701

Milton: *Original Papers illustrative of the Life and Writings of John Milton*, ed. W.D. Hamilton, Camden Soc., 1859

Monluc: *The Commentaries of Blaise de Monluc*, ed. Ian Roy, 1971

Monro, Robert, *Monro His Expedition with the Worthy Scots Regiment called Mac-Keyes Regiment*, 1637

Morant, Philip, *The History and Antiquities of the County of Essex*, I, 1748

Newcastle-upon-Tyne: 'Chorographia: Or, a Survey of Newcastle upon Tine, 1649', *Harleian Miscellany*, III, 1809

Newton, George, *Mans Wrath and Gods Praise*, 1646

Norton, Robert, *The Gunners Dialogue*, 1643

Nye, Nathaniel, *The Art of Gunnery*, 1647

Ogilby, John, *Britannia*, 1675

Ottery St Mary: *The Register of Baptisms, Marriages & Burials of the Parish of Ottery St. Mary, Devon, 1610–1837*, ed. H. Tapley-Soper, Devon and Cornwall Record Soc., 1908–29

Oxford Council Acts 1626–1665, edd. M.G. Hobson and H.E. Salter, Oxford Historical Soc., 1933

Papillon, David, *A Practicall Abstract of the Arts, of Fortification and Assailing*, 1645

Pontefract: *A Journal of the first and second sieges of Pontefract Castle, 1644–1645, by Nathan Drake*, Surtees Soc., 37, 1860

—— *The Booke of Entries of the Pontefract Corporation 1653–1726*, ed. Richard Holmes, Pontefract, 1882

Powell, J.R., and Timings, E.K., eds, *Documents Relating to the Civil War 1642–1648*, Navy Records Soc., CV, 1963

Pythouse: *The Pythouse Papers*, ed. William Ansell Day, 1879

Raleigh, Walter, *The History of the World*, 1687 edn

Reading Charters, Acts and Orders. 1253–1911, ed. C. Fleetwood Pritchard, Reading, 1913

Roy: *The Royalist Ordnance Papers, 1642–1646*, ed. Ian Roy, Oxfordshire Record Soc., XLII, XLIX, 1964, 1975

Rushworth, John, *Historical Collections*, 10 vols, 1680–1722

Sanderson, William, *A Compleat History of the Life and Raigne of King Charles*, 1658

Shropshire: *Orders of the Shropshire Quarter Sessions, I, 1638–1708*, ed. R.L. Kenyon, Shropshire County Records, 14, undated

Simienowicz, Casimir, *The Great Art of Artillery*, 1729

Slingsby: *The Diary of Sir Henry Slingsby, of Scriven, Bart.*, ed. Daniel Parsons, 1836

Smith, Thomas, *The Art of Gunnery*, 1643 edn

Somerset: *Quarter Sessions Records for the County of Somerset, III Commonwealth 1646–60*, ed. E.H.B. Harbin, Somerset Record Soc., 28, 1912

—— *The Somerset Protestation Returns and Lay Subsidy Rolls 1641/2*, eds A.J. Howard and T.L. Stoate, Almondsbury, Bristol, 1975

Sprigge, Joshua, *Anglia Rediviva*, 1647

Sussex: *Quarter Sessions Order Book, 1642–1649*, ed. B.C. Redwood, Sussex Record Soc., 54, 1954

Symonds: *Diary of the Marches of the Royal Army during the Great Civil War: kept by Richard Symonds*, ed. C.E. Long, Camden Soc., LXXIV, 1859

Taylor, John, *A Short Relation of a Long Journey*, 1652

—— *Wanderings to see the Wonders of the West*, 1649

Thirsk, Joan, and Cooper, J.P., eds, *Seventeenth-Century Economic Documents*, Oxford, 1972

Townshend: *Diary of Henry Townshend of Elmley Lovett, 1640–1663*, ed. J.W. Willis Bund, Worcestershire Historical Soc., 1915–20

—— 'Henry Townshend's "Notes of the Office of a Justice of the Peace", 1661–1663', ed. R.D. Hunt, *Miscellany II*, Worcestershire Historical Soc., new series, 5, 1967

Tullie, Isaac, *A Narrative of the Siege of Carlisle, in 1644 and 1645*, ed. Samuel Jefferson, Carlisle, 1988 edn

Turner, William H., *Selections from the Records of the City of Oxford, 1509–1583*, Oxford, 1880

Vere: *The Commentaries Of Sir Francis Vere*, 1657

Vicars, John, *God on the Mount, or A Continuation of England's Parliamentary Chronicle*, 1646

—— *God's Arke Overtopping the Worlds Waves, or The Third Part of the Parliamentary Chronicle*, 1646

—— *The Burning-Bush not Consumed, or The Fourth and last Part of the Parliamentarie Chronicle*, 1646

Wallington, Nehemiah, *Historical Notices*, ed. R. Webb, 2 vols, 1869

Ward, Robert, *Animadversions of Warre*, 1639

Warwick, P., *Memoires of the Reigne of King Charles I*, 1701

Whitelocke, Bulstrode, *Memorials of the English Affairs*, 1732

—— *The Diary of Bulstrode Whitelocke 1605–1675*, ed. Ruth Spalding, Oxford, 1990

Widdrington, Sir Thomas, *Analecta Eboracensia: Or, some remaynes of the ancient City of York*, ed. Caesar Caine, 1897

Williams, Roger, *The Actions of the Lowe Countries*, 1618

Wiltshire. The Topographical Collections of John Aubrey, F.R.S., ed. John Edward Jackson, Devizes, 1862

Wiltshire: Records of the County of Wilts, being extracts from the Quarter Sessions Great Rolls of the Seventeenth Century, ed. B. Howard Cunnington, Devizes, 1932

Winchester: Documents Relating to the History of the Cathedral Church of Winchester in the Seventeenth Century, eds W.R.W. Stephens and F.T. Madge, 1897

Wood: The Life and Times of Anthony Wood, antiquary, of Oxford, 1632–1695, described by Himself, ed. Andrew Clark, Oxford Historical Soc., 4 vols, 1891–5

Worcester: The Hearth Tax Collectors' Book for Worcester 1678–1680, eds C.A.F. Meekings, S.Porter and I. Roy, Worcestershire Historical Soc., new series, 11, 1983

Worcestershire: Diary of Francis Evans, Secretary to Bishop Lloyd, 1699–1706, ed. David Robertson, Worcestershire Historical Soc., 1903

—— *The Parliamentary Survey of the Lands and Possessions of the Dean and Chapter of Worcester*, eds Thomas Cave and Rowland A. Wilson, Worcestershire Historical Soc., 1924

—— *Inspections of Churches and Parsonage Houses in the Diocese of Worcester in 1674, 1676, 1684 and 1687*, ed. Paul Morgan, Worcestershire Historical Soc., new series, 12, 1986

Yorkshire Royalist Composition Papers, ed. J.W. Clay, Yorkshire Archaeological Soc., Record Series, XV, 1893

SECONDARY SOURCES

Acton, F.S., *The Garrisons of Shropshire during the Civil War, 1642–48*, Shrewsbury, 1867

Adair, John, *Roundhead General*, 1969

—— *They Saw It Happen: Contemporary Accounts of the Siege of Basing House*, Winchester, 1981

Adey, K.R., 'Seventeenth-century Stafford: A County Town in Decline', *Midland History*, II, 1974, pp. 152–67

Airs, Malcolm, *The Making of the English Country House 1500–1640*, 1975

Anderson, M.S., *War and Society in Europe of the Old Regime 1618–1789*, 1988

Atkin, Malcolm, and Garrod, A.P., 'Archaeology in Gloucester 1989', *Trans. of the Bristol and Gloucestershire Archaeological Soc.*, 108, 1990, pp. 185–92

Atkyns, Robert, *The Ancient and Present State of Glocestershire*, 1712

Auden, J.E., 'Ecclesiastical History of Shropshire during the Civil War, Commonwealth and Restoration', *Trans. of the Shropshire Archaeological Soc.*, 3rd series, VII, 1907, pp. 241–310

Bailey, D.S., *The Canonical Houses of Wells*, Gloucester, 1982

Barley, Maurice, *Houses and History*, 1986

Barnes, W.M., 'The Diary of William Whiteway, of Dorchester, from November, 1618, to March, 1634', *Proceedings of the Dorset Natural History and Antiquarian Field Club*, XIII, 1891, pp. 57–81

Barry, Jonathan, ed., *The Tudor and Stuart Town*, 1990

Bates, E.H., 'Great Fire at Yeovil, in 1640', *Notes and Queries for Somerset and Dorset*, I, 1890, pp. 69–73

Bayley, A.R., *The Great Civil War in Dorset 1642–1660*, Taunton, 1910

Beesley, Alfred, *History of Banbury*, 1854

Bellett, G., *The Antiquities of Bridgnorth*, Bridgnorth, 1856

Benedict, Philip, *Rouen during the Wars of Religion*, Cambridge, 1981

Bennett, H.S., *English Books and Readers, 1603–1640*, Cambridge, 1970

Benthall, Paul, *Benthall Hall, Shropshire*, 1976

Bewes, W.A., *Church Briefs*, 1896

Binns, J., 'Scarborough and the Civil Wars 1642–1651', *Northern History*, XXII, 1986, pp. 95–122

Blackstone, G.V., *A History of the British Fire Service*, 1957

Blomefield, Francis, *An Essay Towards A Topographical History of . . . Norfolk*, III, 1806

Bold, John, *Wilton House and English Palladianism*, 1988

Borsay, Peter, *The English Urban Renaissance: Culture and Society in the Provincial Town, 1660–1779*, Oxford, 1989

Bramble, J.R., 'Ancient Bristol Documents VIII: Three Civil War Retournes', *Proceedings of the Clifton Antiquarian Club*, II, 1888–93, pp.152–6

Braudel, Fernand, *The Structures of Everyday Life*, 1981

Brett-James, N.G., *The Growth of Stuart London*, 1935

Brown, Cornelius, *A History of Newark-on-Trent*, 2 vols, Newark, 1907

Broxap, Ernest, 'The Sieges of Hull during the Great Civil War', *English Historical Review*, XX, 1905, pp. 457–73

—— *The Great Civil War in Lancashire (1642–1651)*, 2nd edn, Manchester, 1973

Bund, J.W. Willis, *The Civil War in Worcestershire*, 1905

Burke, G.L., *The Making of Dutch Towns*, 1956

Byford-Jones, W., *Midland Leaves: A Travel Notebook*, Wolverhampton, 1934

Carew, Richard, *The Survey of Cornwall*, 1749

Carlton, Charles, *Going to the Wars: The Experience of the British Civil Wars 1638–1651*, 1992

Chandler, George, and Wilson, E.K., *Liverpool under Charles I*, Liverpool, 1965

Chanter, J.F., *The Bishop's Palace Exeter*, 1932

Chatwin, Philip B., 'Edgbaston', *Trans. Birmingham Archaeological Soc.*, XXXIX, 1913, pp. 5–35

Cherry, Bridget, and Pevsner, Nikolaus, *The Buildings of England: Devon*, 1989

Childs, John, *Armies and Warfare in Europe 1648–1789*, New York, 1982

Clark, Peter, 'The Ownership of Books in England, 1560–1640: The Example of Some Kentish Townsfolk', in *Schooling and Society: Studies in the History of Education*, ed. Lawrence Stone, 1976

—— '"The Ramoth-Gilead of the Good": Urban change and political radicalism at Gloucester 1540–1640', in *The English Commonwealth 1547–1640*, eds Peter Clark, Alan G.R. Smith and Nicholas Tyacke, Leicester, 1979

Clark, Arthur, *Raglan Castle and the Civil War in Monmouthshire*, Chepstow, 1953

Cliffe, J.T., *Puritans in Conflict: the Puritan Gentry during and after the Civil Wars*, 1988

Clifton-Taylor, Alec, *The Pattern of English Building*, 1972

Cockle, Maurice J.D., *A Bibliography of British Military Books up to 1642*, 1957

Collinson, John, *The History and Antiquities of the County of Somerset*, III, Bath, 1791

Corfield, Penelope, 'Urban Development in England and Wales in the Sixteenth and Seventeenth Centuries', in *Trade, Government and Economy in Pre-Industrial England*, eds D.C. Coleman and A.H. John, 1976

Cornwall, Julian, *The Revolt of the Peasantry 1549*, 1977

Cunnington, B. Howard, *Some Annals of the Borough of Devizes 1555–1791*, Devizes, 1925

Dallaway, James, *The Parochial History of the Rape of Arundel, in the Western Division of the County of Sussex*, ed. Edmund Cartwright, 1832

Docton, Kenneth H., 'Lancaster, 1684', *Trans. of the Historical Soc. of Lancashire and Cheshire*, 109, 1957, pp. 125–42

Donagan, Barbara, 'Codes and Conduct in the English Civil War', *Past and Present*, 118, 1988, pp. 65–95

Duffy, Christopher, *Siege Warfare. The Fortress in the Early Modern World 1494–1660*, 1979

Duncumb, John, *Collections towards the History and Antiquities of the County of Hereford*, I, Hereford, 1804

Dyer, Alan, 'Urban housing: a documentary study of four Midland towns 1530–1700', *Post-Medieval Archaeology*, 15, 1981, pp. 207–18

Dyos, H.J., *Victorian Suburb, A Study of the Growth of Camberwell*, Leicester, 1961

Eales, Jacqueline, *Puritans and Roundheads: The Harleys of Brampton Bryan and the outbreak of the English Civil War*, Cambridge, 1990

Ellis, Sir Henry, 'Letters from a Subaltern Officer of the Earl of Essex's Army . . .', *Archaeologia*, XXXV, 1864, pp. 310–34

Everitt, Alan, *Change in the Provinces: the Seventeenth Century*, University of Leicester, Department of Local History, Occasional Papers, second series, 1, 1969

Falkus, Malcolm, and Gillingham, John, *Historical Atlas of Britain*, 2nd edn, 1987

Farrow, W.J., *The Great Civil War in Shropshire (1642–49)*, Shrewsbury, 1926

Firth, C.H., *Cromwell's Army*, 3rd edn, 1921

Fletcher, Anthony, *The Outbreak of the English Civil War*, 1981

—— 'The Coming of War', in *Reactions to the English Civil War 1642–1649*, ed. John Morrill, 1982

Fletcher, W.G.D., 'The Sequestration Papers of Sir Thomas Whitmore, Knight and Baronet, of Apley', *Trans. Shropshire Archaeological Soc.*, 4th series, IV, 1914, pp. 265–316

Frank, Joseph, *The Beginnings of the English Newspaper 1620–1660*, Cambridge, Mass., 1961

Friedrichs, C.R. *Urban Society in an Age of War: Nördlingen, 1580–1720*, Princeton, 1979

Gentles, Ian, *The New Model Army in England, Ireland and Scotland, 1645–1653*, Oxford, 1992

—— and Sheils, W.J., *Confiscation and Restoration: The Archbishopric Estates and the Civil War*, Borthwick Papers No. 59, York, 1981

Gibbs, Robert, *A History of Aylesbury*, Aylesbury, 1885

Girouard, Mark, 'Wardour Old Castle', *Country Life*, 14 Feb. 1991, pp. 44–9, 21 Feb. 1991, pp. 76–9

—— 'Wootton Lodge, Staffordshire', *Country Life*, 125, 1959, pp. 522–5, 596–9

Godwin, G.N., *The Civil War in Hampshire (1642–1645)*, 1904

Goudsblom, Johan, *Fire and Civilization*, 1992

Green, Emanuel, *The Siege of Bridgwater, July 1645*, Bath, 1905

Gribble, John Besley, *Memorials of Barnstaple*, Barnstaple, 1830

Hale, J.R., 'Armies, navies and the art of war', *The New Cambridge Modern History*, III, ed. R.B. Wernham, Cambridge, 1968

—— *War and Society in Renaissance Europe 1450–1620*, 1985

—— 'Armies, navies and the art of war', *The New Cambridge Modern History*, II, ed. G.R. Elton, 2nd edn, Cambridge, 1990

Hall, A.R., *Ballistics in the Seventeenth Century*, Cambridge, 1952

Harrington, Peter, 'English Civil War fortifications', *Fort*, 15, 1987, pp. 39–60

—— *Archaeology of the English Civil War*, Princes Risborough, 1992

Harte, W.J., 'Ecclesiastical and Religious Affairs in Exeter 1640–1662', *Trans. of the Devonshire Association*, LXIX, 1937, pp. 41–72

Harwood, Thomas, *The History and Antiquities of the Church and City of Lichfield*, 1806

Hedges, John Kirby, *The History of Wallingford*, II, 1881

Hembry, Phyllis, 'Episcopal Palaces, 1535 to 1660' in *Wealth and Power in Tudor England*, eds E.W. Ives, R.J. Knecht and J.J. Scarisbrick, 1979

Hill, J.W.F., *Tudor and Stuart Lincoln*, Cambridge, 1956

Hinderwell, Thomas, *The History and Antiquities of Scarborough*, 2nd edn, York, 1811

Hine, Richard, *The History of Beaminster*, Taunton, 1914

Hughes, Ann, 'Coventry and the English Revolution', in *Town and Countryside in the English Revolution*, ed. R.C. Richardson, Manchester, 1992

Hulme, E.W., 'History of the Chichester Needles', *Sussex Notes and Queries*, XII, 1948–9, pp. 124–8

Hunt, John Dixon, and de Jong, Erik, eds, *The Anglo-Dutch Garden in the Age of William and Mary*, 1988

Huntingford, G.W.B., 'Church Building and Restoration in North Berkshire in the Seventeenth, Eighteenth and Nineteenth Centuries', *Berkshire Archaeological Journal*, 40, 1936, pp. 94–105

Hutchins, John, *The History of Dorset*, 3rd edn, 1863

Izacke, Richard, *Remarkable Antiquities of the City of Exeter*, 1681

Jenkins, Alexander, *The History and Description of the City of Exeter*, Exeter, 1806

Johnson, A.H., *The History of the Worshipful Company of the Drapers of London*, III, 1603–1920, Oxford, 1922

Johnson, D.A., and Vaisey, D.G., *Staffordshire and the Great Rebellion*, Stafford, 1964

Jones, E.L., Porter, S., and Turner, M., *A Gazetteer of English Urban Fire Disasters, 1500–1900*, Historical Geography Research Series, 13, Norwich, 1984

Jones, T.L., *Ashby de la Zouch Castle*, 1972

Kamen, H., 'The Economic and Social Consequences of the Thirty Years' War', *Past and Present*, 39, 1968, pp. 44–61

Karslake, J.B.P., 'Early London Fire-Appliances', *The Antiquaries Journal*, IX, 1929, pp. 229–38

Kemp, A., 'The Fortification of Oxford during the Civil War', *Oxoniensia*, 42, 1977, pp. 237–46

Kendall, H.P., 'The Civil War as affecting Halifax and the surrounding towns', *Halifax Antiquarian Soc.*, 1910, pp. 21–59

Kenyon, J.P., *The Civil Wars of England*, 1988

Ketton-Cremer, R.W., *Norfolk in the Civil War*, 1969

Killick, H.F., 'Memoirs of Sir Marmaduke Rawden, Kt. 1582–1646', *Yorkshire Archaeological Journal*, 25, 1920, pp. 315–30

Kingsley, Nicholas, *The Country Houses of Gloucestershire*, Cheltenham, 1989

Kingston, Alfred, *East Anglia and the Great Civil War*, 1897

Langton, John, 'Residential patterns in pre-industrial cities: some case studies from seventeenth-century Britain', *Trans. of the Institute of British Geographers*, 65, 1975, pp. 1–27

Latimer, John, *The Annals of Bristol in the Seventeenth Century*, Bristol, 1900

Lawson, John, *The Endowed Grammar Schools of East Yorkshire*, East Yorkshire Local History Series, 14, 1962

Leatherbarrow, J.S., *Churchwardens Presentments in the Diocese of Worcester c1660–1760*, Worcestershire Historical Soc., Occasional Publications, 1, 1977

Liversidge, M.J.H., 'Abingdon's 'Right Goodly Crosse of Stone'', *The Antiquaries Journal*, LXIII, 1983, pp. 315–25

Llewellyn, Nigel, *The Art of Death*, 1991

Lloyd, J.D.K., 'The New Building at Montgomery Castle', *Archaeologia Cambrensis*, CXIV, 1965, pp. 60–8

Lysons, Daniel, *The Environs of London*, III, 1795

—— *Magna Britannia*, I, 1806

MacCaffrey, Wallace T., *Exeter, 1540–1640. The Growth of an English County Town*, 3rd edn, Cambridge, Mass., 1975

Machin, R., 'The Great Rebuilding: A Reassessment', *Past and Present*, 77, 1977, pp. 33–56

—— 'The Mechanism of the Pre-industrial Building Cycle', *Vernacular Architecture*, 8, 1977, pp. 815–19

MacIvor, Iain, 'The Elizabethan Fortifications of Berwick-upon-Tweed', *The Antiquaries Journal*, XLV, 1965, pp. 64–96

Macray, W.D., *A Register of . . . St Mary Magdalen College, Oxford*, III, 1901

Manning, Brian, *The English People and the English Revolution 1640–1649*, 1976

Miller, Keith, Robinson, John, English, Barbara, and Hall, Ivan, *Beverley. An archaeological and architectural study*, R.C.H.M.E., Supplementary series, 4, 1982

Moore, John S., 'The Gloucestershire section of Domesday Book: geographical problems of the text, part 4', *Trans. of the Bristol and Gloucestershire Archaeological Soc.*, 108, 1990, pp. 105–30

Morgan, F.C., 'Local Government in Hereford', *Trans. of the Woolhope Naturalists' Field Club*, XXXI, 1942, pp. 37–57

Morrill, John, ed., *Reactions to the English Civil War 1642–1649*, 1982

Morris, R.H., *The Siege of Chester 1643–1646*, Chester, 1924

Mounfield, P.R., 'The Footwear Industry of the East Midlands: II Northamptonshire', *The East Midlands Geographer*, 3, 1964–5, pp. 394–413

Nash, John, *Collections for the History of Worcestershire*, 2 vols, 1782

Newman, P.R., 'The Royalist Officer Corps 1642–1660: Army Command as a reflection of the social structure', *The Historical Journal*, 26, 1983, pp. 945–58

Nichols, John, *The History and Antiquities of the County of Leicester*, II, 1795

Oliver, George, *The History and Antiquities of the Town and Minster of Beverley*, Beverley, 1829

Owen, J., and Blakeway, J.B., *A History of Shrewsbury*, 2 vols, 1825

Palliser, D.M., 'York under the Tudors: the trading life of the northern capital', in *Perspectives in English Urban History*, ed. Alan Everitt, 1973

—— 'The Unions of Parishes in York, 1547–86', *Yorkshire Archaeological Journal*, XLVI, 1974, pp. 87–102

Parker, Geoffrey, *The Army of Flanders and the Spanish Road 1567–1659*, Cambridge, 1972

—— *The Dutch Revolt*, 1977

—— 'The "Military Revolution 1560–1660" – a Myth?', in *Spain and the Netherlands*, 1979

—— *The Thirty Years' War*, 2nd edn, 1987

—— *The Military Revolution*, Cambridge, 1988

Partington, J.R., *A History of Greek Fire and Gunpowder*, Cambridge, 1960

Peacock, Edward, 'Gainsburgh during the Great Civil War, A.D. 1642–1660', *Reports and Papers of the Associated Architectural Societies*, 8, 1866, pp. 254–79

Peckham, W.D., 'The Parishes of the City of Chichester', *Sussex Archaeological Collections*, 74, 1933, pp. 65–97

Pennington, Donald, 'The War and the People', in *Reactions to the English Civil War 1642–1649*, ed. John Morrill, 1982

—— and Roots, I.A., *The Committee at Stafford 1643–1645*, Manchester, 1957

Pevsner, Nikolaus, *The Buildings of England: Shropshire*, 1958

—— *The Buildings of England: Herefordshire*, 1963

—— *The Buildings of England: Essex*, 2nd edn, 1965

—— *The Buildings of England: Worcestershire*, 1968

—— *The Buildings of England: Nottinghamshire*, 2nd edn, 1979

—— and Hubbard, Edward, *The Buildings of England: Cheshire*, 1971

—— and Harris, John, *The Buildings of England: Lincolnshire*, ed. Nicholas Antram, 1989

Phillips, William, 'The Ottley Papers relating to the Civil War', *Trans. Shropshire Archaeological Soc.*, 2nd series, VII, 1895, pp. 241–360; VIII, 1896, pp. 199–312

Picton, J.A., *City of Liverpool: Selections from the Municipal Archives and Records, from the 13th to the 17th century*, Liverpool, 1883

Platt, E.M., 'Liverpool during the Civil War', *Trans. of the Historical Soc. of Lancashire and Cheshire*, 61, 1909, pp. 183–202

Polisensky, J.V., *The Thirty Years War*, 1974

—— *War and Society in Europe 1618–1648*, 1978

Porter, Stephen, 'Fires in Stratford-upon-Avon in the Sixteenth and Seventeenth Centuries', *Warwickshire History*, III, 1976, pp. 97–105

—— 'Fire Precautions in 17th Century Bath', *Notes & Queries for Somerset and Dorset*, XXXI, 1981, pp. 109–12

—— 'Fire Precautions in Early-Modern Abingdon', *Berkshire Archaeological Journal*, 71, 1981–2, pp. 71–7

—— 'The Civil War Destruction of Boarstall', *Records of Bucks*, 26, 1984, pp. 86–91

—— 'The Fire-raid in the English Civil War', *War and Society*, 2, 1984, pp. 27–40

—— 'Property Destruction in Civil-War London', *Trans. London & Middlesex Archaeological Soc.*, 35, 1984, pp. 59–62

—— 'Fireships in the English Civil War', *The Mariner's Mirror*, 70, 1984, pp. 85–6

—— 'The Oxford Fire of 1644', *Oxoniensia*, XLIX, 1984, pp. 289–300

—— 'The Destruction of Axminster in 1644', *Devon & Cornwall Notes & Queries*, XXXV, 1985, pp. 243–6

Portman, Derek, *Exeter Houses 1400–1700*, Exeter, 1966

Poulson, George, *Beverlac; or, The Antiquities and History of the town of Beverley*, 2 vols, 1829

Prestwich, Menna, *Cranfield: Politics and Profits under the early Stuarts*, Oxford, 1966

Pruett, John H., *The Parish Clergy under the Later Stuarts. The Leicestershire Experience*, Urbana, Ill., 1978

Pugh, R.B., and Saunders, A.D., *Old Wardour Castle*, 1968

R.C.H.M.E., *Herefordshire, III North-West*, 1934

—— *Dorset: V East Dorset*, 1975

—— *Newark on Trent, the Civil War Siegeworks*, 1964

—— *The City of York*, IV, 1975

—— *The City of York*, V, 1981

—— *The Country Houses of Northamptonshire*, 1996

Reddaway, T.F., *The Rebuilding of London after the Great Fire*, 1940

Redlich, Fritz, *De Praeda Militari. Looting and Booty 1500–1815*, Wiesbaden, 1956

—— 'Contributions in the Thirty Years War', *Economic History Review*, 2nd series, 12, 1959–60, pp. 247–54

Roberts, Keith, 'Lessons in revolution: the impact of the London Military Companies', *Cromwelliana*, 1992, pp. 35–47

Roberts, Michael, *The Military Revolution, 1560–1660*, Belfast, 1956

Rogers, J.E.T., *A History of Agriculture and Prices in England from 1259 to 1793*, 7 vols, Oxford, 1866–1902

Roper, John S., *Dudley: The town in the eighteenth century*, Dudley, 1968

Rosen, Adrienne, 'Winchester in transition, 1580–1700', in *Country towns in pre-industrial England*, ed. Peter Clark, Leicester, 1981

Ross, W.G., 'Military Engineering During the Great Civil War, 1642–9', *Professional Papers of the Corps of Royal Engineers*, Royal Engineers Institute Occasional Papers, XIII, Chatham, 1887

Rowley, Trevor, *The Shropshire Landscape*, 1972

Rowley-Morris, E., 'Royalist Composition Papers', *Montgomeryshire Collections*, 18, 1885, pp. 71–92

Roy, Ian, 'The English Civil War and English Society', in *War and Society, A Yearbook of Military History, I*, eds Brian Bond and Ian Roy, 1975

—— 'England turned Germany? The Aftermath of the Civil War in its European Context', *Trans. Royal Historical Soc.*, fifth series, 28, 1978, pp. 127–44

—— 'The Profession of Arms', in *The Professions in Early Modern England*, ed. Wilfrid Prest, 1987

—— and Porter, Stephen, 'The Social and Economic Structure of an Early-Modern Suburb: the Tything at Worcester', *Bulletin of the Institute of Historical Research*, LII, 1980, pp. 203–17

———— 'The Population of Worcester in 1646', *Local Population Studies*, 28, 1982, pp. 32–43

Rudder, Samuel, *A New History of Gloucestershire*, Cirencester, 1779

Salter, M., *The Old Parish Churches of Worcestershire*, Wolverhampton, 1989

Schove, D.J., 'Fire and Drought', *Weather*, XXI, 1966, pp. 311–14

Seaver, Paul S., *Wallington's World. A Puritan Artisan in Seventeenth-Century London*, 1985

Seyer, Samuel, *Memoirs of Bristol*, 2 vols, Bristol, 1823

Sharpe, Kevin, *The Personal Rule of Charles I*, New Haven and London, 1992

Simmons, Jack, *Leicester: The Ancient Borough to 1860*, Gloucester, 1983

Smith, Geoffrey Ridsdill, *Without Touch of Dishonour. The Life and Death of Sir Henry Slingsby 1602–1658*, Kineton, 1968

Steer, F.W., *The Chichester Needle Industry*, The Chichester Papers, 31, 1963

Steinberg, S.H., *The 'Thirty Years War'*, 1966

Stephens, W.B., *Seventeenth-century Exeter*, Exeter, 1958

Stone, Lawrence, and Stone, Jeanne C. Fawtier, *An Open Elite? England 1540–1880*, Oxford, 1984

Stoye, J.W., *English Travellers Abroad 1604–1667*, 1952

Stoyle, Mark, *The Civil War Defences of Exeter and the Great Parliamentary Siege of 1645–46*, Exeter, 1990

—— *Exeter City Defences Project: Documentary Evidence for the Civil War Defences of Exeter, 1642–3*, Exeter, 1988

Sturdy, David, 'The Civil War Defences of London', *The London Archaeologist*, 2, 1975, pp. 334–8

Styles, Philip, 'The city of Worcester during the Civil Wars, 1640–1660', in *Studies in Seventeenth Century West Midlands History*, Kineton, 1978

Symonds, Henry, 'A By-Path of the Civil War', *Somerset Archaeological & Natural History Soc. Proceedings*, LXV, 1919, pp. 48–75

Talbot, C.H., 'Notes on Spye Park and Bromham', *Wiltshire Archaeological Magazine*, XV, 1975, pp. 320–8

Taylor, A.J., *Raglan Castle*, 1975

Temple, R.K.G., 'Discovery of a manuscript eye-witness account of the battle of Maidstone', *Archaeologia Cantiana*, XCVII, 1981, pp. 209–20

Terry, C.S., 'The Siege of Newcastle-upon-Tyne by the Scots in 1644', *Archaeologia Aeliana*, 2nd series, XXI, 1899, pp. 180–258

Thirsk, Joan, ed., *The Agrarian History of England and Wales, V, 1640–1750*, Cambridge, 1984–5

Thomas, Peter, and Warren, Jacqueline, *Aspects of Exeter*, Plymouth, 1980

Thompson, M.W., *Farnham Castle Keep*, 1978

—— *The Decline of the Castle*, Cambridge, 1987

Thorpe, Harry, 'Lichfield: A Study of its Growth and Function', *Collections for a History of Staffordshire*, 1950–1

—— 'The Lord and the Landscape', *Transactions and Proceedings of the Birmingham Archaeological Soc.*, 80, 1962, pp. 38–77

Tibbutt, H.G., *The Life and Letters of Sir Lewis Dyve 1599–1669*, Bedfordshire Historical Record Soc., XXVII, 1948

Tickell, John, *History of the Town and County of Kingston upon Hull*, 1798

Tierney, M.A., *The History and Antiquities of the Castle and Town of Arundel*, II, 1834

Tittler, Robert, *Architecture and Power. The Town Hall and the English Urban Community c.1500–1640*, Oxford, 1991

Townsend, James, *A History of Abingdon*, 1910

Toynbee, Margaret, and Young, Peter, *Strangers in Oxford. A Side Light on the First Civil War, 1642–1646*, 1973

Trevelyan, G.M., *England under the Stuarts*, 1965 edn

Turner, Michael, 'New towns for old? Reconstruction after fires in the South West: the case of Blandford Forum, Dorset, 1731', in *Landscape and Townscape in the South West*, ed. Robert Heigham, Exeter, 1989

Twamley, Charles, *History of Dudley Castle and Priory*, 1867

Tyack, Geoffrey, *Warwickshire Country Houses in the Age of Classicism 1650–1800*, Warwickshire Local History Soc., Occasional Paper No. 3, 1980

Underdown, David, *Somerset in the Civil War and Interregnum*, Newton Abbot, 1973

—— *Fire from Heaven: The Life of an English Town in the Seventeenth Century*, 1992

V.C.H., *Cheshire*, III, 1980

—— *Gloucestershire*, IV, 1988

—— *Hampshire*, III, 1908

—— *Oxfordshire*, X, 1972

—— *Staffordshire*, VI, 1979; XIV, 1990

—— *Warwickshire*, II, 1908; V, 1949; VII, 1964; VIII, 1969

—— *Wiltshire*, VII, 1953

—— *Worcestershire*, III, 1913; IV, 1924

—— *The City of York*, 1961

Varley, F.J., *Cambridge during the Civil War 1642–1646*, Cambridge, 1935

Venables, Edmund, 'A List and Brief Description of the Churches of Lincoln previous to the period of the Reformation', *Reports and Papers of the Associated Architectural Societies*, 19, 1888, pp. 326–54

Verey, David, *The Buildings of England: Gloucestershire, 1. The Cotswolds*, 1970

—— *2, The Vale and the Forest of Dean*, 1970

Walker, J.H., 'St Nicholas' Church Nottingham', *Trans. of the Thoroton Soc.*, XLIV, 1940, pp. 51–67

Warburton, Eliot, *Memoirs of Prince Rupert and the Cavaliers*, 3 vols, 1849

Ward, S., *Excavations at Chester: The Civil War Siegeworks 1642–6*, Chester, 1987

Webb, John, *The Siege of Portsmouth in the Civil War*, The Portsmouth Papers, 7, 1969

Webb, John and T.W., *Memorials of the Civil War between King Charles I and the Parliament of England as it affected Herefordshire and the adjacent counties*, I, 1879

Wedgwood, C.V., *The King's War 1641–1647*, 1958

—— 'The Chief Passages in Middlesex', *Middlesex Local History Bulletin*, 14, 1962, pp. 1–7

Welford, Richard, ed., *History of Newcastle and Gateshead vol. III Sixteenth and Seventeenth Centuries*, 1887

Wenham, Peter, *The Great and Close Siege of York, 1644*, Kineton, 1970

Whiffen, Marcus, *Stuart and Georgian Churches*, 1947–8

Williams, J. Gwynne, 'The Castles of Wales during the Civil War, 1642–1647', *Archaeologia Cambrensis*, CXXXVII, 1988, pp. 1–26

Willis, Browne, *The History and Antiquities of the Town, Hundred, and Deanery of Buckingham*, 1755

Wilson, John Marius, *The Imperial Gazetteer of England and Wales*, 1866–9

Wood, A.C., *Nottinghamshire in the Civil War*, 1937

Wroughton, John, *The Civil War in Bath and North Somerset*, Bath, 1973

Index

Page numbers in italic type refer to illustrations.